What reade

*"Emory John Michael has given us a milestone – an epic work of empower-
ment. His thoughts are brilliant, the narrative inspired.*
Alchemy of Sacred Living *has best-seller written all over it."*
– Metaphysical Reviews

*"So beautifully written ... and so profound. You have such a gift.
Many passages touched me deeply and brought tears to my eyes.
I'm ordering a case to give to my friends and family."*
– Barbara Sheridan, Seminar Coordinator

*"***The Alchemy of Sacred Living*** is a blueprint for living. Read it! Absorb its
life-affirming truths—so clearly and beautifully presented, and you will walk
in the light."*
– Delia Sellers, Editor, *Abundant Living*

*"Thanks for writing such a refreshing and original book.
I want to order ten copies immediately."*
– Barbara Bane, Editor, *Center of Attention*

*"Thank you for a beautifully inspiring book.... such a pleasure to read....
and the voluminous yellow underlining in my copy speaks for itself. I loved it."*
– John Roberts, author, *The Fruit of Your Thoughts*

*"A captivating gift of vital truths, wrapped in the style of a talented writer....
sure to be a best-seller."*
– Mona Feirson, Editor, *Ensoulment Institute Press*

*"As the saying goes: when the pupil is ready the teacher will come. What a
teacher you are! Thank you so much for your* **Alchemy of Sacred Living***!
I am reading it for the second time; the book contains so much wisdom,
so much to remember. I am sure I will pick it up often.
Bless you for writing this book!"*
– Annie Van Mourik, *Midwest Review*

THE ALCHEMY OF SACRED LIVING

Creating a Culture of Light

Emory J. Michael

Mountain Rose Publishing
Prescott, Arizona

THE ALCHEMY OF SACRED LIVING
Creating a Culture of Light

by Emory John Michael

Mountain Rose Publishing
Prescott, Arizona

Copyright 1998 Emory John Michael

Front cover:
Sir Edward Burne-Jones (English, 1833–1898)
The Days of Creation (The First Day), 1875–1876
Watercolor, gouache, shell gold and platinum paint on linen-covered panel
with zinc ground, 102.2 x 35.5 cm (40 1/8 x 14 in.)
Photograph courtesy The Fogg Art Museum,
Harvard University Art Museums
Bequest of Grenville L. Winthrop
Image Copyright: President and Fellows of Harvard College, Harvard University

Mountain Rose Publishing
PO Box 2738
Prescott, AZ 86302
520-445-5056

ISBN 0-9642147-2-5

Portions of *The Alchemy of Sacred Living*
were originally published as *Jewels of Light*

Printed in the United States of America
Graphic Impressions Inc., Prescott, Arizona

Typesetting and layout by The Agrell Group, Prescott, Arizona

Cover design by Lewis Agrell and Emory Michael

Address all correspondence to Emory J. Michael,
c/o Mountain Rose Publishing

PRELUDE

There was once a tiny mountain surrounded by many high mountains. The small mountain looked with envy at the tall, majestic peaks that towered above it. In the winter the large peaks were covered with snow and people came from far and wide to ski on the beautiful slopes. In the summer, adventurers enjoyed climbing the impressive rocks, campers explored the high trails and valleys, and children played in the meadows.

The tiny mountain felt ignored, unappreciated and unloved. She believed herself to be insignificant. Then one day some people came and drilled several deep holes into her interior. They were excited by what they found. Soon many visitors came to see the small peak. It was declared a national treasure, for it was discovered that the tiny mountain was filled with gold, diamonds and all manner of precious gemstones and jewels. The tiny mountain beamed with happiness and pride to know that deep within she had such a vast store of hidden treasures.

Each of us is like the little mountain in this simple tale. Within us is a priceless treasure—the jewels of our soul and spirit. We extract those jewels as we learn to live a sacred life. This book is a tool to help you uncover and express the splendor that lies within you.

CONTENTS

ACKNOWLEDGMENTS

I wish to thank Delia Sellers, Brooke Monfort, Kathryn Agrell and Catherine Freimiller for their valuable help and suggestions in editing the manuscript. Thanks, also, to Katie and Abe for their boundless generosity. To my wife, Mia, a beacon of light and a constant inspiration, and to my daughter, Sera Maria—one of my wisest teachers and a source of wonder and delight—I express eternal gratitude. Thank you for believing.

INTRODUCTION

B eing here is the primal mystery that gives rise to our seeking. Is not our presence more than our bodies? Toward what goals will we strive? How may we live graciously on the Earth?

The ancients taught that the Earth was alive—a pulsating, evolving Being. To them, nature and the elements were ensouled. All matter and substance were permeated with the mystery of divine immanence. To the ancients, it was obvious that divinity was present in the human soul as well as in the elements of nature. From these certainties streamed the essential sanctity of all life.

Every religion gives its prescription for bringing the sacred into daily life. The Native Americans have as one of their most noble ideals that we learn to walk on the Earth in a sacred manner. Yet vast stretches of "civilized" terrain are becoming wasteland. It seems wherever corporate culture and modern technology go, a portion of the Earth dies. Weapons manufacturing is still the world's number one business. The growing deterioration of the world's air and water, along with the steady proliferation of "weapons of mass destruction," threaten the existence of future generations. Even our culture has been described as "toxic," especially to children. It appears we are entranced—like a princess in an enchanted tale—deaf to the spirit calling out to us through our slumber.

Sometimes it takes a life trauma—perhaps even a near-death experience—for an individual to become aware of the deeper wisdom that guides us from within. Our current culture is flirting with an apocalyptic event or series of convulsions that might bring the human race to such a collective trauma. To avoid catastrophe, we will need to embrace a sacred manner of living on the Earth.

Fortunately, the human race is a work in progress. The past is prologue, and the book of human culture has only begun to be written. Though science has produced an extraordinary material technology, we are still childish in our ability to live by the truths taught by the wise men and women who have given humanity its highest cultural and spiritual impulses. To live those truths is the task of the future. Doing so will require a transformation in our understanding and our ways of living. Centuries ago, philosophers gave the mystery of transformation the name *alchemy*.

The word *alchemy* is vaguely mysterious in most people's minds. It might conjure an image of a medieval sorcerer toiling, Merlin-like, in a shadowy laboratory, seeking to discover the secret of making gold. It is true that alchemy refers to an archaic branch of medieval chemistry. Alchemists were the forerunners of modern science. In their research they discovered zinc, created porcelain, and introduced the use of chemical compounds. Alchemists are known to have sought a mysterious substance they called the "Philosopher's Stone" that would give them the power to transmute ordinary metals into gold. In addition, they hoped to acquire the "Elixir of Life," which would grant abundant, perhaps even eternal, life.

Alchemy was not merely the concern of quirky figures on the fringes of society. Historically, many of the greatest names in science, philosophy, theology and art busied themselves with alchemical experiments and writings. These include Paracelsus, the "father of modern medicine," Albertus Magnus—who was himself canonized and is best remembered as the teacher of Saint Thomas Aquinas—and Roger Bacon, a Franciscan, who was one of the most learned and innovative minds of his day. Perhaps most notable is Isaac Newton, the great physicist, who wrote exhaustively of his experiments with the transmutation of metals in his alchemical diaries. It should be remembered that Isaac Newton is widely considered the greatest scientific mind ever to have lived, unequaled by any, save Einstein.

Although the novice might initially scoff at the notions of alchemy, and wonder why such great minds would be interested in its mysteries, modern science has led us into a world where the transmutation of substance is a given. With the advent of Einstein and atomic fusion, the new physics demonstrates conclusively that matter may be transmuted into "essence," or energy. Regarding the alchemical quest for gold, it is interesting that at Harvard University in 1941, famous experiments with the metal mercury (quicksilver)—a key element of the alchemists—were conducted by physicists using a cyclotron. Inside a particle accelerator, the physicists bombarded mercury with subatomic particles and succeeded in transforming the mercury into a small amount of gold. This would seem to vindicate the alchemists' quest. It certainly supports their belief that "The seeds of gold are contained in all substances." Yet it is essential to understand that the traditional alchemical effort to "turn base metal into gold" is an allegory. The Philosopher's Stone and the Elixir of Life are terms representative of states of consciousness. Alchemy was closer to philosophy than pure science.

Alchemists were seeking the secrets of abundant living. They were pioneers of the spirit, who hid their work from the foolish and intolerant by using symbols of turning coarse matter into gold. Although they foreshadowed modern science, they were primarily concerned with transforming the elements of their own souls. Genuine alchemists sought wisdom before wealth.

Carl Jung, perhaps the greatest psychologist of modern times, was instrumental in reintroducing the images of traditional alchemy and interpreting them as metaphors for soul development. Modern depth psychology has integrated alchemical imagery, perceiving it as symbolic of uniting spirit, soul and body in the process of inner awakening and enlightenment. Joseph Campbell, the leading modern interpreter of mythology, also explored the psychological meaning of traditional alchemy. Now, many are discovering that alchemy provides illuminating and suggestive guidelines for the eternal quest toward sacred living and spiritual becoming. The "base metals" that are to be transmuted are human society and the human soul. The "gold" sought by true alchemists is that of spiritual illumination within a new "golden age" of culture.

Alchemy, in the true sense of the word and in the sense it is used in this book, is a process whereby the commonplace becomes special. It is the act of turning ordinary living into sacred living. The alchemy of sacred living is the art of soul transformation that enables us to express the golden light of the spirit in all areas of life.

The essential truths of spiritual alchemy, of human soul transformation, form a philosophy of light that has always existed on Earth, albeit often in a fragmented form. Since primordial times a stream of ancient wisdom has flowed through human culture—a knowledge that seeks to inform us of the divine presence, of the mystery of our being and the purpose of our earthly appearance. Because it has to do with the unknown, and because it grants access into a world previously hidden, enshrouded in silence, it is only natural that this wisdom should be given the name of the Mysteries. Until we can penetrate beyond the veils of unknowing, these truths remain—at least in part—a mystery. As Saint Paul wrote, "Now we see poorly as if through a dark mirror, but then (we shall see) face to face." In coming face to face with the realities of the spirit, human beings find themselves. As we realize the mystery of our own being, we will comprehend our presence and purpose on the Earth.

Many years ago, when I was struggling to figure out what life was all about, I met a teacher of ancient history who influenced me greatly. His specialty was Egyptology and he had been a lifelong student of comparative religion. Though seeming fairly "normal" to casual observation, in his conversation he displayed a ripened wisdom, which was the fruit of lifelong efforts to grasp the deeper truths that are the foundation stone of wisdom underlying human culture. It was the early seventies, a time of great social agitation, and this man was particularly sensitive to the issues of the period. Nonetheless, he seemed to have achieved a degree of serenity and inner contentment that made a deep impression on me.

One day, on the lawn of an old Maryland mansion, I had an unforgettable conversation with him. We chatted for hours beneath the shade of an ancient oak, our faces illumined occasionally by the sun as the breeze rustled the branches. His large black eyes could be alternately piercing, or as soft as those of a dreamy child. We talked about the problems in the world and about the mysterious "hidden splendor" within all people. He said most people lived life as if they were in a dark cave underground and had forgotten about the sunny atmosphere outside the cave, a luminous world that was our true home. Suddenly transfixing me with his gaze, he challenged me to come out of the darkness and discover the bright realm outside the cave of ignorance, a realm he appeared to know intimately. For an instant I felt personally responsible for the state of the world and saddened by my inability to articulate my intuitions of a deeper reality. Perceiving my response, his gentle laughter set me at ease. He claimed that there was a body of essential truths that formed the core of all religions and sacred traditions, both ancient and modern, and that the science of the future would be based on these insights, the essence of which has been called *the perennial philosophy.* He called these ideas the secrets of existence. When we begin to master these truths, he explained, we step outside the dark cave into the brightness of the world that we have forgotten, the land of light from which we have come. I found our conversation exhilarating and enlightening, and was moved that such a distinguished individual would give me the benefit of his free time.

The next day I was further startled when he gave me a lengthy handwritten essay on the very subjects we had discussed. He had apparently spent much of the night writing the material for my benefit. I was touched by his gesture, for I knew he was in the middle of a heavy teaching load. I pored over his writings, finding them illuminating. It was a sketch of ancient wisdom embellished with his personal realizations. He had captured in those few pages the essence of what for me was—and remains to this day—a philosophy of happiness and enlightenment. I have never seen this gifted teacher since, but have often thought of our conversation and the inspiration that he gave me.

In the spirit of the man who wrote those inspired pages years ago for my benefit and instruction, I offer this book as a map of the new consciousness. My hope is that those who read it will find in its pages the eternally living keys to personal and cultural transformation. This work is based on my efforts to build my life on a knowledge of these laws and principles—truths that are the heart of the wisdom of antiquity as well as the foundation of the new spiritual paradigm. They form the golden thread of truth that runs through all the world's religions. Each of these keys is like a letter in nature's alphabet, which helps us read the living book of truth that lies before us each day. When we begin to express these ideas in our lives, we will see unfolding before us the beauty and wisdom that govern life.

The chapters that follow are a kind of toolbox of sacred living. Those who apply these tools will find that they possess a power capable of transforming their inner and outer lives. Within these pages discerning readers will discover a virtual "Philosopher's Stone." If they wish, they may employ it to become alchemists of the sacred, turning the experiences of life into priceless treasures of the spirit.

Those who activate the power of the celestial laws through harmonious living begin to experience a transformation. It is as if they are each handed the keys to a kingdom all their own—a realm of limitless possibilities where they are destined to reign masterfully. They become creative and successful in their lives. Most important of all, they are led to the discovery of life's greatest treasure, the immortal jewel of the indwelling spirit.

May the ideas in this book help you discover the keys to your kingdom.

Emory John Michael – October, 1998

Dedicated

to the Messengers of Light

of all times and places.

MY PERSONAL JOURNEY

In October of 1994, I self-published an autobiographical work of fiction entitled, *Queen of the Sun*. When the book arrived from the printer, I tossed some boxes into my van and drove to bookstores in Arizona and New Mexico, selling my book to whoever would take it. In December and January several book distributors began to supply *Queen* and sales picked up in the independent bookstore market. Just a few weeks later, in mid February, I received a call from a prominent literary agent in California. She told me that she had seen my book and felt it had the potential to be a national bestseller. In short, she wanted to be my agent. I was thrilled, for I knew that she represented several successful writers, some of whose books were on the New York Times bestseller list. Just days later she had to take an unexpected, month-long leave of absence from her work and suggested I not wait for her, because, in her words, "Things happen very quickly in this business." I hired another California agent whom she recommended, and a week later we received a substantial offer from a large publishing house. It was a dream come true.

As part of the preparation for a twelve-city publicity tour to promote *Queen*, my publisher flew me to Los Angeles to receive "media training." I was told that as part of the promotional efforts for *Queen of the Sun,* I would need to "tell my personal story." I found that at first I was reticent about talking about myself in front of groups. Growing up, I had not been encouraged to "promote" myself. Not that I was actively discouraged, but the subtle message was that it wasn't dignified to make yourself the subject of the conversation.

But the fact is that all of us are interested in each other's story. Each person's biography communicates something of the universally human. We learn from each other and from our trials, failures, and successes. Each of us is on the same journey in life, the journey to our deeper selves, which, in the language of mysticism, is also the journey to God.

One memorable event of my early childhood stands out vividly in my mind because of its extraordinary nature. When I was five years old, I lived with my parents and four brothers in a small town in Connecticut. One sunny spring morning I was walking across the parking lot to my red-brick apartment when I became aware of a "presence" behind me. I turned around, but there was no one there. My sense of the "presence" remained, however, and became still stronger. Although there was nothing perceptible to my physical senses, I knew there was someone standing beside me. I felt an overwhelming sense of security and well-being. Whoever this "presence" was, she or he was unimaginably loving and protective. The "presence" then "spoke" to me, not in physically audible words, but in a clear and powerful thought that filled my entire being with an energy and an awareness I had never known before and have rarely experienced since. The presence said simply, "You are on Earth to learn to love."

I stood still for a moment, serenely happy, conscious that the experience was an "unusual" one. Although at that age I did not have a conceptual framework in which to place the event, I knew that something important had just happened. I ran across the parking lot to my apartment, filled with an overwhelming happiness. Even at the age of five, I somehow sensed that I had been blessed with a rare and important experience. I never mentioned the experience to anyone, but filed it away, referring back to it in times of disappointment, loneliness and fear.

In my late teens, when I began to read spiritual and metaphysical literature, I came across the concept of a "guardian angel." I believe now that my guardian angel had drawn close to me, made me aware of its loving presence, and "communicated" that beautiful thought to my childhood mind. I believe that one reason I was given the experience was so that I would develop the conviction that the physical world was not the only reality. It was not until I was nineteen years old that I would again have a similar experience.

It was 1970, and American society was more deeply divided than at any time since the Civil War. The Viet Nam conflict was raging and claiming 250 American lives per week. The so-called "counter-culture" of the disenchanted sixties generation had begun to experiment in Eastern mysticism and "alternative lifestyles." The use of psychedelic drugs, marijuana, and a whole list of other "mind-altering" substances was epidemic, and had spilled over into the mainstream. I had smoked grass a couple of times during my freshman year at college. During the summer of 1969 I got high more frequently and took LSD for the first time at the Woodstock music festival in New York state. During my sophomore year at college, it seemed wherever I went someone was passing a pipe or rolling a "joint." I smoked grass or hashish nearly everyday. At the same time, I started to become interested in mystical spirituality. My psychology professor, a wonderfully intuitive educator named Richard Perls, played to us the taped lectures of Baba Ram Dass—formerly Richard Alpert of Harvard—who had just returned from his sojourn with a spiritual master in India. I knew there was another world, the world of the spirit, that was calling to me. Intuitions from my deeper self told me that I had to leave drugs behind if I wanted to truly live a more spiritual life, but I had become addicted to the experience.

In May of 1970, four students were killed by National Guardsmen who opened fire at an anti-war protest at Kent State University in Ohio. My friends and I were stunned. A huge protest was planned for the University of Maryland in College Park the next weekend. My life was about to change dramatically.

One morning that week I was in the Montgomery College cafeteria in Tacoma Park, Maryland. As I was walking slowly across the floor to leave the building, I was overcome with an awareness of the same benign "presence" that had visited me when I was a five-year-old boy near my home in Connecticut. The "presence" radiated extraordinary power, and again I "heard" a thought ring through my whole being. But this time the message was not so pleasant. "Find your direction or you will not remain on Earth much longer." I knew that the message had to do with discovering my task on Earth, and that it was a specific warning to stop using drugs. Although moved by the feeling of compassion that I sensed from the visiting "presence," who I believed was my angel, I was shaken and disturbed by the angel's warning.

That same week I had an unusually vivid and remarkable dream. In the dream I was riding an old bicycle—the first I had ever owned as a child—past my old high school. I was on the wrong side of the road and a huge truck was coming straight at me. I was unable to get out of the way of the truck and we collided violently. At the moment of "impact," I awoke from the dream, sweating and shaken. Although I had never read books on dream analysis, I knew intuitively what this dream was telling me: change my life direction or lose my life.

That Saturday afternoon I gathered with my friends at College Park for the anti-war protest. In the wake of the Kent State shootings, the mood of the crowd was restless and many people were angry. The National Guard was there in force and there was real danger of another tragic incident. Thousands of people of all ages and walks of life blocked off Route One. I sat in the road in a semicircle with some friends. A young man was playing guitar and someone passed a marijuana "joint" around the circle. With my recent vivid dream and the experience of the "angel presence" still strong in my mind, a sharp intuition told me not to partake. I suppressed the "still small voice," telling myself that one more time wouldn't matter. Moments after inhaling, I began to experience sensations I had never known from marijuana or any other drug. They were somewhat pleasurable, but accompanied by a touch of nausea. When the joint came around a second time I took another long inhale. Moments later, I knew I had made a mistake.

The feelings of nausea increased and became unbearable. I felt a dreadful pressure in my head. The sound of the guitar grated against every cell. Never had I felt so terrible. Shortly thereafter I passed out of external consciousness and entered an inner world of horrific darkness. I was certain that I had died and had entered the very pit of hell. It felt as if I was being ground up and pulverized into tiny fragments.

Slowly I rose from this dark region toward a place of greater light. The terrible feelings left me, although I still felt that I was in limbo, suspended between darkness and light, heaven and hell. Slowly I was drawn upward into the region of light, and as I entered this atmosphere I was engulfed in a sea of blissful happiness I had never known before.

After a brief time in this world of divine rapture, I lost consciousness completely. When I finally awoke, perhaps twenty minutes after the experience began, my friends were overjoyed, for they were afraid that I would never regain consciousness from my bizarre reaction to the joint, which had apparently been laced with some chemical. No one else had been adversely affected, but I am convinced that if I had taken another "hit," I would have died.

Since that time I have read dozens of books that describe the "classic" near-death experience. Although I wish I could say I encountered a "being of light" and had seen my entire life pass before my eyes, I must admit that my experience was different. But I did become aware—when I entered the region of light and happiness—of the "presence" that had come to me when I was five years old and had warned me just days earlier that I needed to "change my path."

I radically altered my life in the months following my brush with death. I became a vegetarian and began to read every book on spiritual matters I could find, from virtually all of the world's wisdom traditions. I was astonished to learn of an ancient tradition of enlightened philosophy, often called the sacred Mysteries. This stream of wisdom can be traced through the various civilizations of antiquity. With these discoveries, my life took on an exhilarating new meaning. I felt that we were on Earth to discover the divine in ourselves and create a sacred culture. With zealous enthusiasm I began to pray and meditate every day. Shortly before my twentieth birthday, I read the *Bhagavhad Gita*, the great spiritual epic of India, four times in a month. It felt as if a curtain was being opened before my eyes and I was discovering the spiritual world of light for which I hungered. I also read many classics of Christian mysticism, including *Dark Night of the Soul* by the Spanish mystic St. John of the Cross and the anonymously written, *Cloud of Unknowing*. I was profoundly impressed with these works. Although I didn't stop using marijuana and psychedelics overnight, within five months I no longer felt the desire for drugs. The practices of prayer and meditation had enabled me to stop. Although I did not define it as such then, I later realized this was an experience in soul alchemy—the process of inner transformation that changes us forever.

In the spring of 1971, I felt I needed to have the kind of mystical revelation I had been reading about. I decided to go into the forest by myself in hopes of having a transforming inner experience. As part of my preparation I gave away virtually all of my possessions other than some books, clothes and a minimum of equipment that I would need for camping. I then headed into the woods of Virginia and camped for several days, fasting, praying, and reading illuminating books, spending most of my time with *The Cloud Of Unknowing* and a tiny book containing all the words of Christ from the New Testament.

On the second day I heard a loud crashing in the woods. I had heard of the Native American practice of the vision quest, and was aware that during the traditional four-day vigil one was often visited by an animal, which became of great importance to one's life. Consequently, I wasn't sure if I should be amused or disappointed when I discovered my "power animal" was a large Virginia wild turkey.

The next day I had another visitor, this time a large tawny animal that I glimpsed through the screen of underbrush in front of me. The animal made a strange grumbling sound in its throat and slammed its front paw or hoof hard into the ground. It seemed a bellicose gesture, a sign that this creature didn't want me there. The frightening image of a mountain lion flashed in my mind, but I had never heard of one coming so far east.

Moments later a large stag deer with threatening antlers crashed through the underbrush just a few feet away from where I sat cross-legged on a blanket, then bounded into the woods. Although at first I didn't attach much importance to the animal visitations, their significance increased as time wore on. It was several years later that I discovered that in the Native American tradition, the turkey represents the "give-away." It symbolizes generosity and the ability to give of oneself, knowing that the universal supply will always bring you what you need. This seemed remarkable in light of the fact I had given away all my material possessions just days before leaving on my "vision quest" into the Virginia forest. I also discovered that a male deer was a symbol of strength and independence. Years later I learned that antlers and horns, whether they appear in symbolism or in art, represent the development of higher faculties of perception, the clairvoyant gifts of the spirit that exist potentially in all human beings. In retrospect I can see that these two animals in their symbolic natures have been significant throughout my entire life. "Giving" seems to me the essence of the fundamental moral law on which this universe rests. And my entire adult life has been an effort to awaken awareness of the deeper self, which leads to the unfolding of clairvoyant and intuitive gifts of spirit.

That summer, I hitchhiked across country from Maryland to California and back, having marvelous experiences and meeting extraordinary people along the way. Immediately upon my return to the East Coast, I made preparations to leave for Peru. I was intent on finding an ancient spiritual retreat, a veritable Mystery school, which I had read of in the unusual book, now out-of-print, entitled *Secret of the Andes* by Brother Philip. I journeyed with two friends, Ed and Charles.

That experience in the Andes deserves a book of its own, and in many ways became the inspiration for *Queen of the Sun*. My experience in the Andes left an indelible mark on my life and character. Driven by a desire to find a sacred culture—a community where people lived in harmony with each other and with nature—I was willing to leave everything I knew and risk my life on what proved to be a perilous quest. The effort of hiking in the high Andes for weeks at a time was both transformative and exhausting. Ed returned to the states first and my parents sent me a plane ticket about a month later. Charles intended to remain in Peru and continue his search for the valley. In the charming town of Juliaca, over fourteen thousand feet above sea level, I gave Charles the last of my money and hugged him goodbye.

During the next several months, I received several letters from Charles in which he described his experiences and the people he encountered. In particular, he mentioned a young woman named Sal, who was also in search of the valley and with whom he had met up. Then the letters from Charles abruptly stopped. I had a vague intuition that something unpleasant had happened to him.

That summer, while I was working in a natural foods restaurant in Washington, DC, called *YES!*, I gradually became aware of a peculiar phenomenon. On numerous occasions my attention was drawn to a particular, dark-haired young woman. I would see her walking along the streets, browsing in shops, even passing in cars. The experience was uncanny, for it was unusual to keep noticing the same person in a variety of places and situations in a sprawling city of more than a million people. It was as if I was being prepared to meet her. One day she and I actually met for the first time in *Yes!* We were astonished to learn that we had both recently returned from Peru. The shocker came when we finally exchanged names. She was Sal!

In a few breathless minutes I caught up on the events in Charles' life since I had left him in the high Andes several months earlier. To my dismay, I learned why the letters from Charles had abruptly ended. He had gone down a llama trail against the pleading of the Quechua Indian guide and the others in the group, which included Sal. Charles was never seen again.

Both Sal and I felt intuitively that Charles was no longer alive, but we needed confirmation. We had heard of a reputable medium who lived in Washington, not far from the Capitol building. We made an appointment to see her.

A stocky blondhaired woman with a German accent met us warmly at the door and ushered us into her apartment. Her name was Irmgard. She knew nothing about the reason for our visit and we had told her nothing about ourselves or about Charles. We sat at a small table and Irmgard said the Lord's Prayer, then entered into a meditative state, though remaining fully conscious. Within moments of my handing her Charles' letter she began to tell us in great detail exactly what had happened to him. She said Charles had stumbled on the trail and fallen to his death on the mountain side. He had died instantly and was "in the light." He was happy except for the fact that his parents missed him. He regretted leaving Earth without having healed his relationship with his father. Now his father was about to hire private detectives and organize a search for his missing son. Through the mediumship of Irmgard, Charles asked Sal and I to visit his parents and "tell them what had happened." Sal and I were absolutely convinced of the authenticity of the message. We were certain that we had spoken with Charles.

Visiting Charles' parents, whom we had never met before, was one of the most difficult things I have ever done. They were cordial and happy to meet two young people who had recently spent time with their missing son. It was obviously difficult for them to have lost contact with him. They were practicing Roman Catholics and we wished to respect their beliefs. We did not feel it appropriate to simply blurt out that "Charles had spoken to us" through a medium. In 1971, young people who professed to communicate with "spirits on the other side" were a rather suspect group. Nonetheless, we felt compelled to tell them our intuitions, now confirmed in the session with Irmgard, and to honor Charles' request to us through the medium. With as much delicacy as we could muster, we shared our conviction that Charles had "died," but was "alive and well" in the spiritual dimensions.

Years later, when I was living outside Rome, Italy, I was alone one autumn night in my apartment. As I sat at my desk, preparing lessons for the fifth grade class I was teaching in a small, English-speaking international school, I had a vivid sense of Charles' presence in the room. I felt that he wanted me to communicate with his parents. That night I wrote a long letter to his mother, stating again my conviction that Charles had left this Earth life while hiking in the Andes. I also expressed my beliefs that life on Earth was a reflection of the greater existence of which we are a part, and that in our soul and spiritual nature we can never die. Some months later I received a letter from her in which she thanked me and stated her intuition that Charles had indeed passed on. I also realized, in retrospect, that the night that I had been so filled with a sense of Charles' presence in my apartment was November first, the eve of All Soul's Day, the time when it is traditionally believed that the spirits of the departed are allowed to communicate with those on Earth.

Throughout my adult life I have felt close to the spiritual dimensions that interpenetrate the familiar world of the physical senses. For me the "real" and true world has always been the "hidden side"—the "higher realms" from which we have come. We live our earthly lives on the borderland of luminous eternity, yet much of our current civilization appears enmeshed in "outer darkness," ignorant of the great mystery. To transform our culture into an image of the sacred may be a daunting task, but the alternatives are not pleasant to contemplate.

In ancient times, special places were set aside by all cultures as focal points for the intersection of the spiritual world with the physical.

These were the temples and sacred sites. The Greek word for a shrine or temple is *temenos*. The modern world has had its sense of the sacred severely blunted by five centuries of progressive materialism. If our civilization is not to end in a series of dramatic convulsions, either man-made or natural, we will have to rekindle awareness of the sacred. The Earth is not a dirty ball hurtling blindly through meaningless space. Nor are we haphazard arrangements of chemicals. Science has yet to find a worthy explanation for the sublime intelligence that has organized the enormous complexity of life. In the age to come, it is likely that a new spiritual science will emerge as human beings unfold their innate capacities for spiritual perception. With these new faculties will come a new culture and a new civilization.

The task of humanity in the future will be to make living a sacred experience. The experience of *temenos*, of the sacred shrine or temple, will expand to include every aspect of daily life. We will discover the secret of bringing sacred elements into all that we do. When we live in accordance with the deeper truths, we infuse light and harmony into every area of life. Kindling a new sacred culture is the task of the future. To accomplish this great work we will need to build on the ancient wisdom or "primordial tradition," which teaches that humanity is an extension of a divine order of being.

In my personal quest for illumination and the creation of a better world, I have found that the ideas of alchemy provide a striking and practical metaphor for the work of personal and cultural transformation. Although alchemy suggests the pursuit of a formula for condensing gold, true alchemy is the quest for spiritual illumination. Alchemy is the art of soul transformation, of turning inner and outer darkness into light. Soul alchemy means bringing the sacred to life by infusing the spirit into our work and our play. It requires finding the balance between inner striving and practical efforts. It is not easy to find the golden thread of the sacred while living in an often harshly materialistic world. But it is possible when we discover and apply life's dynamic underlying principles. When we live these truths, we awaken our "hidden self," the sleeping giant of our immortal spirit.

In fact, our deeper self is already awake. The path of inner unfolding consists largely in shrugging off the cultural trance in which our personalities slumber. We dissolve the mist of illusion—the "cloud of unknowing"—that lies between our conscious mind and our "divine spark" when we comprehend and apply the eternal laws of sacred living. May the ideas in this book help readers discover the secrets of transformation and in so doing help them find their own "heaven on Earth."

PRAYER TO A GUARDIAN ANGEL

Be thou a shining star above me.
Be thou a shepherd to protect me.
Be thou a guiding light to lead me.
Be thou a rose of love within me.
Be thou a beauty shining through me.
Be above, below, beside, before, behind me.
Be all around about me.

– Traditional Celtic

CHAPTER ONE

THE ALCHEMY OF THE SEED

"As is the gardener, so is the garden."
– Jewish proverb

"Give and it shall be given unto you."
– Jesus

Thousands of years ago, many centuries before Christ, holy ones of India told a touching story. In the tale, the divine prophet Krishna tells his youthful friend, Narada, to fetch him a glass of water. Narada does as Krishna tells him, crosses an open field and knocks on the door of a farmer's house. An enchanting girl with almond eyes as deep as the night answers the door and invites Narada into her home. Narada is entranced by the loveliness of the girl, the eldest daughter of the household. One thing follows another and soon Narada asks for the young girl's hand in marriage. Her parents approve and a festive wedding ensues. Before long, Narada and his young bride have their own brood of beautiful children. Their sons and daughters grow up to be wealthy and powerful landowners, with many prosperous estates. The valley in which Narada lives is full of his relatives, all of whom shower him with honor and affection.

The idyllic beauty of his life is shattered when a terrible flood sweeps through the valley and destroys everything in its path. All of Narada's family, his beloved wife and all his wealth vanishes. Narada is left alone with his sorrow. As he stands on a hilltop, he hears someone chuckling behind him. Angrily, he turns to see who dares mock him in his grief. Astonished, he beholds Krishna, peacock feather in his hair, smiling kindly but with a gleam in his eye. "Narada," the prophet asks, "where is my glass of water?"

This tale speaks timelessly to the heart of the human condition. The sages of India remind us not to forget our purpose on Earth. Krishna represents the Godhead, the divine creative impulse that has impelled us into Earth experience. Like Narada, we have become entranced and have forgotten our mission and purpose. Many of us have scarcely a notion of what to be looking for. We have forgotten about "the glass of water." Might this be the same water of which Jesus spoke when he said to the woman at the well, "I will show you how to drink of water such that you will never thirst again?" Might Narada's forgotten water represent the *water of life,* the eternal wisdom which governs life?

Most people are unaware that they are unaware. Awakening itself is a mystery, a miracle of unfolding. Experience gently nudges us toward the threshold of deeper knowing. We cross that threshold as we discover that the world is less outside us than it is within us. This process of discovery and unfolding is the essence of alchemy.

Alchemy conjures mystery and magic. The medieval alchemists were famous for trying to change base metals, such as lead, into gold. This is not the true quest of alchemy, however—though some alchemists pursued this as a hobby. "Transforming base metals into gold" is a metaphor for the most dynamic and fundamental spiritual process— changing destructive thoughts, emotions and behavior patterns into luminous, loving ones. True alchemists worked less on external nature than on the "substance" of their own personalities. The treasure they sought was the "gold" of spiritual wisdom and illumination. Alchemy, then, refers to the science of human transformation. When we release the past and embrace new thought and emotional patterns, we are engaging in soul alchemy. Those who discover the secret of soul transformation grasp hold of an awesome and mysterious power. The medieval alchemists called this power the Philosopher's Stone. The Philosopher's Stone is an image of the inner magic that enables us to transform our lives. This power begins to work when we shift our feelings and thoughts from darkness to light, from bitterness to love. In an ancient tale from *The 1001 Arabian Nights,* this power was symbolized in the image of Aladdin's Lamp.

FINDING ALADDIN'S LAMP

An old man at the end of his years sits and rummages through the mementos and artifacts of his life. Gazing at old letters, papers and photographs, he becomes increasingly wistful. Tears fill his eyes. He feels that despite the richness of his experience, some secret of happiness has eluded him. He cannot shake the heavy sense of emptiness— almost a feeling of despair—of having missed out on some essence or insight into life that could have brought fulfillment.

An image comes to the old man of one of his favorite boyhood stories, the tale of Aladdin and his magical lamp. "If only such a lamp had actually existed!" he laments. Perhaps then, if he had found such a lamp, his fondest dreams would have been achieved. The old man never realized that such a lamp was always within his reach.

So many go through life as if asleep or in a dream, unaware of the deeper laws and principles upon which life is organized. As the years pass, the regret and bitterness accumulate. This may be the dark side of our vaunted "age of information." There is such an overwhelming outpouring of disconnected "facts" that it is easy for the essential truths to get lost in our culture's information labyrinth.

Like the old man in the above example, each of us has within our grasp an Aladdin's lamp of limitless power. Those who discover this power gain the secret of alchemy—the ability to revolutionize the conditions of life. What is this mythic force, this "Philosopher's Stone," with which we may fashion the world of our dreams?

Modern physics claims that our galaxy came into being through the activity of "super novas," the mysterious birth of stars. The physical matter of which our bodies are made—the atomic elements of which our organisms are composed—originated in these fiery nuclear reactions within stars. In our physical constitution we are literally "star dust." Paralleling this material view of modern science, the wisdom of the ancient teachings of both Western and Eastern spirituality state that each individual is endowed with a "divine spark"—a spiritual flame fashioned from the primordial Light by those creative Spirits who brought the universe into being.

The lamp of the old man's dreams represents this extraordinary power hidden away within our minds and souls. The genie of the lamp signifies the spiritual spark, which is the core essence of all individuals. Socrates, the wise Athenian philosopher who gave so much to civilization, called this deeper self his "daimon." St. Paul described it as "Christ in us, the hope of glory." Today this spiritual spark is called by some the *higher self* or "indwelling presence." Regardless of the terms we use, this mysterious core identity is the source of life, energy, love and power, which lights all human beings that come into the world. **The way to invoke the genie of the lamp lies in the way we live.** Each person holds the key of destiny in his or her hands. When we discover and apply the secrets of soul alchemy, not only do we transform our own lives, but we become emissaries of a culture based on the laws of love and light that underlie the world.

Divine Law versus Human Laws

Despite the many conflicting views regarding an ultimate Higher Power in the cosmos, it is obvious that a remarkable intelligence has organized the world. The universe in which we live is fashioned out of a profound genius and a measureless love. There is an underlying wisdom in life—a system of celestial laws or principles not created by humans—which all of us may discover if we so desire. These are the laws of our own being and are the building blocks of the manifested universe.

Running throughout history like a golden thread is the enlightened conviction that there is a higher law—sometimes called natural law or cosmic law—that organizes and disposes life. Humanity's best thinkers consistently affirm that human law, to be just, ought to reflect as much as possible these benign guiding principles that are the foundation of the physical world. In 1750 an American clergyman named Jonathan

Mayhew delivered a sermon that had tremendous influence in shaping the thinking of the time. John Adams said that it was "read by everyone." In the sermon Mayhew affirmed that there was a higher, transcendent moral law that was woven into the very fabric of life. This law came from the Creator and was above laws devised by human beings. Mayhew's ideas were a restatement of an ancient belief—that there is a moral code, or underlying law, implicit in life. Religion is essentially an effort to identify and live by these higher principles—laws not made by humans, but woven by higher beings into the fabric of the universe. We cannot alter these laws, only discover and align ourselves with them.

Man-made political laws are called *statutes*, meaning *regulations*. Statutes are often created to protect or benefit special interest groups and may have little or nothing to do with the higher laws that govern life. This realization by the founders of American government led to the Bill of Rights, which sought to insure individual liberties and guarantee freedom from tyranny. It may even be the moral position to willfully break oppressive and unethical political statutes, as demonstrated in the lives of Henry David Thoreau, Gandhi and Martin Luther King.

But no one may break the higher divine laws with impunity. Unlike statutes made by legislative bodies, these are the laws and principles that are the underpinning to creation. If we disregard these principles in our behavior, we will eventually suffer the consequences. When we live in accordance with these higher laws, although it may take time, we benefit and prosper.

No doubt, Cosmic Intelligence would like us to succeed—to be healthy, happy and fulfilled. But the universe will not simply give us what we want without effort on our part. We are free to create the kind of life we desire, but there is a price to pay. The universe demands that we live in harmony with the essential principles that govern life. A magical awakening takes place in all those who aspire to comprehend these open secrets of nature.

THE ESSENTIAL LAW OF LIFE = THE ALCHEMY OF THE SEED

Nature is lavish in her lessons. She displays the truths of life in the open book of her countless manifestations. The living book of nature contains more eloquence than all the libraries of the world. In the presence of nature's rhythms and cycles, we contemplate the mysteries of existence. The sacred laws of life are revealed in the script of natural events. The fundamental law of life has been given many names. Perhaps the most descriptive is simply *the law of the seed.*

No other manifestation of nature's creative process so perfectly displays the miracle of alchemy as does the unfolding of a seed. From a tiny hard kernel—looking to untutored observation like a lifeless stone or pebble—a new plant springs into existence. The light and warmth of the sun beckon the hidden life-force within the seed to germinate and come forth. A tender sprout pushes outward into the soil. Soon a pair of leaves emerge in the air, turning toward the light. With the right combination of the elements—of water, air, earth and sun—the miracle unfolds. From a simple seed emerges a flowering plant. Through nature's mysterious alchemy, a fragile acorn becomes in time a majestic oak.

In like manner, each of us has a spirit-seed within our souls—an unquenchable divine spark. Just as an acorn might never dare imagine that it could become an oak, so do we fail to comprehend the awesome creative might within us. Yet if we provide the proper "elements" in the form of inspired thoughts, warm feelings and constructive activity, we find that we begin to blossom in the sacred garden of our limitless potential. Perhaps life's profoundest secret—the most sacred revelation—is that each of us is an immortal spirit-seed manifesting through physical embodiment. Our spirit-self is the dynamic seed-potential of our being. We unfold the potential of our spirit through action in life.

Through nature's artful language, the law of the seed teaches us how best to live our lives. Gardeners were, perhaps, the first philosophers. They contemplated the mystery of the seed. They drew conclusions from the wisdom of nature's school of life. Gardeners understood that they can only harvest what they have first planted. They knew that it is no use bemoaning fate if there are no carrots to harvest at the end of the growing season. If they want carrots, they must plant them. Thus they gained insight into the laws of the soul. As it is in the garden, so it is in life.

Each life is like a garden, and we can only reap what we have sown. Our experiences are a fertile field in which we are always planting seeds. The seeds we sow each day in the soil of our lives are our thoughts, words, feelings, decisions and deeds. Just as gardeners can only harvest what they have first planted, so can we only take out of our lives what we have put into them. The kinds of seeds we sow will determine the harvest.

The alchemy of the seed reveals the law of causation. Our harvest is the consequence of our planting. Our lives bear the fruits of the seeds we sow. In physics this law is expressed as Newton's third law of motion: for every action there is an equal reaction—equal in force and opposite in direction. Our deeds set up a current, a force, that first influences the world around us. Thereafter, there flows a reciprocal current or force that enters our personal life experience. Like a boomerang, what we give out, comes back.

Action does not mean physical action only. Whenever we think, feel or speak, we set in motion the delicate mechanism of reciprocity. Thus we are always planting seeds. If not with our hands, then with our minds and our hearts, our words and our decisions. In the short term, our behavior impacts those around us. In the end, our deeds come home to roost. We receive into our lives the very currents we ourselves have released into the ocean of existence.

For every action, there is a consequence; every decision we make leads to a whole string of ensuing events. Every deed plants a seed, every consequence of action is the fruit of the seed. Sowing and reaping are linked together as two aspects of the same operation. Everything we receive in life is directly connected to the forces we have set in motion by what we do. All reaping is a direct consequence of the actions of head, heart and hands. All that we obtain in life is rooted in our behavior. The first step in soul alchemy is to sow seeds that bring a harvest of light.

Maturity in life begins when we start to take responsibility for the circumstances in which we find ourselves. This is no easy task, for as one wit put it, "To err is human, to blame others is even more human." We step onto the path of wisdom when we take charge of our own affairs. Truly, there is no one to blame. No matter how rough or how peaceful the seas, each one of us guides the rudder that steers our ship through life.

WE LIVE IN A UNIVERSE OF LIGHT

Modern physics is beginning to corroborate what sages taught in the temples of ancient times, that our universe is a universe of light. Quantum physics now recognizes that matter is really the energy of light in a more condensed or "concrete" form. Physicist Davis Bohm says that "All matter is frozen light." We live in a light wave universe. Knowing this, it is easier to comprehend what the ancients taught— that all things are recorded in the light-sensitive ethers.

There exists everywhere a delicate recording mechanism, a subtle luminous membrane that interpenetrates all things physical. Upon this sensitive layer or energy field—called the *quintessence* by ancient Greek philosophers, *akasha* in Sanskrit, and "the Book of God's Remembrance" in the Bible—all thoughts, feelings, words and actions are imprinted, just as you leave footprints when you walk on the beach. The universe records all things and keeps a just account of all our sowing and reaping throughout time. We might think of this subtle recording mechanism as a kind of universal bookkeeping system, which records infallibly every transaction of our lives. The condition of our "account" will determine our circumstances, including the status of our relationships and the level of our prosperity.

In the East, the balance of one's account is called *karma*. The word karma comes from a Sanskrit root, *kriya*, meaning action. Karma is the sum of the consequences of our actions from the dawn of our existence. In the West we call it destiny, fate, or fortune. If you don't like where "the wheel of fortune" has stopped, you can give it another turn. It is not a frozen wheel. No one ever condemns another person to an unhappy life. Each of us pronounce our own sentence. If you feel that life has dealt you a bad hand, you may deal yourself a new hand. You can start to create better conditions now by setting in motion currents of constructive force through positive, helpful thoughts and acts.

Knowledge of this dynamic truth is an essential element in the "Philosopher's Stone," the long-sought magic talisman that transforms us. It may not instantly turn lead to gold, but it can begin to transform our lives from dullness and frustration to expectation and success. By comprehending and applying this principle, we can establish our lives on a new footing and free ourselves from the negativity of the age that is dying.

WE ARE THE SOURCE OF OUR EXPERIENCES

Virtually everyone falls short of their ideal of what, or *who*, they'd like to be. Our culture puts such an emphasis on external beauty that nearly everybody feels a bit *less than* on occasion. Most women aren't naturally drop-dead gorgeous. Most men resemble Moe, Larry or Curly more closely than a heart throb from the soaps. But the source of life experience is within us. Not only does intelligence spring from within, so also do authentic beauty, spiritual understanding, and—ultimately—happiness. It has been said that happiness is an inside job. The same may be said for beauty, intelligence and success—however we may define them. They are all "inside jobs." When we change our thoughts, feelings and attitudes, we change our life experience from within. Those fortunate individuals who truly grasp and embrace the alchemical secret of the law of the seed gain the power to completely transform their health, their finances, their relationships, their career and their spiritual understanding. An acquaintance of mine turned his fortunes around by applying this principle.

Tom's life had spun out of control as a result of his drinking and his habitual negativity. He lost his job and his wife left him. Nobody liked to be around him for he seldom had a good word to say about anything. He was in a downward spiral when he wandered into the public library one day to get out of the rain. He fell to reading the classic book by James Allen, *As a Man Thinks*, which a friend had once recommended. He spent the entire day absorbing the book, then bought a copy of his own the next day. He was so influenced by the book's message that he arranged with a bookstore to buy fifty copies at a discount. These he began to give away to people on the street, in stores, to whomever he got in a conversation with. Through Alcoholics Anonymous he began getting sober, and as a result of his reversal in attitude, he gradually reversed his fortunes. He volunteered his time helping out in a bookstore and soon got a job there. When I knew him, it was difficult to imagine the straits in which he had once been trapped, for he was widely admired and respected for his sincerity and generosity. Tom learned that the alchemy of the soul begins as we comprehend and apply the law of the seed.

The law of the seed is life's central and most dynamic principle. Without a comprehension of this truth, life is a bewildering maze of haphazard and unrelated accidents—all "sound and fury, signifying nothing." A knowledge of this truth is the golden thread that can lead one out of the labyrinth of ignorance, into the clear light of understanding. Our thoughts, intentions and deeds in the present have value and importance for all time to come. Regardless of where we find ourselves in the stream of life, we can begin now to remold ourselves in the image of our idealism by applying the law of the seed.

We Master the Law of the Seed by Giving

When my wife, Mia, and I started our first bookstore in California, it was the realization of a dream. Nevertheless, the first few months were a harsh awakening. We had very little capital and virtually nothing to spend on advertising. Business was slow. In desperation, I liquidated our IRA accounts and sold the few gold coins I had just to keep the business going. Every morning at four a.m., I drove across the San Francisco Bay to deliver bagels for five hours before opening the store so that we would have some spendable income. When I had to leave this part-time job due to exhaustion, we had no real personal income, for every penny the store made went to pay bills or buy new inventory. When I applied for a bank loan, the loan officer literally laughed in my face. With an infant child and house payments, it seemed our dream was about to become a nightmare. That's when Lee entered our life.

Lee came into the store as a customer and became one of our best friends. He was tall, strong and kind, with deep blue eyes and a ready smile. He was one of the most gentle men I've ever met. Mia and I called him "our angel" because he was incredibly supportive and helpful in those difficult times when we were just getting the business on its feet. When he sensed that we were a little discouraged, he would always have positive words and solid practical advice.

If we needed help moving things around, Lee would always be there. If we needed boxes opened, (we still couldn't afford employees), he would cheerfully volunteer. One of his practical suggestions was to give customers a free gift with every purchase. So we started to give little pieces of amethyst, rose quartz or carnelian—even sticks of incense—along with every purchase over ten dollars. Within a year, we had a flourishing business with a loyal and appreciative clientele.

Until we sold the store to move to Arizona, Lee always seemed to be there when we needed someone to help out. He had a knack for making the ordinary sacred. Lee lovingly applied the law of the seed in virtually all he did.

The law of the seed is the law of reciprocal action. This law becomes the soul's transforming power when we acquire the attitude and habit of giving. Soul alchemy is the miracle of our own unfolding that comes as we give from our hearts. Giving is the happy habit, the victorious addiction that sets us free. In the game of life, givers win and takers lose. The hand that gives, gains. The winning strategy is the generous strategy.

As a consequence of this fundamental law of life, it follows that our environment and affairs are the result of the sum of our giving-ness throughout all the years of our existence. Those who take more than they give are living on borrowed time. Eventually the piper must be paid. It may appear that the selfish and deceitful prosper while the industrious and generous fail to make progress. But this is a tempo-rary condition. In the alchemy of reciprocity, everyone must eventual-ly experience the consequences of their actions. Giving with a spirit of love multiplies the good that comes into our lives. "There are those who have but little and give it all," wrote Kahlil Gibran. "These are the believers in life and the bounty of life, and their coffer is never empty."

An Ancient Lesson in the Magic of Reciprocity

From ancient Rome comes a charming story that artfully captures the magic of reciprocity. Two thousand years ago in Egypt, a youth named Androcles is a slave, the property of a cruel landowner named Casca. Loving freedom above all else, young Androcles plots his escape. Late one starry night he makes a daring getaway, hiding out in fields, swamps and forests as he travels toward unknown western lands. Closely followed by bounty hunters, he takes refuge in a dismal cave. To his horror, he finds out that the cave is the dwelling of a ferocious lion, who confronts Androcles in the fading evening light. Instead of devouring Androcles, the lion holds out its massive paw, in which is embedded a painful thorn. Trembling with fear, Androcles removes the thorn and the beast gratefully licks the fortunate youth in the friendliest lion fashion.

The lion and boy spend several weeks together before soldiers stumble upon Androcles in a field. They take him back to Egypt, where he is eventually returned to his master, Casca. As punishment, Casca sells Androcles to Roman slave traders and after months of hardship he is taken to Rome. His fate is sealed when he is selected to be fodder for lions as a spectacle in the Coliseum. On the fateful day, guards lead Androcles into the arena and leave him to die in front of the bloodthirsty crowd. A gate is flung open and a lion rushes toward Androcles. To the crowd's astonishment, the beast stops dead in its tracks, then rolls and plays at Androcles' feet. The trembling youth recognizes the very lion from whose paw he had removed the painful thorn. The Romans are moved by the spectacle and Androcles is given his freedom. He receives the lion as a gift from the emperor himself, and the lion and the lad live out their days together as honored residents of Rome.

As this lovely tale illustrates, the good we do returns to us, often in ways marvelous and unexpected.

WHEN WE ACT, THE UNIVERSE RESPONDS

Many people have an intellectual comprehension of the sacred law of sowing and reaping. Yet for this understanding to work its transforming magic we must absorb it in our hearts and express it in our deeds. Living the law of the seed requires discernment in our thoughts so that we anticipate the consequences of our behavior before we act. "In every affair," advised the Greek philosopher, Epictetus, "consider what precedes and what follows."

East Indian mythology illustrates this pictorially. Saraswati, the beautiful goddess of wisdom, is often accompanied by a swan. According to tradition, the swan is able to separate milk from water as she drinks from a bowl containing both liquids. This represents the faculty of discrimination in action—perceiving in advance the consequences of our deeds—one of the hallmarks of enlightened living. By exercising discernment, we can plow the fields of life wisely and plant seeds that bring a joyful harvest. If not, we may all too often "sow the wind and reap the whirlwind."

One of the most charming and well-liked people I know is a woman named Marie, who never goes anywhere empty-handed. She is always writing cheerful cards, giving gifts or flowers, or taking fresh baked goods to her friends and acquaintances. Marie gives spontaneously and lovingly, not because she hopes to receive something in return, but because she loves to make other people happy. She exemplifies the highest attitude in giving: that we give not with personal gain in mind, but as a spontaneous outpouring of the heart. As a result of her loving and generous approach to life, Marie's own life is full of love. She has mastered the first principle of living a sacred life—the secret of the seed, the power of giving.

The alchemy of the seed is mastered as we learn how to give. Every gift carries the seed of its fruition, returning ultimately to enrich the one who gives. In order to receive benefits in life, our actions must provide benefits to others. We improve our conditions mentally, physically and spiritually in direct proportion to the manner in which we have assisted those around us. We are the recipients of the forces we ourselves originate in the stream of life. The more we give of all that is good, the more of all that is good will flow into our lives. Ultimately, we give to ourselves and we withhold from ourselves. Suffering is self-inflicted, happiness is self-bestowed.

The most valuable gifts spring from the selfless and loving human spirit. They may be so subtle—or perhaps even commonplace—that the one who gives may be unaware that he or she is giving. The mother who lovingly teaches her child how to make something, the father who plays wholeheartedly with his children, the teacher who carefully crafts a lesson or passes on a skill, or the stranger who dispels the shadow of depression with a funny or inspiring tale; these are gifts of measureless value. A kind word or a helpful thought may be of far greater significance than a monetary or material gift. The point is that everyone can give something, even if it only be their prayers, which may be the most valuable gift of all.

A knowledge of this truth bestows great power, but it would be a mistake to approach the practice of giving as a kind of "bargaining with God." We should examine our intent in giving. Our generosity should truly benefit those to whom we give and not be simply to make ourselves feel good. Nor should it make others dependent and weak. Misplaced charity can turn people into unproductive parasites—lazy and ungrateful—who think society owes them something. Charitableness that is egotistical in nature—that is prompted by a desire to appear superior or to curry favor—is tainted and devalued. To make a spectacle of giving, or using it as an attempt to bribe people or buy favors, is to diminish the good that comes from it. Giving that is manipulative or that has strings attached is not true giving. One way to eliminate egotism in giving is, whenever possible, to give anonymously. The highest value in a gift is the love that prompts it.

Giving does not mean becoming emotionally or physically drained, sacrificing time that you really need for yourself, or being somebody's doormat. It is not a call for martyrdom or overnight sainthood. The impressive literature that has grown up around the issue of codependency provides eloquent testimony that there is a wrong way to give. What is emphasized here is a primordial fact of nature, an existential law established not by human caprice, but by divine authority. When we act, the universe reacts. As we give, the universe gives back. If my life is less than satisfactory, to find the cure I must first look in the mirror.

Breathing is nature's image of a healthy approach to the concept of giving. Just as the lungs cannot always expel air, but have to inhale after each outbreath, so do we need to know when to seek our own restoration and renewal. If the atmosphere—the air and sky—did not draw water from the oceans and the soil through evaporation, it would have no rain to give back to the Earth.

Times of recreation and personal renewal are essential if we are to have anything worthwhile to offer·others. We need to know when to take care of ourselves. One of life's greatest pleasures is to be able to enjoy solitude. Solitude and quiet time are necessary if we are to have strength for life and for giving.

THE GREATEST GIFTS ARE NOT MATERIAL

Regardless of intentions, there is only so much one can do to help people externally. The spiritual teacher, Mikhael Aivanhov learned this as a boy. While growing up in Varna, Bulgaria, he and a boyhood companion became friends with an old beggar who sat in front of the Church of the Holy Trinity. The two boys decided they would help the old man. They persuaded the director of an "old folk's home" to take in the aging vagrant. The boys were proud of their humanitarian act as they led the old man to his new home. Soon he was shaved, washed, fed and given new clothes. They could hardly recognize him. Several weeks later they came upon an old beggar in the familiar spot in front of the Church of the Holy Trinity. Coming closer, they realized to their surprise that it was the same man they had befriended. He kindly explained to the boys that he preferred his life outside the confines of the old folk's home. He felt free and happy begging in front of the Church. This anecdote illustrates the limitations of "helping people on the outside." Only as individuals improve their inner life will their external conditions change for the better.

The most important gift we can bring to others is the effort we make to improve ourselves. "If the rose adorns itself," wrote the poet, Goethe, "does it not also adorn the garden?" Self-education and personal development are the foundation for the expression of service. We cannot remove dirt from someone else's eye if our own hands are soiled. To heal and help others, we must first heal and help ourselves. The soul's innate impulse is to evolve into something greater. Far more valuable than any material gifts are the benefits that flow to others through the progress we ourselves make toward the light of wisdom. Every new skill we gain, every new insight we discover, becomes a building block in the creation of our own temple of expanding life. When we grow and expand as persons, we weave light into the fabric of our souls. Like the caterpillar that becomes a butterfly, we give our most precious gift as we change ourselves for the better.

WE GIVE THROUGH THE RADIANCE OF OUR INNER LIFE

The forces we set in motion by our actions develop a mysterious momentum all their own. The universal fabric of life is a seamless tapestry and the causes we originate by our deeds extend outward in all directions, much as a pebble tossed into a pond creates widening ripples. We do not know how far-reaching the effects of our giving will be. We might think of this as the "domino effect" of all action. Our deeds in life have consequences far beyond those of which we become aware.

When camping in the mountains with his students, the Bulgarian mystic and saint, Peter Deunov, would tell them to pour water on a stone or plant, for no apparent reason. In this way he tried to make them aware that even seemingly insignificant gestures have ongoing effects and far-reaching influences—that everything in the subtle web of life is interconnected. Modern physics calls this web of life the "unified field." We are all creating ripples in the same "pond."

To comprehend the full significance of the law of the seed, we must realize that our thoughts and feelings are as real and enduring as any physical action. Not only what we do, but *who we are* is constantly setting forces in motion that return to us in the form of experiences, circumstances and conditions. To grasp this fact, we must realize that our physical body is only a fraction of our total self. Our personality manifests through a web of feelings, thoughts and emanations that create a force field around us—our personal "energy field," or aura. The nature of our emanations—the full spectrum of one's inner life and external actions at any given time—sets up a "resonance" that stimulates a sympathetic response from the universal life in which we are imbedded. Our consciousness at any moment elicits a vibratory response or current from the larger life in which we live. This current flows into our lives as a sense of well-being or otherwise, depending on the quality of the force we emanate from our thoughts and moods. We give out constantly, not only through physical gestures and the performance of "service," but by every impulse of our inner lives.

The path of happiness and sacred living begins with a comprehension of the alchemy of the seed. When we become benefactors—literally, "doers of good,"—our own life will be gradually transformed for the better. Each helpful, generous action—each good thought and sacred feeling—becomes a seed planted in the garden of our personal well-being. In time, we will be astonished and delighted at the harvest of abundance that comes streaming into our personal world.

In the age to come, to be miserly, greedy or selfish will be seen as a form of illness that blocks the circulatory flow of abundance and blessing. Giving will become a science and an art. In the words of the saintly American spiritual teacher, Hilda Charlton, "A life is worthless that does not reach out a helping hand to others."

From deep within us comes the impulse to become greater and better. Our deeper self—the spirit-seed in our hearts—prompts us on our journey of transformation. The motivating principle at the heart of the spirit-seed is desire. The essence of this desire is love. As we manifest love through our actions, we come to know that our essential nature, the seed of our spirit, is love itself. By expressing love in our actions and our thoughts, we gradually come to know the truth of our being—that we are love. The greatest gift we can offer is the radiance of heart that springs from our contact with the divine in ourselves and the world. They give the most who radiate the light of understanding in their minds and the warmth of love in their hearts. When our actions are imbued with wisdom and love, we walk in harmony with the sacred laws that govern life. We become emissaries for a new culture of light and beauty on the Earth.

We begin to live a sacred life when we start to become a source of blessing through our actions. As we apply the dynamic power of the alchemy of the seed, we set in motion the wheels of a better life. A transformation takes place in our inner life of thought and feeling. The wisdom of reciprocity becomes the key to our own soul's liberation. In time, we will reap the harvest of our sacred seeds and life will crown each of us the master of our personal destiny.

Exercises in Sacred Living:
Activating the Alchemy of the Seed.

Activity Number One

For one week perform the following experiment: Every day think of at least a half dozen actions that you can perform that will enhance your own and other people's lives. These can be any constructive deed: writing a cheerful letter, cleaning out closets and giving charitable donations of clothes you no longer need or use, surprising a friend with a gift, taking someone to lunch, smiling at all the children you see. Keep a record of your sowing. Make a note of each "seed." Consider them as deposits in your heavenly treasury, the balance of which will determine your future circumstances. Get into the habit of releasing constructive currents into the ocean of life. Give those you meet a "flower," even if it be only in the form of a kind thought. Remember that thoughts, words, and feelings are also seeds. Become a benefactor to those you contact. Begin now to recreate the garden of your life; transform your future by applying the magic of the seed.

Activity Number Two

Think of something that you have always dreamed of doing, but for some reason never have. Perhaps it is visiting Europe, spending a week in Acapulco, or taking a voyage on a cruise ship. Or perhaps you've been meaning to enroll in an art or drama class at the junior college, go on a wilderness vision-quest, or climb a nearby mountain. Make a commitment to doing something that will bring you pleasure and expand you as a person. Think of it is a gift of love to yourself. Remember that as we become more generous in our lives, we expand our own consciousness of deserving.

Affirmations

"Giving opens the way for receiving. I master the law of the seed by giving constructively to all who can benefit by my actions."

"I transform my life into a beautiful garden by sowing positive seeds each day."

"The more I give to others of that which is beneficial and helpful, the more I will receive."

CHAPTER TWO

THE ALCHEMY OF THINKING

"What a man thinketh, that is he; this is the eternal mystery.
...Man becomes that which he thinks."

– *The Upanishads*

"There is nothing fashioned by man that is not first
fashioned by his thoughts."

– Joan Grant, *Winged Pharaoh*

One day a man of about sixty came into our book shop. I greeted him and told him that if he needed any help would he please let me know. He paused a moment, then with a half smile and a gleam in his eye replied, "All I need is a sack of jewels and a second chance."

I loved his response, and have always felt that those few words speak volumes about the human condition. Virtually all of us would like to have a "sack of jewels" with which to "finance" our lives, whether we conceive of those "jewels" as being in the form of money, health, position, beauty, education or talent. And virtually everyone would like to be able to relive certain experiences or periods of life, for nearly all of us carry regrets or feel that we've "botched" at least a few things along our path.

Soul alchemy teaches us that the greatest "jewels" and the most valuable treasures in life are not of a material nature. They are the insights and understanding—the gems of wisdom—that we gain through living. They are a comprehension of the sacred laws and principles that govern life, the "pearls beyond price" of higher understanding.

Though it's true we can't go back into the past and relive our lives again—except in our imagination—we can begin anew each moment to fashion the kind of future we want. It's never too late to begin applying the truths that make life sacred. In Tennyson's poem *Ulysses*, the aged hero embarks on another quest. Ulysses stands on the deck of his ship, still seeking wisdom and adventure. Bidding his shipmates to strike the oars, he passionately tells them that "It's not too late to seek a newer world." We can find this new world when we realize that we are both captain and navigator of our ship through life. We "set our sails" by the habitual trend of our thoughts. We direct our progress by the goals and ideals that prompt us.

THE SOURCE OF ALL EXPERIENCE

"I am not all contained between my hat and my boots," wrote Walt Whitman, expressing his conviction that the source of his consciousness and power was within his deeper self—of which his physical body was the outer expression. The poet's intuition has now been confirmed by modern science. In the words of Max Planck, the famed physicist, "Mind is the matrix of all matter." His statement supports one of the fundamental assertions of the ancient wisdom—all things in the universe have been shaped by mind.

One of the great discoveries of the new science is that human beings do not stand outside of nature as some kind of uninvolved observers. According to the famous Heisenberg Principle of quantum physics, our observation of events *influences* those events. We are not

hallpark; we are playing in the game. Ours is a partici-
participate by our very presence and perception.
's creates circumstances. Awareness is power.

led on the realization that the origin of
e's consciousness. It is absolutely essential
ner world of thought and feeling creates
onment and relationship. The nature of
ne the kind of experiences you draw to
's possible when we perceive the inde-
sness and circumstances.

Ms. Cindy Lepzinski
6140 Puma Pt.
Littleton, CO 80124

show that our inner, subjective world
or conditions our perception of life and events.
Take the example of four people hiking together in a forest. One is
completely absorbed in personal problems; all he can think about is
a recent argument with his girlfriend. He barely notices the forest at
all. Another constantly complains about the dampness, the insects,
the possibility of wild animals; for her it is a miserable experience. A
third hiker observes the trees and speculates to himself the number of
board feet of lumber in each, and how much profit could be made by
logging the forest for timber. The last companion is absorbed in poetic admiration of the magnificent plants and vegetation. She is transported into a reverie of wonder and admiration at nature's splendor—awed by the vista of teeming life. The experience of each hiker is
the result of his or her inner life of consciousness. Hence the saying
of the Indian teacher Hari Dass Baba: "If a pickpocket meets a saint,
he sees only his pockets." Our ideas, attitudes and beliefs condition
our perceptions.

Although we often tend to be preoccupied with sensory stimulation, we actually spend most of our waking life immersed in our
thoughts, moods and emotions. Only a small portion of our total
being lives exclusively in the physical world. The life of the senses is
only a fraction of experience, while our inner world of consciousness
is where we encounter our true selves. If you examine yourself closely,
you will see that you spend much of your life in your consciousness—
in the inner experience of thoughts, sentiments, moods and imagination. In this sense we might truly say that we live in our souls.

Mind Is the Womb of Creation

Socrates, the great Athenian philosopher, said that "The unexamined life is not worth living." Self-knowledge begins as we become conscious of our inner lives. The first step on the road to enlightenment and sacred living is to become aware of the thoughts that pass through our minds. The alchemy of personal growth and life improvement—our path of illumination—originates in the awareness of our thoughts and feelings, which are the building materials of life.

Our spiritual progress accelerates when we become present in our thoughts. Our thoughts and feelings are like a river—a stream of consciousness. If the current is muddy, we cannot see to the depths. As we watch our thoughts, clarifying our mental images, the stream becomes clear—the psychic "flotsam and jetsam" is dispersed. With awareness comes the ability to gently guide the stream of our thinking. Gradually we learn to see to the depths, to the ground of our being.

Nonetheless, soul alchemy requires more of us than merely watching our inner states. We must apply a "higher temperature" to the ingredients of the inner life. Fire was an indispensable ingredient in traditional alchemy. Those who would be alchemists of the soul ignite a "fire" in their minds in order to spark the process of transformation. Our desire to remold ourselves is the spark that ignites our inner fires. Our wish to grow as individuals continually feeds our spiritual aspiration. As we seek to live a sacred life, the fire of our spirit "raises the temperature" in our mind. As a result, our thoughts increase in intensity, clarity and power. Sacred influences stream into us from a world of inspiration of which we formerly knew nothing. Our activities in the world take on new color and meaning. Through the presence of sacred elements in our mind, we begin to have a beneficial influence in the world.

An exact explanation of how the mind shapes substance is beyond the scope of this book. The essential thing is to acknowledge that it does. A striking image of this process comes from Indian mythology. The god Vishnu is asked by Indra, the king of the gods, to create a potion that will grant eternal life. Vishnu sets about stirring up the vast Ocean of Milk. Out of the milk come all manner of marvelous creations—extraordinary gems, an elephant, a wish-fulfilling tree and cow, a magnificent white horse. Finally the beautiful goddess, Lakshmi, emerges—created from Vishnu's churning of the cosmic ocean. Lakshmi becomes Vishnu's consort and the two are virtually inseparable.

In this story, milk is a symbol of the life force. The Ocean of Milk is the universal etheric sea out of which manifest existence springs. Vishnu's churning of the ocean represents the process of thinking and imagination. Out of this activity come material forms. The eventual result of right thinking is the birth of wisdom within us, represented by the goddess, Lakshmi. The marriage of love and wisdom—of Vishnu and Lakshmi—leads to eternal life.

Although this mythological imagery deals with gods and goddesses—beings of the divine world—the same principles of creation apply in our lives also. When you think, you "churn" the subtle "ocean of existence," creating "divinities" or "monsters," depending upon the nature of your thoughts. Thus, your thinking is the point of origin for what comes into your life. If your thoughts are positive, they will produce positive, beneficial effects. In other words, if you think wisely and lovingly, you will constantly create your own miracles. You will be fashioning the conditions in your mind for a life on Earth of happiness, fulfillment and love. Those who learn to guide their thinking, find that everything else starts to fall into place.

To become alchemists, we must apply the sacred law of the seed in the realm of thinking. Our minds are a fertile garden and each thought is a seed. A seed-thought takes root and begins to sprout, grow, and eventually produce fruit of its own kind. A successful gardener is selective in his or her use of seeds. This enables one to gain command of thoughts, focusing on the positive and constructive ones. Conscious gardeners need to nurture the beneficial plants and weed out the harmful ones. This means "taking hold" of our inner world of thoughts, and guiding our mind stream in channels of our own choosing. We can create an inner garden of beautiful roses, or a field of worthless weeds that choke out the sunlight. Ultimately, our lives are shaped by our minds.

Mind is the universal womb that gives birth to all material forms. No one can escape the consequences of their thoughts and feelings.

There is an unbreakable connection—an indivisible link—between the inner world of consciousness and the outer world of events. Ultimately, our environment is an image, or reflection, of our mental activity. All of us live in circumstances we have created for ourselves.

SACRED THOUGHTS PRODUCE A SACRED LIFE

Given the gravity of problems facing the world today, it appears that our many gains in material comfort and convenience have not been matched by our spiritual progress. The argument can be made that we moderns have diminished our sense of the sacred, our admiration for the noble and profound. If we are to develop our sense of wonder and respect for the natural world, we must revitalize our love for beauty, goodness and truth—the philosophical trinity so prized by the ancients. We will need to rediscover the sublime truths that once were called the Mysteries. Only people who love the light can create a sacred culture.

Since ancient times, the religions of the world have emphasized the importance of pronouncing sacred prayers, verses and formulas. Many people think that to read spiritual literature—to pray, meditate, or think about "higher realities"—is a waste of time. But without understanding the higher truths, our existence lacks depth and meaning. Ideas that do not give us enthusiasm and strength for living—that only clutter our minds with "facts" or information trivia—lead gradually to apathy. Commonplace thoughts cannot provide the spark to light our inner fires.

In order to introduce sacred elements into our lives, it is essential to spend time immersing ourselves in thoughts that lift us out of the ordinary—ideas and insights that were true thousands of years ago and will be true a thousand years from now. Sacred thoughts belong to eternity.

Mikhael Aivanhov relates a fable about a king who went for a stroll in the marketplace and found a merchant shouting, "Wisdom for sale! Wisdom for sale!" Curious, the king asked the "wisdom merchant" what price he was asking for his peculiar wares. The man answered that he had wisdom available for 1,000 crowns, some for 5,000 crowns, and still more valuable wisdom for 10,000 crowns.

Amused, the king agreed to buy the wisdom valued at 10,000 crowns, whereupon the merchant said to him, "Do what you do, but think of the consequences." Despite paying dearly for what seemed trivial advice, the king returned good-naturedly to his palace. Because he wished to extract "full value" from his purchase, he mentally repeated over and over the advice given him by the merchant.

The next day the king visited his barber for his customary morning shave. As the barber sharpened his knife, the king decided to share his expensive wisdom with his subject. "Do what you do, but think of the consequences," the king declared, half expecting the barber to think it were a joke. But to his surprise, the barber fell to his knees and cried out, "Forgive me your majesty, it was not I who wished to kill you. The ministers put me up to this crime!" The king, realizing the gravity of the situation, maintained a stern demeanor, as if he knew all about the plot against him. The barber proceeded to reveal all the details, whereupon the king was able to punish the guilty.

This fable, though perhaps implausible, illustrates the power of our thoughts. The king's wisdom, for which he paid so dearly, represents the gems of truth that we make our own. When we fill our minds with knowledge of the heavenly laws—uplifting "advice" that comes from the enlightened teachers of the human race—we can ward off all manner of potential harms. The ideas we continually affirm in our minds become the blueprint of our lives. These thoughts will either protect us or lead us into harm, depending on their content.

We Mold Ourselves in the Image of Our Thoughts

Lily was in her late forties when she discovered the truth that thoughts are the blueprint of life. She had been an unwed teenage mother in a small town during an era when there was great social stigma attached. Consequently, she became socially ostracized and gave her child up for adoption. Suffering from dismally low self-esteem, she went through a series of relationships and marriages that ended unhappily. Seeking spiritual help, she was counseled by numerous clergymen. Although assured by a priest that "God doesn't make junk," she had difficulty believing it applied to her.

For years Lily suffered from chronic illness. In her mid-forties her third husband moved out, leaving her sick, troubled and disconsolate. The awakening came for her when she met an older woman, a healer and herbalist, who was part Cherokee. Lily studied herbal healing with the woman and her health improved gradually. But she continued to hold a grudge against life for all the hardships she had endured. The old healer told her that she would have to change her attitudes about herself and about life if she wanted to completely heal and "start life afresh." Lily began to record her thoughts and beliefs and kept a journal for writing ideas that inspired her. Her knowledge of herbal remedies steadily increased and she began leading nature walks to identify and gather edible plants and healing herbs. Her opinion of herself improved dramatically as she saw how others appreciated the way she shared what she was learning. She became interested in traveling, something she had never done, and began visiting some of the world's sacred sites. She became so enthusiastic that she helped organize several tour groups to visit these sites. Lily discovered that thought is the dynamic force that shapes the experience of life, and that the source of enthusiasm and inspiration is in the ideas she holds in her mind.

We create ourselves in the image of our thinking. The mind is a lens through which we focus the remarkable power of our intentions and our dreams. The stronger and clearer our focus, the more rapidly do we achieve what we seek. The offspring of your inner contemplations will be your deeds. Each of us shapes our lives by our thoughts, just as a sculptor shapes the clay into the image he holds in his mind.

The Road We Travel Is Paved with Our Intentions

Perhaps there is no force on Earth greater than a strong intention that is backed by intense mental focus. A time-honored method of goal-achievement is to write down your intentions and read them aloud every day, taking practical steps to reach those goals. The longer you hold an intention in the mind, the more powerful it becomes. A strong intention can rearrange circumstances, as if magically shuffling the actors and scenery in your personal life drama. If you are sincere enough, eventually the opportunity will arise to accomplish your goal.

When Mia and I decided we wanted to start a book and gift shop, we wrote down in detail our goals. At the time, we were both teachers and had neither the time nor the money with which to realize our intention. But we knew that one day the dream would materialize if we wrote down our goal and focused our thoughts upon it. We created a "book of dreams" and we called our plan, "Project Omega." We wrote a declaration, or mission statement, which captured what we wanted our shop to be like. And we envisioned the kind of storefront we would like to have. I bought several copies of my favorite books and placed then in a special place. This was the beginning inventory of our store. The books were the starter seeds for our "garden."

Years later we were living in another town. Project Omega still seemed an impossible dream. One day Mia drove past a dress shop on a side street near the commercial center. The dress shop was located in a building that seemed to her ideal for a book and gift shop. She took me to see it and I agreed that the dress shop was located in a perfect place. "This or something better," we affirmed together.

Over a year later I was driving in town doing errands. To my dismay, I could not find a parking place near my destination, a street where there was usually abundant parking. I finally parked on a side street five blocks away. As I got out of the car, I realized I had parked in front of the dress shop we'd visited the previous year. I noticed a sign that said "going out of business sale." Curious, I entered the shop and spoke to the owner, a charming woman from South America. She confirmed that they were, in fact, going out of business. My heart leaped in expectation, realizing this was the opportunity for which we'd waited.

I drove home and told Mia. Our daughter was only six weeks old, but we agreed this was our chance. We said a prayer and decided to take instant action. I called the landlord and met him that very day. Although we had little capital and no prior business experience, our energy and enthusiasm apparently convinced the landlord to take a risk and we signed a three-year lease. Our intention had become a reality.

Thoughts Weave the Pattern of Our Lives

Thoughts are really living things. Our thoughts take wing and journey through space, returning to us in the form of conditions that are in accord with their nature. When you fashion an idea, you give birth to a child on the plane of thought. Over time, one's thoughts crystallize into character and circumstance. We become what we think. Because all physical manifestations are the result of thought, it follows that by working with these ideas we can begin to mold the kind of life we desire. If you think constructively, you will create your own miracles. Those who formulate noble intentions amass an enormous power to do good in the world.

Manuel was forty-five years old and unhappy in his work as a Spanish-speaking translator on the East Coast. He spent a lot of time brooding, and although he loved his family, he would often explode into angry tirades at home. A friend invited him to a seminar on personal growth and empowerment, and he began to apply the principles of universal law that he learned there. Manuel purchased a quantity of "self-help" books and read them voraciously. He copied inspiring passages out by hand and spent hours studying and affirming the truths he discovered.

One summer, he went with a friend to a Church picnic. Before the softball game, which was the highlight of the occasion, Manuel stole off into the Church and sat quietly in a rear pew, reflecting. The pastor noticed him as he left the building and a few minutes later they met at the softball game. The pastor of the Church was also the dean of a small religious college. He was so impressed with Manuel that he offered him a position as instructor of Spanish, even though Manuel had no previous experience as a teacher. Manuel accepted and spent the summer preparing to teach introductory Spanish to freshman.

Manuel worked diligently at his new position. Students appreciated his warmth and friendliness. He offered his services as a tutor in the afternoons and became one of the most popular instructors on campus. He continued his own education at the college level and soon obtained a master's degree in psychology. Manuel remained in his late-blossoming career for years, always one of the most liked and respected teachers. His life transformation was made possible by the changes in his mental attitude. It has been said that the one thing over which everyone has control is their mental attitude.

THE LAW OF ATTUNEMENT

Thought is the greatest power in life, for it determines the direction we take. We live in a sea of energies—a universe of forces and frequencies of almost infinite variety. We benefit ourselves when we are selective in what we focus our attention on. Imagine thoughts as being wave forms or frequencies, analogous to radio and TV waves, but much more subtle. Like radio receivers or televisions, our minds may be attuned to many and varied frequencies. When we select a channel on a television set, it emits a particular frequency signal, which then pulls in that frequency from the larger broadcasting station. In like manner, when the frequency or wavelength of our thoughts resonates at a high vibratory level, we synchronize our subtle thought field with the higher dimensions from which stream inspiration and joy. This is an aspect of the law of affinity, or attunement—one of the sacred laws of creation. A fundamental principle of soul alchemy and sacred living is that we can "tune our receiver" to "broadcasting stations" of wisdom, love, and truth. By so doing, we become a force for good in the world.

Our inner life does not occur in a vacuum. We are constantly bombarding the space around us with our emanations. Each of us is a miniature transmitter, ceaselessly broadcasting thoughts as well as receiving them. One's presence is never neutral. We are always sending out signals that have an influence on those around us. "One person thinking truth," said Alice Bailey, "can revolutionize his or her environment." Though it may be difficult to imagine, the activity of your mind has an influence that reaches to the farthest star.

Because many people are mentally attuned to that which is discordant and chaotic, their lives mirror these characteristics. If you choose, you can become instead a receiving station for the angelic vibrations of harmony, peace and happiness. Mental attention is your tuning device—the focal point of consciousness. Good, positive, loving thoughts have a very high frequency. Like the ultra-violet rays of the electromagnetic spectrum, they have a short wave length and a rapid oscillation. When you tune your instrument to loving, positive frequencies, you become a broadcasting station for that which is luminous and helpful. Your thoughts of love and goodness create an impression in the subtle dimensions around you and draw corresponding forces or frequencies that bring about health and happiness. In this way, your life will gradually reflect the qualities of your thinking. By focusing attention on thoughts that embody the qualities we seek, we develop those qualities in our personalities. This is the essence of soul alchemy—the miracle of inner transformation.

Once we realize the indestructible link between our inner world of thought and our outer world of experience, we realize that no one is a victim of circumstance. We create our circumstances by the mental scenarios we entertain, habitually and persistently. We bring to life the scenes on which we focus our attention. When we concentrate upon a particular "landscape," we give reality to the very images we picture. Take advantage of this truth by making a list of things you want to do that make your life better and improve you as a person. Begin and end each day reflecting on these objectives. This is a simple way to enhance our efforts in sacred living.

Even one's physical body is a creation of thought. Your body is a hieroglyph or image of your consciousness. Our bodies, in their good or ill health, will reflect the mind images upon which we habitually dwell. Thoughts—and the feelings they stir up—are to our souls what food is to our physical bodies. The higher the frequencies of thought and feeling that we create in our minds, the more perfect will be our physical well-being. One's physical features reveal character, the inner life of soul.

It may be true, as some quantum physicists have suggested, that the human body itself is a projected image, a holographic picture, created by our thinking spirit. Perhaps the brain is a kind of screen upon which the mind projects images. It may be that each of us first existed as an image in the mind of God. Regardless of what the science of the future may reveal to us about our origin and destiny, you can gain command of your life right now by controlling your mind.

IMAGINATION—THE GATEWAY TO SACRED LIVING

One of the most wonderful attributes of the mind is the power of imagination. This is a truly magical instrument in our repertoire of life-building tools. So little is really understood about the imagination's power. Yet it is unbelievably great. The secret of creation lies in the imaging faculty of the mind. Imagination is a key ingredient in the inner alchemy of the spirit. Because of its power to transform our souls and our lives, the great psychologist Carl Jung called imagination a "transcendent function." Our imagination alters the contents of our inner lives and magically influences our environment.

The alchemists sought to transform the "base" or ordinary metals into gold. This process was symbolic of the transformation of the human soul to its most noble stature. The superior metals were gold and silver. Gold was often called *sol,* meaning the Sun. Silver was referred to as *luna,* meaning the Moon. All of the primary metals—which also included copper, mercury, iron, zinc and lead—were symbolized by one of the seven traditional planets: Sun, Moon, Mercury, Venus, Mars, Jupiter and Saturn. To the alchemists, the planets and the metals were representative of the dynamic forces of the human soul. The transformation of the metals signified the unfolding of the soul into its pristine, divine nature. The higher nature of the soul—illumined by the spirit—was represented by gold, or *sol,* the Sun.

Silver was next to gold in importance. Silver was the Moon, *luna,* and it represented the imagination. Through the imagination we are able to pictorialize. It is revealing in this regard that silver is used to coat mirrors, and is also an essential element in the creation of light-sensitive photographic solutions.

In the alchemy of sacred living, imagination plays a central role in the evolution of the human soul. This refers to imagination in its highest meditative use, not in commonplace daydreaming or vague musings. By harnessing the imaginative power we increase the soul's luminosity, making it brilliant with inner radiance. In alchemical symbolism, the soul transformed by sacred living becomes gold. *Luna* becomes *sol.* The splendor of the divine self enters the soul and personality through spiritualized imagination.

Many educators regard imagination as the cornerstone to creativity and philosophical insight. The power of imagery and pictorial thinking to develop genius and reveal truth was recognized by Albert Einstein. When asked how to educate so as to produce intelligent children, he responded, "Tell them fairy tales." When asked how to produce *really* intelligent children, he replied, "Tell them *more* fairy tales."

The imagination has also a more concrete influence in our lives, in that it impacts our environment in an almost magical fashion. When you visualize a scene or a picture in your mind's eye, you are forming images out of the substance of your soul. In time, these pictures will crystallize into actual physical realities. In this manner we fashion the world in which we live. Our material surroundings mirror our minds. Your environment comes to reflect your inner world of consciousness.

TRANSMUTING SUBSTANCE AND CRYSTALLIZING SPIRIT

Two of the processes that occupied the efforts of ancient alchemists were the *transmutation of substance* and *the crystallization of spirit*. We "transmute substance," as we free ourselves from habits and practices that tie us down and limit our potential. When we "crystallize spirit," we are manifesting—that is giving form and concrete reality to—our dreams, goals, plans and aspirations. Imagination is essential to both these processes. Let's look at each of them in turn, beginning with "crystallizing the spirit."

Whenever we take steps to realize our goals in any area of our lives, we are bringing wishes, hopes and ideas into form. This is how we materialize, or *condense*, spirit. This is the eternal process of "real-ization," of bringing spiritual qualities and awareness to life. Every time you act out of inspired idealism, you bring the spirit into expression. Every deed that flows from a loving heart contributes to the coming culture of light. When we picture our goals and objectives and focus on what we want in our lives, we are using the magical power of imagination to manifest our dreams.

The "transmutation of substance" refers to changing limiting habits and behavior patterns into new, constructive ones. As we expand ourselves and grow beyond self-imposed limitations, we release the awesome power of the spirit. Through faulty education or cultural conditioning, our deeper self may be trapped inside narrow belief systems. When we liberate our creative potential and expand beyond limitations, we raise ourselves to a higher level of awareness. Even the activity of losing weight by dieting and exercise is an expression of this alchemical act of transmuting substance. A helpful factor in successful dieting is the ability to picture yourself as you would like to be.

In its highest expression, the "transmutation of substance" refers to replacing negative, destructive habits of thought and emotion with harmonious and constructive ones. When we elevate our thoughts and feelings—that is, our consciousness—we are altering "the substance" of our inner lives. Thus we are transmuting ourselves. We then experience greater mental clarity and deeper happiness. As we release ourselves from limiting habits and discordant inner states, we experience the liberating influence of the spirit. Using the imagination in contemplation or meditation changes us inwardly. One might say we "polish our souls" so that, like a perfectly silvered mirror reflecting sunlight, our souls come to reflect a true image of the divine self.

Our striving for illumination lights the fire in our soul that frees us from frozen habits and icy feelings. Many today call this "the ascension process." Anyone who has ever mastered a limiting habit or overcome an addiction has engaged in the soul alchemy of transmuting substance. The alchemy of sacred living releases our imprisoned splendor.

Imagination is an essential key to inner renewal and life enhancement. Our lives reflect the beauty we create in our minds. Not only can imagination help materialize our fondest dreams and wishes, it can give wings to our soul and lift us to a higher plane of being.

The Golden Thread

The ability to think pictorially and symbolically is a doorway to a subtle form of intelligence. Much of the wisdom of the human race has been stored up in the form of the imaginative stories we know as mythology, legend and parable. "It would not be too much to say," writes Joseph Campbell, the modern popularizer of the wisdom in folklore, "that myth is the secret opening through which the inexhaustible energies of the cosmos pour into human cultural manifestation."

The great mythologies of the world are the "dream images" of the human race. Myths are the soul of humanity speaking to us from out of its wisdom-filled depths. Myths and parables convey truth on multiple levels and always have more than one valid interpretation. Mythic imagery provides spiritual nourishment for all, regardless of one's stage of inner readiness, while revealing a deeper message for those wise enough to comprehend. The scriptures of the world are filled with allegories and pictorial tales. Jesus taught in parables because these imaginative stories convey truths and moral lessons to all listeners, regardless of their point of spiritual attainment.

Consider an example of imaginative wisdom from Greek mythology—the story of Ariadne's golden thread. Ariadne is the daughter of King Minos, the ruler of Crete. Under the palace of King Minos is a famous labyrinth wherein dwells a Minotaur, a monstrous creature—half man, half bull. No one who enters the labyrinth comes out alive. Theseus, the heroic son of the King of Athens, volunteers to go into the labyrinth, courting certain death.

On his way into the dark maze, Ariadne, who loves Theseus, gives him a ball of golden thread. Theseus ties the thread to the door of the entrance into the labyrinth, then unwinds it as he makes his way through the underground passages. He finally meets the dreaded Minotaur and slays the beast in mortal combat. Theseus finds his way back through the confusing maze thanks to Ariadne's golden thread. Theseus and Ariadne then depart for Athens to be married.

Theseus represents the human individuality that must find its way through the confusing labyrinth of earthly experiences. The Minotaur represents the many dangers in life that would harm us. In particular, it symbolizes the soul-destroying influence of materialism. The ball of golden thread represents the light of wisdom that emanates from our soul, or higher self, symbolized by Ariadne. This ancient story from the Mystery schools of Greece teaches us that we must discover the golden thread of wisdom in order to find our way in life. The thread of wisdom comes from the deeper self, which radiates the light and love that guide us. Stories like Ariadne's golden thread depict the intuitive wisdom that comes through inspired fantasy and mythic imagination.

Our imagination has immense importance for our spiritual lives. We imbue our minds with sacred influences when we immerse ourselves in imagery from the world's wisdom traditions. Sages have taught that through the wise use of imagination, in periods of meditation and prayer, we may gradually become aware of higher spiritual dimensions that are interwoven with the physical earthly life. According to the sacred literature from many traditions, at the time of death the soul departs the physical body and becomes conscious in these higher dimensions. The soul finds itself in the higher ethers surrounded by its own thought creations. Thus, we are drawn in the afterlife to the "levels" of universal vibratory substance that correspond to our dominant trend of mind while on Earth.

By cultivating a positive, healthy imagination we can begin to unlock the deeper mysteries of life—the *meaning* within our experiences. This ability to discern meaning leads to the development of intuition and inspiration. Imagination is a key that can open the gates of the celestial worlds. With it, one can unlock the hidden powers of the soul and the mind. The developing of an imaginative consciousness is a step toward unfolding wisdom in our lives. We can build a light-filled future for ourselves—and those whose lives we touch—by the radiant weavings we create in our imaginations now.

THE SUBCONSCIOUS: AN AWESOME ALLY

The work of soul alchemy—of inner transformation—is a process of refining our patterns of thought, feeling and action. To free our consciousness from the oppressive memory of past error, we need to enlist the support of the subconscious dimensions of the mind and the emotions. The subconscious—what the Huna shamans of Hawaii call *ku*—is a tremendous ally in our growth toward spiritual maturity and enlightenment. We influence the subconscious by repetition of positive acts and thoughts, and by developing a conviction of the sure outworking of universal laws. The more powerful our feelings, the greater our capacity to activate the support of the subconscious.

The subconscious mind has awesome power and an extraordinary intelligence, far exceeding that of the conscious mind. Consider that it is the subconscious power of the body-mind that oversees all the complex functions of digestion, assimilation, metabolism, growth, all the organ functions, the operation of the endocrine system, reproduction, circulation, breathing and heartbeat. It is the subconscious wisdom operating through the body that enables the physical organism to heal itself of injuries.

The conscious mind has virtually no knowledge of how this incredibly complex system works. If it did understand and tried to interfere, it would probably only botch up the smooth interworking of all these processes. It is not surprising that traditional metaphysics teaches that what we call the subconscious mind includes superconscious influences that are the work of higher beings—known for millennia as the divine Hierarchies of angels—which include Archangels, Cherubim, and Seraphim.

We do know that one aspect of the subconscious mind is to work as a recording device, and that it records all messages from the conscious mind and will act on these "orders." When we feed good, constructive suggestions to the subconscious, we gain the assistance of a prodigious ally. This aspect of the subconscious is like a mighty giant that is entirely obedient to our conscious command.

The subconscious may be compared to the basement of a huge castle. It contains all the records and treasures of all our experiences. When we organize our subconscious through feeding it positive commands and affirmations, and when we put our house in order by constructive actions, we begin to harness this power to be used for our benefit. When we establish our life on constructive lines, the positive suggestions we give our subconscious will start to take effect. Though this work takes time, it is not difficult. It is delightful and satisfying to see the steady improvements that gradually unfold in one's life.

The subconscious works through our habits. We change our habits by first changing our thoughts. Our thoughts influence our feelings and desires which in turn lead to action. Repeated actions become habit, and habits crystallize into character. Character is the lightning rod of destiny. This process has perhaps never been summarized better than by James Allen when he gave the classic formula:

"Sow a thought, reap an action,

Sow an action, reap a habit,

Sow a habit, reap character,

Sow character, reap destiny."

THOUGHT IS THE DYNAMO OF LIFE

We begin to revolutionize our experience when we acknowledge that thought is the most dynamic power in shaping our lives. It is true that our deeper self—our indwelling spirit presence—is pure joy, bliss, and love beyond any concept of the mind. But we can build a bridge to our immortal spark through enlightened mental activity. When we become fully present in our thoughts, we begin to weave a garment of light out of the bright substance of our souls. If we invite the sunlight of wisdom to be the guest at our table, we can commune with the angels themselves.

The mind is the portal through which we allow experiences to enter our lives. Each of us is our own gatekeeper, or sentinel. Vigilance is the power that enables us to be present within the activity of our own minds. When we invite warm and friendly thoughts into our dwelling, we discover the power to be happy in ourselves, regardless of what may be going on around us. As we send out loving messages to the world, the universe responds with a flow of blessings into our lives. Thoughts arising from a mind attuned to the light create a ceaseless stream of miracles. The mind is an instrument of incalculable power.

Life is essentially a process that is set in motion by the dynamo of thinking. Your circumstances tomorrow will be a reflection of your thoughts today. Each person's life is a mirror of his or her mental activity. Those who think great thoughts will accomplish great things. You can never be greater or better than your thoughts.

Our thoughts are the magnets that draw experience to us. We can set ourselves up for success or failure by our customary attitude of mind. If we set in motion constructive forces through our thoughts, actions and words—forces that benefit and uplift—the effects will take care of themselves. As our thoughts become inspired and loving, we master the art of sacred living. The Hunas—native shamans of Hawaii—have an expression that captures the right attitude in regard to thinking about one's life. "Bless the present. Trust yourself. Expect the best."

We transform our lives into gardens of love and happiness as we learn the indispensable alchemical secret to sacred living. That secret is to fill our minds with kind and light-filled thoughts. The sanctification of culture begins with the transformation and renewal of our minds. In time, we will find that the physical environment in which we live will reflect the garden we have created within.

Exercises in Sacred Living:
Activating the Alchemy of Thinking

Activity Number One

Perform the following experiment: For one week go on a "mental diet." Allow yourself to think only positive thoughts. Negative thoughts will come to your awareness, but resist them by replacing them with positive, constructive thoughts. Keep a record of your success. If you think negatively, begin again on "day one." When you can go a week with only positive thoughts, you will have taken a giant stride in transforming your life.

Activity Number Two

Many people are surprised to learn that observation of one's surroundings is a great way to sharpen the mind. During the course of the day, be mindful of what you see in your environment. Notice what people are wearing—their shoes, the colors and style of their clothing. Pay attention to the nuances of their speech. Wherever you go, look carefully at your surroundings. Notice the details of color, architecture, and furnishings.

At the end of the day take five or ten minutes and recall in your mind the details of what you observed. If you can't remember particulars—such as the color of the woman's sweater just ahead of you in the supermarket checkout line—then imagine a color. It's all right to fill in the details for what you can't fully recollect. This exercise creates mental alertness. It is helpful in developing memory, as well as enhancing moment by moment awareness during the day. (A note of caution: be careful not to judge people critically according to dress, speech, etc. The purpose here is simply to sharpen observations skills and thereby sharpen your mind.)

Activity Number Three

Make a list of at least five thoughts or affirmations that embody qualities you would like to develop more strongly—virtues or strengths you would like to express in your life. They may be thoughts you find in this book, read elsewhere, or that you composed yourself. They should have meaning and importance to you.

Read these thoughts aloud until you have committed them to memory. Affirm them silently in your mind each day as often as you can. These thoughts are seeds that will eventually blossom into features of character. It is important to think these thoughts, with intensity and feeling, at least once every day.

Affirmations

"I transform myself by the renewal of my mind. I fashion my mind into a temple of wisdom and truth."

"All my thoughts are positive, loving and light-filled. I create a better life for myself now by my bright and luminous thinking."

"My mind is a fountain of understanding, blessing and enlightenment."

"My thoughts are inspired, considerate and helpful. I transform my mind into a garden of beauty and success and my life reflects this transformation."

CHAPTER THREE

THE ALCHEMY OF FEELING AND DESIRE

"Great is my joy when you ask from your heart."

– Anonymous, *Turning*

"The fragrance of the flowers is their prayer."

– Peter Deunov

In the ancient world, feelings of wonder and reverence were considered the starting point of gaining true knowledge. "It was through the feeling of wonder that humans now and first began to philosophize," said Aristotle. The ancients would be appalled by anyone seeking to know truth who first did not love the world. Modern science places little value in feelings of devotion, reverence and wonder—failing to see any connection between such sentiments and the acquisition of knowledge. Yet our minds cannot really grasp the marvels of the world if we can't appreciate beauty. We will begin to kindle a sacred culture on Earth as we restore a sense of wonder to our perceptions of the world. Such a view recognizes the importance of educating the feelings as well as the thinking process.

If you ask someone to point to themselves, they will almost always point to their heart, almost never their head. A great truth is revealed by this gesture. Although the wellspring of consciousness is in our thinking process, the mystery of our soul—our deeper identity—is bound up with our feelings. It is our feelings and our desires that give life and energy to our thoughts. Feelings bring our thoughts down to Earth and provide the spark of motivation. Without feelings, life would be dull, bland and lifeless.

Thoughts are a subtle frequency far removed from the densities of material substance. The bridge between ideas and material objects is the world of feelings. Feelings include moods, emotions and desire. It is in the womb of desire that our intentions are conceived. And the mind ever dwells on that which the heart loves.

Desire is the motivating impulse that gives energy to our thoughts and direction to our imagination. Desire is the spark that ignites our will into action. It is also the fuel that feeds our dreams of what we want to accomplish in life. Feelings compel us to get up and go.

Without feelings, life would be sterile. From this it follows that the most sublime feeling is also life's most compelling element. This element is *love*. Thoughts and feelings of love are the world's irresistible driving force. Those who work lovingly and harmoniously with universal law find that the universe seemingly works with them in realizing their good intentions.

Some people say that feelings are neither right or wrong, good or bad; they are just feelings. This is true in part, for feelings seem to well up from an unseen fountain, with an irresistible pressure from within us. Nonetheless, emotions are not neutral. Different feelings produce vividly different effects. Our feelings are the gateway into the soul world. They impact all of our experiences. In fact, to a large extent, our feelings about an experience *are* the experience. Though feelings will always tend to have a "life of their own," as we awaken to our deeper self and contact the shining source behind our feelings, we can begin to direct their course.

In their quest for the secrets of nature and the spirit, alchemists sought to procure the Elixir of Life—a mysterious distillation of life force. Alchemists realized that feelings were of special importance in this work. The soul world, the world of feelings, was sometimes designated allegorically as *mercury*, or quicksilver. Mercury was one of the alchemists' fundamental trinity of substances, which also included *sulfur*—representing the fire of spirit—and *salt*, which represented the physical body and the material world. As we live a sacred life, our inner world of feelings becomes not our master, but an essential ally on our quest. We come to realize, as did the alchemists, that by revitalizing our feelings we distill the Elixir of Life.

THE RAINBOW OF FEELINGS

Perhaps the best analogy to the diversity of human feelings is the great variety of colors in nature. Goethe, who was a scientist as well as one of the world's great poets, said that "Colors are the joys and suffering of the light." The same may be said of our emotions—they reflect the joys, sorrows and dramas of life. Most of the time we experience a mixture of feelings. Our emotions are like a palette of colors of every shade and hue.

Feeling, moods and emotions are not just comparable to color in a poetic sense. They are *literally* color. The world's wisdom traditions have always referred to the fact that the inner life of soul becomes objective as a rainbow of colors displayed around us in the form of our energy field, or aura. The word *aura* comes from the Greek *Aurora*, who was the goddess of morning light. The aura is the field of light projected by an individual's thought and feeling emanations. The science of human vibration is intimately related to the electromagnetic spectrum of colors ranging from violet to red. Our feelings send out a stream of hues that we project around us. Different feelings and emotions create very different colors in one's auric field. Positive emotions create bright, lucid colors that reflect the pure shades of the electromagnetic spectrum. The story in the Bible of Joseph's rainbow colored jacket, which was the envy of all his brothers, is a symbol of the radiant, healthy aura.

Feelings, by their nature, conjure mystery. We sense that they connect us to something vast, awesome, barely comprehensible. It is true we must honor our authentic feelings, not deny or suppress them. Feelings are the substance of our souls, and are an immense source of strength. But it is important to discern between those that lead to a happier life, and those that hold us back—between emotions that liberate and those that pull us down. In our journey to the light, we can strive to create a beautiful tapestry of rich, vibrant feelings with which to paint the landscape of our experience. The ultimate work of art is one's own life. The colors in our palette are our moods and feelings. We can make our life an expression of beauty—a masterpiece that illustrates our path toward enlightenment and self-realization—if we are careful in the colors we choose.

There are two portals into our world of feelings. One is the familiar gateway of the senses. Through the impact of our environment, feelings are awakened—either of like or dislike, sympathy or antipathy. The other gateway is our thoughts, which include imagination. The ideas we hold in our minds stimulate feelings that correspond to the nature of these ideas.

We can never control completely what comes to us from our environment, although we can learn to manage our responses. In this lies our freedom. Freedom is found in our ability to guide our responses to circumstance. By consciously taking the lead in determining the way we react to events, we can shape the direction of our experiences, and ultimately the very course of our lives.

The area in which we have the most freedom is in our thinking process. The spirit is greater than the mind. It is the spirit that thinks, using the mind as its instrument. We must be spiritually active in order to guide our thoughts, and thereby get a handle on our emotions. Until we become present in our mental process, selecting thoughts we want to think, we are at the mercy of what comes to us through the gateway of our senses. The best way to get a handle on your inner life of feelings and moods is to be *present* in your thoughts.

Harmonious Feelings Heal

Our feelings are connected to our organs, glands, tissues and cells. Every thought or emotion we experience sends electromagnetic signals through our nervous system. Feelings of doubt, suspicion, worry, anger or hate, trigger responses in our cells. Discordant feelings produce metabolic wastes and toxins that build up in the blood stream. As a result, the immune system is weakened. Our blood vessels constrict, making us listless. We thus become illness-prone. Without our conscious intent, we gradually paralyze our good intentions.

Conversely, emotions of happiness, hope, belief, faith, friendship, love and joy trigger an entirely different chemical response in the body. When our feelings are uplifted, our nerve cells secrete chemicals called *neuropeptides*, which bring health to our organisms. Neuroscience has identified more than 50 neuropeptides, some of which are hormones that directly influence behavior. The body's chemistry is directly linked to our emotions and attitudes. A cheerful, optimistic attitude improves the functioning of the endocrine and immune systems. Positivity expands our blood vessels, enabling our bodies to eliminate metabolic wastes more easily. Our blood becomes healthier and our complexion improves. Our health is linked directly to our emotional states.

Discordant emotions—such as those of anger, envy and jealousy—wreak havoc not only in our own bodies, but also in our relationships. Many people feel they have the right to express their angry feelings, regardless of consequences, in the spirit of being open and direct. Although this may be better than bottling up negative feelings—which then become simmering resentment—great care must be taken in expressing our emotions in relationships. It is helpful to keep in mind the law of the seed, for when harsh words are expressed in moments of anger, we cast forces to the wind that will one day return to the sender. There is a fine line between being open and communicative, thus "clearing the air," and tactlessly expressing volatile emotions. There is a difference between feelings and *emotionalism*. We may thoughtlessly arouse the furies when we express harsh feelings in our relationships.

Our thoughts, moods and emotions are to our inner life what nutrition is to our physical bodies. Feelings are the food that nourishes our souls. Angry and negative feelings poison our hearts. This "inner toxin" gradually becomes manifest in our physical bodies. On the other hand, loving, kind and enthusiastic feelings are a tonic that elevates us. Like the fabled ambrosia of Greek mythology—warm and happy feelings are a divine elixir that lifts our hopes and gives strength to our dreams.

There is still an enormous amount to be learned about creative ways of transmuting discordant feelings into positive and creative ones. We know it is useless to deny emotions. Yet discharging harsh feelings such as anger will only cause harm to ourselves and others. Dark emotions show where we have been hurt in our lives. Emotional healing begins when we can go beneath the armor of our hurt feelings and discover our essential nature. Beneath the mask of our wounded feelings shines the light of the spirit, whose nature is love.

In his book, *Being Peace,* the Vietnamese Buddhist monk, Thich Nhat Hanh, gives an example of how practitioners of Zen approach the transmutation of anger.

> "In the case of a minor irritation, the recognition of the presence of the irritation, along with a smile and a few breaths will usually be enough to transform the irritation into something more positive, like forgiveness, understanding, and love. Irritation is a destructive energy. We cannot destroy the energy; we can only convert it into a more constructive energy. Forgiveness is a constructive energy. Understanding is a constructive energy. Suppose you are in the desert, and you have only one glass of muddy water. You have to transform the muddy water into clear water to drink, you cannot just throw it away. So you let it settle for a while and clear water will appear. In the same way we have to convert anger into some kind of energy that is more constructive...."

Understanding helps to transform anger and other harmful emotions. "Anger is born from ignorance and is a strong ally of ignorance," states Thich Nhat Hanh. As we transmute destructive emotions into the warmth of love, we weave light into our souls. It takes time to change habitual emotional patterns, but with persistence, we alter the circuitry of our energy fields.

If we get caught up in the small discomforts and petty inconveniences of life, we may find that irritability saps our energy. A facet of living wisely is to discriminate between serious issues and trivial matters. My daughter once gave me some good advice on how to respond to small disturbances. One day when she was seven years old, we were playing "restaurant"—one of her delightful make-believe games. I sat in a chair at the kitchen table while she pretended she was the waitress at a fine restaurant. As she set a heavily-laden tray on the tablecloth by my place, the glass of water tipped and spilled. With perfect calm and complete sincerity she said, "Dad, pretend that didn't happen." Benjamin Franklin would have endorsed my daughter's remark. One of his personal life precepts goes as follows: "Be not disturbed at trifles, or at accidents common or unavoidable." Allowing petty disturbances to get under our skin deflects us from more important matters and robs us of inner peace.

One of the characteristics of our soul life is that there tends to be an oscillation—an ebb and flow—between polarities of feelings. It's as if our emotions are tied to an invisible pendulum that shifts between contrasting states or "pairs of opposites:" sadness and happiness, intimacy and aloofness, tension and relaxation, confidence and fear. By breathing, relaxing, smiling and dwelling on themes that uplift us, we can balance our feelings in the still place of peace at the center of our hearts. It will help us to find this equilibrium if we focus our minds on images of beauty from art or nature. This quiet focusing on elevating themes and images is the essence of contemplation. When we find the place of peace in our hearts, a door swings open into a higher state of consciousness. By relaxing inwardly we achieve equanimity.

Harmonious feelings are a gateway to the deepest secrets of the spirit. Beneath our feelings lives the extraordinary power of the deeper self. Behind even the darkest and most frightening feelings lies an ocean of love. As we heal ourselves, relax, and open to love, we tap into a fountain of joy.

THE DIVINE FEMININE AND THE ANGELIC KINGDOM

According to what is often called the *Ageless Wisdom*—the body of teaching presented in the ancient temples, which is resurfacing today through a multitude of books and teachers—the emotional realm is related to what is known in traditional theology as the Holy Spirit. The Holy Spirit is closely connected to the Divine Feminine, and also to those spirits comprising what alchemists called the Hierarchies of angels. Herein lies a clue to a distinctive path of emotional healing.

In the early days of Christianity, St. Paul taught in the city of Ephesus, located in modern day Turkey. Ephesus was one of the principal centers of learning in the ancient world. The ancient Greek Temple of Diana at Ephesus was so spectacular and beautiful that it was considered to be one of the seven wonders of the world. Although this and other ancient Mystery temples were later destroyed, much of the wisdom taught in these schools seeped into early and mediaeval Christianity.

A student of St. Paul—mentioned in the Bible and known to history as Dionysius the Areopagite—is credited with writing several books which codified in Christian form much of the teaching of the Mystery schools regarding that class of glorious beings known as angels. Following an ancient precedent that we may presume is based on clairvoyant perception, Dionysius listed nine classes or levels of angels. They range from those luminous spirits that are very close to the lives of human beings, called guardian angels, all the way to the Seraphim angels who stand before the "throne" of the universal powers and "ceaselessly chant the holy name of God," In ascending order they are called Angels, Archangels, Principalities, Virtues, Powers, Dominations, Thrones, Cherubim and Seraphim. These have been known for centuries as the angelic Hierarchies.

Simply listing groups of angels may not accomplish much, but humanity has always been fascinated by the existence of these luminous spirits. To my knowledge, there is not a single comment from any ancient writer up until the nineteenth century suggesting any opposition to the universal belief in the existence of these benign spirits. Rather, there exists an extensive body of lore regarding them. The word angel means "messenger." The angelic Hierarchies are messengers to Earth from sublime realms. Alchemists believed that angels sought to influence human beings by uplifting our feelings.

Throughout history, people have described angels. Joan of Arc said that they were so beautiful that she wept when they departed and begged them to take her with them. Emanuel Swedenborg saw them often and spoke to them singly and in groups. Soldiers beheld them on the battlefields of the First World War. After Frances Sydney Smith climbed Mount Everest in 1933, he said that an angel had assisted him during his ascent. In recent years, there have been innumerable sightings of angels and a large body of literature has developed on the subject.

When we acknowledge the presence of angels, there is a change in the way we view the world. When we recognize that we are part of an immense universe of divine life, a link in a chain of beings that includes those who have completed their evolution, life takes on a different flavor. If we can open ourselves lovingly to the existence of these higher beings, they become our companions in spirit. At the very least, awareness of higher levels of divine life can give one's inner life a boost.

In addition to the angels, there is a group of highly evolved beings even closer to humanity. In his writings, St. Paul made reference to the mysterious Order of Melchizedek. The Order of Melchizidek is that group of individuals known in metaphysics as the Masters of Wisdom. In Christianity they are known as the "community of Saints," and in the Hebrew Cabala they are called the *Ishim*, or "perfect men." According to the teaching of the Mystery schools, which was known to St. Paul, the Order of Melchizidek is that class of human beings just below that of the lowest rank of angel. Some writers—notably the alchemist, Robert Fludd—include them as a tenth rank of angels, just above the human. These are the "glorified souls"—highly evolved masters and saints who act as intercessors between mankind and the angelic world. When Jesus said "Be perfect as your Father in heaven is perfect," he was instructing human beings to so harmonize their inner and outer lives that they could eventually become a part of the human "hierarchy" of perfected souls, that illustrious group of initiates called by St. Paul, the Order of Melchizidek.

Within this order, there are as many women as there are men. Traditionally, at the highest level of initiation the men are called Masters of Wisdom and the women are called Daughters of Wisdom, or Daughters of Light. The leader of the Daughters of Light is the heavenly spirit known as the World Mother. This being has many names, including the Divine Sophia, in Greek, and Shekinah, in Hebrew. The psychologically minded may prefer to think of her as an archetype, but in the ancient Mysteries she was thought to be an actual being of the most exalted stature—one of the celestial host of angels. It may be helpful to picture the Mother of the World as an archangel.

Throughout history there have been many representatives on Earth of the Heavenly Mother. I had an experience in which the sacred feminine became more than merely a concept, but an actual presence.

Mia and I were living in San Rafael and our book and gift shop was located near the San Rafael Mission, one of the original Spanish missions in California. When I had the chance, I enjoyed sitting quietly in the tiny chapel of the restored mission building. I was not raised Catholic, and Mother Mary was little more to me than an image in Renaissance art. But as I developed my thoughts on the subject, I began to think of her as a representative of the divine mother, a human embodiment of the sacred feminine. In my meditation one autumn afternoon in the mission chapel, I asked her to make herself known to me. As I left the chapel, I grabbed a handful of small pamphlets with her image on the cover and stuffed them into my shirt pocket over my heart.

I was the only one working that evening in our store and felt unusually fatigued. Just before closing, a man came in and hovered around the book cases. He asked me if I could recommend a book to him that would be a good gift for his girlfriend. Although he seemed a trifle scruffy, nothing in his demeanor caused me to be on my guard. A few moments later he walked to the counter with the book, as if ready to make a purchase.

He hesitated when I told him the price of the book, then reached into his trouser pocket and drew out a handgun. He pointed the gun at my heart and demanded that I give him the money in the register. I suddenly knew what it meant to "jump out of one's skin." I stepped back in shock, my heart pounding fearfully. My first impulse was to give him the money and not provoke him in any way. But a growing sense of outrage eclipsed my fear. In what was probably a very stupid thing to do, I told him that I'd already pressed the emergency alarm button, which notifies the police of a holdup. It was a complete bluff, for we had no such button. The gunman walked around the counter and hit me over the head with the butt of his gun, then he reached into the cash box. I fell to my knees with the impact of the blow, then stood up beside him. A power from within took hold of my mind and body. Terror vanished, replaced with a feeling of absolute righteousness and authority. Grabbing the cash box from the man's hands, I heaved it over the counter onto the floor, money scattering everywhere. Then I shouted at him to leave.

The gunman hurried around the counter and headed for the door, stooping to snatch a few coins on the way. I chased after him, grasping on my way—of all things—a crystal ball. I raced into the parking garage and hurled the crystal ball at the gunman as he made his escape. I missed and he got away.

A customer who had been the only other person in the store had crawled from her hiding place and called 911. The police arrived within minutes, but the thief was never found. When I came down from the rush of adrenaline, I began to sob. The thought of my three-year-old daughter nearly becoming fatherless was more than I could bear. I had a strong sense that a presence had protected me through the holdup. Remembering the gun pointed at my heart, I reached impulsively for my shirt pocket. There, over my heart, were the little pamphlets with Mother Mary's image that I had stuffed into my shirt when leaving the mission chapel just hours earlier, moments after my prayer request that she make her presence known to me. My belief then and now was that she had protected me.

The World Mother, however we may conceive of her, can be viewed not only as a *symbol* of the emotional healing that we as individuals must accomplish, but as a *living force* to assist us in the process. All human beings have been wounded by earthly life. The resurgence of interest in the divine feminine is part of the healing taking place in the world. This healing must occur first in our emotions and our feelings before we can heal our relationships and the Earth itself. The divine mother can be seen as both source and symbol of the healing force that restores the lost harmony of our souls.

In the great myth of ancient Egypt, the divine Isis restored to life the body of her husband, Osiris, which had been cut into fragments by the wicked Set. This is one of the earliest recorded stories of resurrection, and represents the fact that it is the wisdom of the sacred feminine—love in action—that must heal and re-enliven the wounded spirit. Our souls have been damaged and torn by the materialism of modern life, symbolized in the myth by the evil Set. We revitalize our lives when we begin to heal our wounded emotions. Emotional healing is an essential element in the alchemy of the soul.

Whether or not one is disposed by personal temperament to acknowledge the sacred feminine and the existence of angels, all of us must work in our own fashion to heal our emotional selves. This healing begins when we learn to transform feelings from negative to positive. We heal our wounded hearts when we begin to love—despite all the good reasons that our minds can find *not* to love. We heal our souls when we embrace the alchemy of forgiveness. When we forgive, we unite ourselves with a healing force within nature.

Gravity and Levity

When we walk in nature, we can perceive two contrary streams at work in all things. One is the stream of decay and death, the other is that of life and growth. The force of gravity is related to the stream of death and decay. There is another force in nature—opposed to gravity—which is associated with the stream of growth and unfolding. One might call it the force of lightness and levity. It is a benign influence that draws the plant sunward and helps a young child to stand upright.

This force of lightness and levity—corresponding to the life-bestowing impulse of advancement and growth—is related to our positive thoughts and feelings, just as gravity is associated with our discordant ones.

Negative emotions are subject to the law of gravity. They pull us down, literally and figuratively, and open us to the destructive processes in nature. "Toxic thinking" releases toxins in our cells, which weaken them, ultimately causing the cells to die. These toxins enter the bloodstream and undermine our bodily resistance and immunity. Destructive frequencies of consciousness undermine our constitution, reduce our resistance, and render us susceptible to illness. Every negatively charged thought and emotion is a blow to the health and integrity of our physical body.

Positive emotions lift us toward the light, giving us strength, energy and health. We overcome gravity when we overcome negative thoughts and emotions, replacing them with luminous, positive ones. Emotions of love and enthusiasm are the Elixir of Life, the universal panacea that leads to health and happiness. When we focus our minds on that which is good, beautiful, and true, we awaken emotions that heal, bless, and prosper.

ALCHEMISTS OF NATURE

Replacing discordant thought and emotional patterns with harmonious ones is comparable to exchanging old, worn-out garments for bright, colorful new ones. Nature has several metaphors for this path of inner transformation, the way of soul alchemy. One of the most compelling is that of the oyster, which transforms an irritating grain of sand into a precious and valuable pearl. The oyster is a highly advanced alchemist and we can learn much from this creature's perseverance and artistry. We too can take the pains of life, experiences that might torment and destroy us, and use them as the raw materials for an inner work of great beauty. Just as the oyster produces a beautiful substance out of itself in order to overcome the painful grain of foreign matter, so can we weave thoughts and feelings imbued with understanding and love—transforming challenges into inner strength.

Another image of alchemy from nature is the diamond, which through tremendous pressure has evolved from a state of raw carbon into an incomparable gem, possessing everlasting brilliance and worth. At this time, most human beings are like amber, a lovely organic mineral that is still evolving. Amber is halfway between the state of raw carbon and that of diamond. Amber is valuable, but not nearly so refined as a diamond, a genuine marvel of nature. Diamonds can look like imitation glass to casual observation. But once put to the test, glass is easily shattered. Diamonds, by contrast, will withstand the most crushing pressure. The alchemy of the soul is to develop the diamond heart. Our souls will become shining jewels when we can use the raw material of our experiences and condense them into a soul substance of imperishable value. This is the sacred path of the new culture, the path of wisdom and love. In the words of Peter Deunov,

"We need the high temperature of the fire of love and the great pressure of wisdom in order for our souls to become divine."

Those who would be alchemists must acknowledge where work needs to be done. We grow by gently replacing unkind thoughts with friendly ones—by tirelessly employing constructive affirmations and prayers. When love becomes the mantra of our hearts, slowly but surely we will change the circuitry of our inner lives. As troubled emotions are transmuted to the warmth of understanding, we absorb light into the substance of the soul. We weave new luminous "garments" to replace the old ones that no longer fit us. In this way one becomes an alchemist of the soul, a fashioner of "diamonds"—imperishable jewels of the spirit.

MUSIC IS FEELING MADE AUDIBLE

In our work of soul alchemy, music can be a great ally. Music has a powerful link to the feeling dimension—the soul world. Music can be used to "educate" our feelings. But here, too, soul alchemy requires that we be selective. Much of contemporary art and music may more likely irritate than inspire. The touchstone of the influence of a piece of art or music on our spiritual lives is simply to observe its effect on us. Does it make us happy? Does it expand us and make us better people? Does it prompt us to acts of goodness or creativity? In art, just as in nutrition, we can imitate Saraswati's swan. We can discriminate before we swallow.

Many people have changed their lives by falling in love with the music of a great composer. Inspired music can be a gateway into the higher worlds. An experience of mine was just such a gateway. It was a time when my musical fare consisted mostly of the Rolling Stones and Led Zeppelin. I was working in a bookstore that played mainly classical music, a situation that didn't excite me. One day a Mozart Concerto was streaming through the speakers. I clearly remember carrying a pile of books across the room when a lovely strain caused me to stop in my tracks. I felt transported by the impact of the music's beauty. Those few bars were for me a portal into an "altered state" of consciousness. It became a defining moment in my life. From that day on I listened to every piece of Mozart's music I could purchase or borrow. Discovering

Mozart altered my perceptions about beauty and awakened me cultur-ally. For me, listening to Mozart was musical alchemy.

Music can harmonize the soul and is often a prelude to the experi-ence of a higher level of awareness. The ancients taught that music originated in the songs of angels. The Greeks believed that the nine Muses inspired all the arts, including music. In fact, *music* comes from the Greek name for these graceful, angelic spirits. Schubert said that he heard his musical compositions in the atmosphere around him before writing them down. For many centuries it was commonly believed that those who remained unaffected by beautiful music were opening themselves to harmful influences. In Shakespeare's words, "The man that has no music in himself, nor is not moved with concord of sweet sounds, is fit for treason, stratagems and spoils."

Inspired music is a reflection of harmonies that originate at very high levels of universal vibration. Music has the capacity to heal and transform wounded emotions. Perhaps this is why Beethoven said that people who listened to his music would never need to suffer again.

Music has been known to move an entire people to heroic deeds. In the mid-nineteenth century, Guiseppe Verdi wrote his great opera *Nabucco* as a thinly veiled metaphor of the political situation of his beloved Italy, which at the time was controlled largely by foreign pow-ers. This fact was not lost on his compatriots, who were inspired when they heard the memorable lyrics and melodies. Verdi's music helped unite the Italian people behind the efforts of Garibaldi to bring inde-pendence and unity to his country.

Music can transform sorrow into understanding and be an impe-tus to our growth. "As long as you can sing," said Peter Deunov, "you can find your way out of sorrow." Singing uplifts us emotionally and puts us in touch with the joy of the spirit. Devotional singing and chanting have always played an important role in spiritual practice. "Those who sing, pray twice," wrote St. Augustine. Inspired music forms a protective aura around an individual, which influences him or her toward harmonious decisions and actions. Beautiful music puts us in direct contact with higher worlds from which emanate inspiration and spiritual light. Singing and music create powerful vibrations or sound frequencies, which have a tremendous influence on the substance of our bodies. This directly impacts our emotional states and our physical health.

Our emotions are closely linked to our memory, and the connection between memory and music has long been recognized. Through the mysterious power of association, certain songs or pieces of music will awaken dormant images of long-forgotten memories. Music conjures imagery and emotion because music is a facet or expression of feeling. Music is feeling made audible. By immersing ourselves in music that moves our soul, we can link ourselves to the light. Great music fills us with beauty and helps us grow and expand as individuals. The power of music to heal and inspire will be used much more commonly in the enlightened therapies of the future.

A sacred culture is characterized by sacred music. Popular music of today is searching—groping blindly at times—for a passageway into the music of the future. The current worldwide fascination with Celtic music is a facet of this search. There are other symptoms of a longing for a renewal of sacred music. In the late 1970s and early eighties, America rediscovered Pachelbel's *Canon*. It seemed everyone all at once fell in love with this distinctively lovely and harmonious baroque piece. Similarly, in the mid nineties there was a resurgence of interest in Medieval Gregorian chants. The fantastically popular pop release *Enigma* featured haunting Gregorian chants interlaced with an upbeat, otherworldly blend of passion and spiritual yearning. Shortly after, monks from a monastery in Spain released their CD, *Chant*, which sold millions worldwide in a matter of weeks. It is likely that an entirely new form of sacred music will emerge in the years ahead.

Our Best Feelings Link us to Heaven

Our consciousness can be thought of as a song—a composition we create in our souls. Our thoughts are the lyrics, our feelings are the melodic accompaniment. Our actions are the steps we take in our dance toward liberation and happiness. Just as plants die if exposed to dissonant music, so do our souls and bodies wither if the "song" of our consciousness—formed by our thoughts and feelings—is dissonant and discordant. We choose the lyrics of our song. We create the melody that lives in our heart. If we wish, we can sing a divine song that brings joy to ourselves and others. We change our lives when we "change our tune."

Feelings are the gateway of the heart; they are the substance of our souls. Feelings give depth to character. People of shallow feeling do not arouse much response in others. People with strong feelings, such as poets, mystics, saints and artists, invariably have an impact upon their fellows. In order for thoughts to have a direct impact in the physical affairs of daily life, they need to be linked to strong feelings.

It is also true that thoughts alone, no matter how lofty, no matter how positive, are unable of themselves to create happiness. Our best thoughts must penetrate into the emotional dimension, stimulating and awakening corresponding feelings, before we can experience happiness. Happiness comes to those who awaken love in their hearts. Feelings of affection, kindness, love and appreciation of beauty are the angels that open the gates of contentment. Our finest feelings give wings to our soul.

The higher emotions of love, compassion, joy and serenity are the passport to a deeper state of consciousness—the awareness that life is a seamless tapestry of interrelationship. The wellsprings of genius lie in the cultivation of these elevated feelings that remain slumbering in most people. Ancient cultures realized that feelings of wonder, reverence and devotion formed the inner foundation for the quest for truth. Such emotions may be kindled by contemplation of inspired art, by listening to the works of the great composers, or by love of nature. They may be awakened by literature, poetry, or by the study of the spiritual teachings of the world. One's feeling response to an inspired thought is as important as the idea. Your best feelings become a bridge into a more generous and exalted state of understanding and wisdom. They are the gateway to a happy, creative and fulfilled life.

We choose our direction in life by that which we introduce into our consciousness. Soul alchemy consists of choosing thoughts and activities that awaken feelings of happiness and light. In feelings of harmony, inspiration, joy and love, the Elixir of Life lies concealed. We say "yes" to life when we nourish our souls on the ambrosia of radiant feelings. When we transmute ordinary emotions into the warmth of love, we are engaged in the highest form of soul alchemy. Every time we transmute discordant emotions into understanding and compassion, we are distilling in our souls the Elixir of Life.

In each moment of life we have a choice. We can express a grievance, or see the positive, hopeful element. We can curse the weeds, or rejoice in the flowers. The choice is ours each moment of every day.

Exercises In Sacred Living:
Activating the Alchemy of Feeling and Desire

Each day for a week set aside at least five minutes for the following exercise. Find a quiet place where you will not be disturbed. Close your eyes, relax your body and your breathing. Visualize yourself standing beside a beautiful mountain waterfall. See yourself stepping into the crystal cascade of the falls. The water is the perfect temperature for you. Imagine that this water has special healing, rejuvenating properties. All darkness of negative, discordant feeling is being removed by this magical, refreshing cascade. Feel all fatigue and resentment vanishing. All bitterness is washed away in the ceaseless torrent from the falls.

Imagine that entirely new and wonderful feelings are pouring into you. Picture yourself as you were at one of the happiest moments of your life. See yourself smiling. Tell yourself that it is natural to experience happiness. Know that the degree of happiness you experience is a result of your habitual emotions. Your thoughts give birth to your feelings. The waterfall represents the positive current in nature that uplifts, restores and heals. See yourself leaving the waterfall and sitting on a comfortable bench by the falls. Imagine that a sun of warmth is shining in your heart. Feel the happiness and smile!

Along with this exercise, notice what you are feeling as often as possible during the day. Try consciously to replace negative feelings with the warmth and light of a higher emotion.

Affirmations

"Happiness comes to those with love in their hearts. My path is a path of love."

"My feelings are a tremendous power. I honor my true feelings by filling them with the light of wisdom, the warmth of kindness, and the power of truth."

"All my emotions are becoming positive and life-bestowing."

"I realize that my desires are the fuel that feeds my actions. All my desires are becoming constructive; they are leading me to a happy and fulfilled life."

"My life continually gets better. I am happy and fulfilled even now."

CHAPTER FOUR

THE ALCHEMY OF ACTION
AND SACRED SPACE

"One grows most tired by standing still."

– Chinese proverb

"....charity isn't a matter of fine sentiments;
it means doing things."

– St. Therese of Lisieux

When we first become aware that our inner world of thoughts and feelings is the supreme influence in creating our experience, we may have a tendency to discount the importance of physical activity. But this would be a mistake. No progress in life is possible without action.

Many spiritually-minded people have a deeply held belief that God will take care of all their needs and they need not exert themselves in any way. I believe that this is a distortion of a profound life truth. It is true that Divine Intelligence will take care of our needs— if we work with it by living in accordance with the universal sacred laws. This means learning to become co-creators, not simply passive "watchers."

There is a gigantic difference between working *with* cosmic intelligence and simply expecting everything to drop in our hands. The vital power in the seeds of the vegetable kingdom originates from cosmic intelligence. But we can only have a garden if we till the soil and plant the seeds. No true healer will say that they are the source of the healing power. But for this healing energy to work through them, they must cooperate with it. The healing force that mysteriously repairs a broken bone comes from God, but we must first properly set the bone or risk becoming crippled. The Hindu saint Ramakrishna told the following story to illustrate the idea of working with universal intelligence. A man sitting in a jungle tree sees a rogue elephant stampeding and calls down to a traveler walking along the trail. "Get out of the way, a rogue elephant is coming!" The traveler replies, "There's no need for concern. God will take care of me." Moments later, he is injured by the wild elephant. As he lies on the jungle floor, the traveler complains aloud to God for not protecting him. The man in the tree calls down: "Why didn't you listen to God warning you to get out of harm's way?"

This anecdote illustrates the need for involvement in life. The forces of the universe come to our aid as we translate thoughts, dreams and desires into action. The alchemists represented the physical body and environment metaphorically as "salt." This element also represented the acting power—the will. In order to perform the "great work" of transformation, which resulted in increased vitality and illumination, alchemists knew that they must engage their wills. There is simply no substitute for action. Like it or not, no lasting reward comes without effort. No great thing was ever achieved without exertion.

Nonetheless, much wasteful and unessential activity can be eliminated by conscious effort in the realm of thought. The game of golf teaches us the importance of economy of energy—of reducing nonessential efforts. Unlike most games, in golf *less* is best. In order to reduce wasteful activity—to take "strokes off your game"—it is necessary to think through one's goals and devise a strategy that will lead to success. Guidance in life comes from within—from our mind, our heart, our soul and our thinking spirit. In formulating our plans, it is always helpful to commit goals and objectives to writing. Once a course of action has been decided upon, it's time to "get into the act."

On ancient Egyptian art one can sometimes see the image of the sun with many rays extending to the Earth. A remarkable thing about these rays is that they have a hand at each end, in a gesture of blessing. This image has great significance. The sun has always been a symbol of the spirit. The hand represents action—the power of will. One interpretation of the sun with the many hands touching the Earth is that thinking must be expressed in deeds. It's not enough to have good ideas, you have to get involved to really make a difference. Real commitment is always expressed by action. It is through our "hands," that is, through our work, that we transform our lives. Idealism can only make a practical difference if we live it. In alchemical terms, when we realize or actualize our ideals through our actions, we are "crystallizing the spirit."

The fact that the hands of the solar rays, in the above-described Egyptian image, have a soft, caressing gesture is also significant. It represents the fact that enlightened deeds bestow blessings and assistance. Our actions are best when warmth and light shine through them. You can fulfill your purpose and your destiny only if you give fully of yourself. Loving actions are the foundation of a sacred culture.

THE MAGIC OF THE ACTING POWER

No matter how much we do inwardly with thoughts and feelings, we must also take action in order to produce results in the material world. From where do we draw the inner strength to act? Emerson said, "Do the deed and you shall have the power." Just as no one can eat for you, so no one can perform the deeds that you alone can perform. Each of us is the miracle-working power in all that we desire to have done. The capacity for dynamic action springs from the inner reservoir of our soul. The springboard of action lies in the feelings and desires that prompt us to be up and doing. The more powerful and intense our desires, longings and aspirations—one might say "our dreams"—the more powerful will be our capacity to act. Intention is the seed that gives birth to the deed.

In the desire to avoid stress, some people have lost sight of the fact that activity is often not the cause of stress at all. Frequently, stress is rooted in emotional and subconscious factors connected to procrastination, that is, the *avoidance* of activity. The source of stress in many cases is having *not done* the tasks that need completion. In this event, no amount of massage or "R and R" is going to relieve the stress. There are times when the best form of stress therapy is getting motivated.

It is valuable to write down in detail our goals and intentions, but we can only realize our aims if we follow up goal-planning with action. The combination of intention with practical effort often produces surprising results. When I left my teaching position, I had almost no money and needed a job. A friend of mine, named Robert, was painting houses at the time and I asked him if he needed an assistant. He told me that if I could find a house to paint, I would have a job.

That night I wrote out a short "telephone script," which in essence stated that my professional painting company offered excellent service at reasonable prices. We would be in the area the next day, and if the homeowner wanted their house painted we would be happy to make an offer. Then I picked up the phone book, opened to the "B's," and started calling. The third person I called was a building contractor who was just completing a large home in an upscale neighborhood. The house needed painting—inside and out—and he invited me to come by and make a bid. I called Robert and the next day he drove by the house. He made an offer, got hired, and I had a job.

We dynamically create our own lives when we live at the origin of experience, that is, at the point of causation. The Greek philosopher, Archimedes said "Give me a lever and fulcrum and I will move the world." We all possess these tools. The fulcrum is our mental focus—our field of attention—which we can use to select the kind of experience we desire. The lever is the ability to consciously act in accordance with universal laws and principles. A simple way to express this idea is that "You get what you set." Not only can we start to consciously create what we want, but we can remove obstacles from our path—just as a lever and fulcrum can remove a large boulder—if we understand these truths.

Stephen Jobs, the legendary founder of Apple Computer, knew the importance of taking action. As a teenager, Jobs was brilliant and charismatic, but he was unsure of what he wanted to do with his life. In 1974, at the age of nineteen, he journeyed to India in quest of spiritual inspiration and enlightenment. Upon his return to California, he and Stephen Wozniak built preassembled computer circuit boards in Jobs' parents' garage. On April 1, 1976 they formed the Apple Computer company and began marketing the Apple I personal computer. Other companies had designed similar systems, but were not making significant efforts to market their product. Steven Jobs realized the extraordinary potential of the new technology. It was a combination of his and Wozniak's innovations, along with their bold and enterprising marketing efforts, that led to Apple's legendary success. Steven Jobs envisioned the possibilities and he acted with swift and sustained enthusiasm.

BALANCING "EAST" AND "WEST"

In the past several decades there has been a tremendous outpouring of ancient spiritual literature from the East. The ancient teachings of the Vedas—India's earliest sacred scriptures—and the sacred writings of Japan, China, and Tibet have become readily available in America and Europe. Hundreds of spiritual teachers and gurus have come to teach, and many eager students have benefited from their instruction. The East has contributed enormously to the spiritual awakening in the West that has transformed so many people's lives. But it also true that the West has much to offer the East. In the East, the tendency, at least in the past, has been to place great emphasis on inner experience and to place far less importance on the perfection of the environment. In the West the tendency has been to seek to perfect the environment, and the emphasis historically has been on the external, often to the detriment of the inner life. The two contrasting tendencies can be seen in the images of the East Indian sadhu, or holy man—who seeks spiritual ecstasy in a decrepit, neglected environment—and the wealthy Western businessman who has every external comfort, yet is driven to suicide by spiritual emptiness.

Both of these are extremes that represent an imbalance. A harmonious approach would be to seek to improve the environment by applying spiritual idealism to one's affairs, while working at self improvement that gives spiritual meaning and fulfillment to life. The ideal of the future will be the pursuit of spiritual accomplishment in a harmonious and beautiful environment. The physical body will be recognized as the temple of the spirit. Physical beauty and health will be the foundation of a harmonious life of spiritual growth. In the sacred culture now dawning, each man will be his own priest and each woman her own priestess. Our environment will be seen as a sacred shrine—what the Greeks called *temenos*—and the body will be seen as the holy temple of spirit.

Illusion or Revelation?

From ancient India comes the concept of the world as *maya*, or illusion. Because the material world is impermanent, it therefore has no ultimate reality. Hence, in ultimate terms, it is an illusion. Although soul alchemy recognizes the impermanent and therefore illusory character of the physical world, it places a different emphasis on understanding nature. An alchemist looks at nature as the handiwork of higher beings. Behind the visible world lies the world of divine causation. Nature is an image of this higher world, concealing the divine presence from the ignorant, yet revealing it to "those who have eyes to see." Alchemists often spoke of being able to perceive the influence of celestial bodies and angelic beings or nature spirits within the processes of nature. The stamp of a higher influence was called a "signature." In this view, one might say that the whole of nature bears the "divine signature"—the stamp of its divine authors. To the spiritual alchemist, nature becomes more than simply an illusion. It is a divine revelation.

To the alchemist, nature is a living book of great wisdom. Everything in the world bears the stamp of its divine authors. Nature reflects and reveals a higher intelligence that is apparent everywhere. In soul alchemy, the ideal is not to escape an illusory world of painful conditions. The goal, instead, is to permeate the world with sacred influences. Just as the Hierarchies of angels infused matter with their substance and intelligence, so can human beings seek to put a divine signature into their affairs by bringing the spirit into expression in the world. The alchemist seeks to perceive the divine signature in all things. She or he becomes an extension of a higher divine order and actively attempts to create sacred conditions in the world. In traditional theological terms this might be described as bringing about the "Kingdom of God" on Earth.

CREATING SACRED SPACE =
THE REDEMPTION OF THE SENSES

The material environment is the arena for our physical actions. The highest motive in action is to seek to make the world a better place by what we do. This means that the world we live in ought to gradually come to express the trinity of spiritual qualities that make up the ancient philosophical ideal: beauty, goodness and truth. The current interest in creating sacred space reflects a yearning on the part of many people to make life spiritually meaningful and to transform the physical environment into a reflection of an imaged beauty.

Our home and work space have a tremendous effect on our experience of who we are. From earliest childhood, the environment has a profound influence in shaping who we become. "We shape our buildings; thereafter, they shape us," said Winston Churchill. Our environment reflects back upon our inner life and affects our moods, thoughts and disposition. In the view of soul alchemy, the noblest approach is not to escape painful conditions in the world, but to transform the world into the image of the divine.

Our technological world bombards our senses with stimulation that can be overpowering. The constant impact from electronic media, long hours in traffic, the cacophony of machines, the radiation from computer and television screens, and the sheer volume and dissonance of much of modern music can desensitize us to the subtle rhythms of nature and the quiet voice of the soul. These modern "techno-influences" can coarsen our senses, dampening awareness of more subtle beauty. In some folk tales, a princess is spellbound by the enchantment of an evil sorceress. It takes the kiss of the prince to release the princess from her bondage. Another variation of this motif is the prince who has been changed into a frog by an evil curse. The kiss of the princess transforms him again into his true nature. These folk tales are imaginative renditions of soul alchemy, the miracle of inner awakening and transformation. Such tales have meaning for us today.

Modern life can cast a spell upon our senses, rendering us unconscious of the wonders of the spirit. To free our senses from bondage to a purely material and utilitarian lifestyle, we need the liberating "kiss" provided by beauty and sacred space. This is a higher kind of enchantment that comes from feeding the senses with colors, music, rhythms, scents and scenery that nurture our appreciation of the divine in ourselves and the world. Walking in nature, listening to uplifting music, gazing upon the splendors of a flower garden are all activities that can heal our senses and *sensitize* us to the spiritual forces behind and within physical life. Appreciation of beauty is one of the most exalted qualities of the spirit. This is one reason we feel drawn to nature, for the beauty of the natural world inspires us with wonder. Reflecting on the beauty of great art or the masterpieces of nature can provide "the kiss" that stirs our sleeping spirits.

When we seek to make the objects of our homes and surroundings more beautiful, we encourage the deeper impulses of the soul. Beauty in the environment not only reflects inner beauty, it draws out wonder, admiration and reverence for life. Beauty lifts us out of the prosaic into the lasting dimensions of the eternal spirit.

Everything in our environment influences us. By becoming conscious of this fact and filling our homes with objects that have a favorable influence, we make our environments sacred. The senses are the gateways into our souls. Everything we allow to enter us from outside has an effect on our mental and emotional states. That is why it is a good practice to open ourselves to the beneficial influence of flowers, uplifting fragrances and beautiful art. When we cultivate beauty in our environment, we awaken beauty in our souls. Alchemists know that flowers exist not only in nature, but also within us. When we cultivate a love of beauty in art or nature, we stimulate and awaken energy centers in our subtle fields—portals into higher states of awareness and happiness.

Simple steps to creating sacred space include using incense, potpourris, sage and "essential oils." Essential oils are the pure liquid extracts of plants. The art and science of employing essential oils goes by the name *aromatherapy*. The use of pure fragrances is an integral part of uplifting our sensory experiences. It is a basic ingredient in soul alchemy. Uplifting scents can transform an atmosphere and harmonize our moods. Since ancient times people have used incense and uplifting plant fragrances to ward off harmful influences and attract beneficial ones. Most ancient cultures believed that the fragrant scents of flowers and certain plants invited the influence and protection of the angelic kingdom.

My wife, Mia, has taught me much about creating sacred space. She turns a free bit of counter or table space into an altar to beauty. With a piece of colored silk, a candle, a flower or crystal she will transform an ordinary area into a reminder of the beauty that uplifts life into the realm of poetry. She will use a greeting card, a photo, an antique book, crystal or pretty shell—or perhaps a feather or leaf snatched from the garden by our daughter—to create a shrine to the sacred. Mia made a seasonal nature table for our daughter that is a delight to us all. Every room has some small shrine to beauty. By burning incense, sage and essential oils daily for years, we have noticeably transformed the atmosphere in our home. Creating sacred space is environmental alchemy.

In the culture of the future, people will make their homes into temples—shrines reflecting the good, the true and the beautiful. When we consecrate our homes, or dedicate a particular room or area for a sacred activity, we attract beneficial influences. I knew a family who kept up a week-long prayer vigil in their home. They had at least one, and usually several, people praying, chanting and meditating twenty-four hours a day for an entire week. A native American shaman told them that they had attracted an angelic influence into their home by their effort. He advised them that henceforth their home would be blessed and protected. It was no longer merely a dwelling; it had become a temple.

Every home benefits by having an altar or sacred place dedicated to a high being, saint or divinity. Those who feel no connection to one of the world's sacred traditions may wish to dedicate their little shrine or altar to nature, beauty, truth or any high ideal that inspires them. A room takes on the influences of the activities that take place there. All our thoughts, feelings and actions leave subtle impressions in the etheric substance that underlies physical matter. Everything we say, do, think and feel is recorded in the luminous membrane, the "akashic light," in which we are immersed. By performing uplifting activities in our homes, or in a space dedicated to our spiritual life, we emanate a stream of positive influences into our subtle environment. Places become sacred when we consecrate them to noble, beneficial purposes.

When we seek to make the home a sacred place, we are mimicking the action of the divine world when it first infused light into creation and established divine proportion in space. Ancient people believed that the god, goddess or divinity in whose honor the temple was built actually came to live in the physical and etheric space of the temple walls. We attract sacred influences by our efforts to invite wisdom and love into the matrix of our dwellings.

Creating sacred space is not limited to an altar, the garden, or an area set aside for spiritual efforts. Even one's office and work desk become more effective and enjoyable if we establish order and beauty. We might not think of an office or business environment as especially sacred. But even simple efforts to organize tasks to get things done effectively can reduce emotional stress and lead to greater effectiveness, and consequently a greater sense of happiness and well-being. When you can organize your time and space so as not to be acting from crisis management, you have greater ability to make conscious choices that enhance the quality of life.

The time will come when each of us realizes that the most important influence in our environment is our own presence. Each of us individually is the most powerful force at work in our personal world. The most important space in an individual's environment is the space he or she occupies. Each person's aura or field of consciousness is a talisman for good, or otherwise, based on the influences one emanates. By working to illumine our inner world and projecting light and kindness from within us, we influence the world around us in a sacred manner.

WHAT MATTERS MOST IS HOW WE LIVE

Activity is not limited just to our physical bodies and external environment. In the *Bhagavad Gita,* India's beloved sacred book, Krishna reminds Arjuna that a wise individual knows "the *action* that is in *inaction,* and the *inaction* that is in *action.*" This cryptic saying refers to the fact that we can be intensively active in our minds when our bodies are still, and conversely, our minds can find a calm resting point of peace and tranquillity even while we are engaged in strenuous external labors.

Everyone is faced with the task of finding the right balance between inner and outer action. The energy of will can work outwardly in the world, or it can turn the gears of consciousness and lead to inner accomplishments of thought, study or prayer. We must come to rely on our own actions, knowing that the seeds we plant must eventually bear fruit of their own kind. By action and effort we liberate ourselves from inertia, which would lead to inner and outer death.

We reveal ourselves through our work. Through good work, or right action, we allow the law of causation—the alchemy of the seed—to work to our own benefit. Your deeds in the world are a revelation of your inner life. Henry David Thoreau said that, "If one advances confidently in the direction of his dreams, and endeavors to live the life which he has imagined, he will meet with a success unexpected in common hours." To live wisely is to demonstrate a harmony in your thoughts, feelings and activities. The ultimate test of any philosophy or worldview is how you live your life. The thing that matters most is not what you profess to believe, but how you actually live. For this reason Gandhi said, "Show me how a man lives; that is his religion."

The sacred literature of the world reminds us that the highest attitude in action is to perform to the best of our ability and not be anxious about results. The results will take care of themselves in their own time. This is not indifference, but a wise detachment that allows equanimity to take root in our souls. We are then not impatient for results and can rest assured that the law always works. We will reap the consequences of what we sow, not in *our* time, but in accordance with a mysterious hidden wisdom that organizes and disposes all life in a rhythm orchestrated by angels and higher beings. This perspective suggests that it is best not to act out of a desire for the fruits of our labor, but rather to act out of love for the work itself because it is the right thing to do. This attitude may seem paradoxical, but it can be emotionally liberating and spiritually enlightening. This approach to living in sacred service to life, without being concerned about the fruits of one's deeds, was highly prized in the ancient sacred texts of India, which gave it the name of Karma Yoga—the path of enlightened action.

Karma Yoga recognizes that our work is most successful and beneficial when we allow the results to take care of themselves in accordance with the mysterious cycles of life—rhythms that are beyond the control of humans. Our work is to plant the seeds and till our fields; the seeds will come to fruition in God's time.

ACTIONS REVEAL OUR INNER LIFE

Truth is revealed through our actions. Not only do actions speak with more eloquence than words, actions reveal the truth of who we are inwardly. Our inner life cannot be hidden. It is exposed for all to the world to see. Our outer conditions and environment are the mirror of what lives in our minds and hearts. What you are on the inside is reflected in your deeds and in what habitually surrounds you on the outside. In the words of Kahlil Gibran, "Work is love made visible."

Some people seem to think that it is enough to "just be." But our "beingness" will always shine through the actions that are prompted by our deep-seated feelings, wishes and aspirations. Thoughts and feelings not expressed in deeds are like works of art that are hidden away in a damp museum cellar. Much of their value is lost. The truth of who we are is revealed in what we do.

Action reveals character just as the full-grown plant reveals the nature of the seed. We transform ourselves and break the chains that enslave us by engaging in constructive efforts. The value of life lies in the wise use of each moment. "Holiness," says Mother Teresa, "does not lie in doing great things. It lies in doing little things with great love."

Actions can be as subtle as a look, a glance or a gesture. Volumes can be spoken through a loving look or a piercing stare. The eyes are truly the windows of the soul and through our eyes we release powerful forces into the world by our gaze and our glance. A hateful stare can be as destructive as a physical blow. I have seen children burst into tears when looked upon derisively. The legendary "evil eye" was a deliberate glance so full of malice that the "victim" was known to be stricken as if with a material poison. A gesture of the hands, a nod of the head, a sincere smile—all of these are actions that release forces into the world. An approving look can communicate more in an instant than the most eloquent speech. In fact, the word "countenance," which refers to the face, also means "to grant approval."

A young man once asked the Vietnamese Zen Buddhist teacher, Thich Nhat Hanh, for a good method to begin the spiritual path. Thich Nhat Hanh told the young man he should keep his mouth in a very slight, barely perceptible smile. Although seemingly insignificant, there is wisdom in this advice, for our mental states are closely connected to our physical gestures and facial expressions. It is difficult to remain unhappy if one makes the effort to smile. Moreover, as Thich Nhat Hanh explained to the young man, when you make the conscious effort to smile, you realize how often you may actually tend to be frowning.

In his profound book entitled *Holiness,* Donald Nicholl describes how a man's life was saved by a face. Olivier Clément was an atheist going through a sorrowful part of his life. His chronic depression made him contemplate suicide. Nicholl writes that Clément took an unhappy walk one day by the shores of the Mediterranean when "his attention was riveted by the face of someone who was passing by. The person's face was radiant with meaning, full of such goodness that can only come about by years of cultivating a loving heart. In a twinkling Clément's suicidal thoughts were dispelled and a seed sown in his heart that was eventually to transform him into an ardent believer." This story is a testimony to the fact that one's facial expressions release forces into the world that can benefit or hurt. It has been said the spiritual life begins with the education of the glance.

ACTION DOES NOT MEAN STRUGGLE

Many people have an approach to activity that leads to burnout. The eighties were a period of cultural fatigue for a large segment of society. The go-go lifestyle of that era—the "splash, dash and crash" syndrome—is a distortion of harmonious activity. Living an active life does not mean running frenetically on all cylinders until we collapse. In fact, when we learn to simplify our lives by eliminating non-essentials, we may find we have masses of time on our hands. Modern media culture, with the all-pervading seduction of advertising, creates an exaggerated pace. So many people are running after an elusive *something* that they believe will fix their lives. Commercial propaganda takes a huge toll on people's emotional and physical well-being—not to mention their finances.

In many ways, our culture contributes to a distorted view of physical action. The Darwinian view that evolution is "the survival of the fittest" has influenced many people to feel that they must "struggle" to obtain things—that work implies stressful, competitive labor. Life does require that we exert ourselves, that we put forth our best efforts, but this does not mean that we must necessarily fight or struggle. Consider the activity of heart and lungs. Through the efforts of these organs our blood circulates and we breathe ceaselessly throughout life. Yet the heart and lungs almost never tire. Only in exceptional instances are we forced to push these organs to the point of exhaustion. Even then, their recovery is quick. The activity of the heart and the lungs is virtually effortless because it is *rhythmic.* This gives us a clue of how to live without struggle. There needs to be balance and rhythm in our activities and our lives. We will discuss the place of rhythm in a harmonious life in Chapter Ten. It will suffice here to call attention to the principle of rhythmic alternation of activities, for it is a key to transcending the struggle for existence.

TRUTH MUST BE LIVED

The saintly teacher, Peter Deunov, once remarked that it is impossible to know the truth solely by one's thinking process. "In order for truth to be known," he declared, "it must be lived." This reflects the fact that wisdom must be expressed in our actions if it is to have real meaning. Love also remains an abstraction unless it is applied. St. John the Divine, the Evangelist who wrote the *Book of Revelation,* says in one of his letters that "Whoever does the truth, comes to the light." Perhaps that is why Jesus considered a hypocrite to be worse than the lowliest of sinners. For to say or pretend one thing and do another is to engage in spiritual deceit. No doubt, the truth will make us free. But truth is not something that the intellect alone can fully grasp. To grasp higher truths they must be expressed through the heart and through right actions.

When Pilate asked Jesus, "What is truth?" Jesus remained silent. He knew that any answer he might give would not have enlightened Pilate, for the Roman official was not living a life that was inviting to truth. Truth comes and dwells within us when we reveal light and love in our relationships and our life. Light and love are the divine artisans that will re-fashion our rough souls until they shine with diamond brilliance.

Our words lose much of their value if not backed by the living power of action. Gandhi demonstrated this principle when a woman brought her son to him and asked Gandhi to tell the boy to stop eating sugar and sweets. Gandhi told the woman to come back to him with the same request in two weeks time. The woman went away puzzled, but returned with her son two weeks later. She again made the same request of Gandhi. This time he told the woman's son to refrain from eating sweets. The woman then asked why he had not done so two weeks before, on her first visit. Gandhi replied that at that time he still ate sweets himself. Gandhi realized that in order for his words to have spiritual power, they must be backed by congruent actions. Gandhi knew that the power of truth, what he called *Satyagraha*, is a force that comes about when we close the gap between our ideals and our actions.

Realistically, there will always be something of a gap between our ideals and where we are in terms of living our ideals. Our current level of realization lags behind our internal perception of where we are going. Although it can be argued that this reveals at least an element of hypocrisy, it accomplishes little if we become too hard on ourselves. What matters is the sincerity of our efforts, the direction we are going. More important than our past is who we are today. More important than who we are today is who we are becoming. Despite our inability to live up to our highest expectations of ourselves, we can continue to plant good seeds and allow the natural course of our efforts to run their course. In time we will note progress if we persist.

THE MAGIC OF PERSEVERANCE

Thomas Edison understood the importance of persistent effort. He is known as a man of genius. He himself said that his discoveries were the result of hard work—"one percent inspiration, ninety-nine percent perspiration." He once told a colleague that during his experiments with electricity, he failed in one experiment more than eighty-one times before finding the right combination of factors that led to success. His colleague was amazed at his perseverance, and exclaimed that it must be like hitting one's head against a brick wall. "Not at all," Edison answered. "You speak of actions that would be painful. I think of challenging excitement. You must see that I always believe I will be successful on the next experiment."

We may not aspire to be inventors, but we can all learn from Edison's perseverance. In pursuing our goals and dreams in life, it's always too early to stop. Perseverance is a master key that eventually proves irresistible. It has been said that "persistence alone is omnipotent."

Many of our activities are based entirely on habit and the expectations of others. We grow as we develop the power of individual initiative—to decide upon a task and do it. Deliberately changing a habit, even one as simple as reducing the time we sit in front of the television, or taking a walk instead of a nap, can be liberating and strengthening. Altering small details in our lives is a part of the soul alchemy of transmuting substance—uplifting the frequencies in our energy field. The capacity to act is essential in the alchemical work of bringing new ideas to life in the world—that is, in manifesting the spirit. Each success leads to a stronger soul and a more supple will. The capacity for decisive action is a characteristic of successful people. It may take courage to overcome habitual inertia and do something new and vital, but the results may be electrifying. The famous words of Goethe capture like no other the extraordinary nature of the acting power:

> "Whatever you can do or
>
> Dream you can, begin it.
>
> Boldness has genius,
>
> Power and magic in it."

Many people become discouraged by disappointments. These experiences sap their energy and their desire to "try again." But failure isn't falling down; it's not getting up. Really, there is no such thing as failure, so long as we continue to learn. We can only learn through being involved with life.

Through action we meet our destiny. By giving fully of ourselves we fulfill our purpose in life. Life cannot be deeply experienced, nor can we develop properly, unless we act. Only through action are we really involved in our own lives. One's inner life of soul is awakened through contact with the world.

Without the possibility of testing ourselves in the arena of life, we have no real way of measuring our progress. Almost anyone can be gentle if they live in a remote cave, avoiding contact with other people. The measure of our growth is the manner in which we respond to challenges and difficulties. The specific nature of the events and incidents that come to try us is of secondary importance. How we respond to events is the primary issue—and the test of our maturity.

Ultimately, the most powerful stimulus to action lies in our emotions and desires. By focusing on what we want in life, we stir our feelings and this triggers the will. When we understand this process, we become effective alchemists, consciously sowing the seeds of a sacred life. Action is essential to growth, for it is through our experiences among people that we learn the lessons of life and give expression to our aspirations, hopes and yearnings. Only through inspired actions can we bring about a sacred culture on the Earth.

Only through deeds can you *live* your dream.

Exercises In Sacred Living:
Activating the Alchemy of Action

Activity Number One

Make a "to do" list of daily and weekly goals and objectives. Stretch yourself by including things that aren't easy for you, or which you have some resistance to doing. Think of it as a game. Make it a challenge. Remember that emotions are the dynamo that sets the will into motion. Try to generate a feeling of enthusiasm for achieving your goals. At the end of each day, check off tasks you've completed. Review your weekly list at the end of seven days. Reflect back on your accomplishments. If you've met your goals, celebrate. Treat yourself to something special. If you've failed to meet expectations, make note of your progress and take courage from all that you did manage to accomplish. Create a new list for the next week.

Activity Number Two

For challenging long-term goals it is helpful to create a "book of dreams." This can be a notebook, a diary or a photo album. Create affirmations that capture in powerful words what you envision for yourself. Place these in the book along with photographs of yourself in the desired situation, whether it be a new home, a new profession, or perhaps an ideal relationship. See yourself in your mind's eye actually reaching your goals. Visualize the details. How will you feel in the moment of achievement? Imagine yourself in that instant and feel that feeling. What would you be thinking? Imagine thinking those thoughts. What clothes might you be wearing? See yourself dressed in them. Picture the surroundings as you imagine they might be.

Remember that at no time should you ever infringe upon the freewill or sovereignty of another person when seeking your personal goals in life. The use of affirmations and visualization in regard to situations that might impose on the freewill of another is, to say the least, unethical, and should be absolutely avoided.

The feeling that arises from successful completion of goals is one of life's sweetest. It becomes fuel for further achievements. Consistently accomplishing tasks that you have set for yourself makes you a winner in the game of life.

Activity Number Three

The following is an activity that works in a subtle way to strengthen our will and also our inner "time organism," so that we are not dependent on alarm clocks. We can train our inner time organism, the etheric body, to trigger us to wakefulness at the appropriate moment. Tell yourself before you fall asleep exactly when you want to wake up. The subconscious mind, which is linked to the etheric body, knows exactly what time it is, even when the conscious mind is soundly asleep. You can program yourself to arise on schedule. This may take some practice, but after several days, you will wake up when you want. You will also give your jangled nerves a break from the "shock" of the alarm. "Where there is a clock, there is no soul," goes an old Hasidic saying. When we free ourselves from the enslavement of the clock, our feelings "breathe" more easily.

Activity Number Four

There are two extremes of unbalanced physical activity that hinder the harmonious application of physical effort. The first is a paralysis of will. Despite good intentions, you simply don't do what you have decided upon. The other is engaging in constant and frenetic activity that is almost a way of filling or ignoring an inner emptiness of soul. As to the first extreme, here are two simple exercises that are helpful in strengthening the capacity to get things done:

Each day choose a simple task—an apparently meaningless action—that has no bearing on your conscious professional goals. It must not be an essential part of your life or something you would normally do for personal pleasure. It may even seem slightly ridiculous, for instance, switching the wrist on which you wear your watch, or bending to your knees, as if to lace up your shoes. Other possibilities are standing on a chair, walking up and down the steps (when you don't need to), or opening a window. With regular practice, exercises of this nature serve to strengthen the will, especially if they are done at the same time each day.

Another simple technique is to act upon an idea as soon as it enters your mind, without hesitation. These two exercises will work to strengthen the acting power so that we are more capable of realizing our goals in life. An added benefit is that a strong will eventually shows itself in a stronger, healthier and more youthful body.

As to the second extreme, if one is prone to hyperactivity, it is helpful to set aside short periods, once or twice daily, even if for only five minutes. During this time avoid all sensory stimulation, close the eyes and perform a simple exercise in visualization. Picture yourself in a beautiful natural setting, possibly relaxing in a lovely garden, seated on a bench in a majestic forest, or upon a mountain with a magical vista. Envision the scenery in minute detail. If at first this is too difficult, try listening to uplifting music while perceiving yourself achieving some of your most cherished life ambitions.

Affirmations

"I am the miracle-working power in everything I desire to have done."

"I create beauty in my environment by love-filled activities."

"Every day I get stronger, more decisive, and more effective."

"I can accomplish all things through the miracle-working power of the spirit within me."

CHAPTER FIVE

THE ALCHEMY OF THE SPOKEN WORD

"Words are the dress of thought."

– Samuel Johnson

"Out of the abundance of the heart the mouth speaks."

– Jesus

The three-pointed crown is an ancient emblem of authority. Although the age of monarchy is over, the symbol of the crown still holds meaning. It represents *sovereignty*. The word sovereignty means "the right to rule." Each human being has that God-given right—the right to govern one's own life—the right to become a free individual.

"One who conquers himself," said Gautama, "is greater than another who conquers a thousand times a thousand men on the battlefield." Every man and woman is meant to exert dominion in his or her life. This dominion represents royal authority—kingship and queenship within our personal world. The crown is a symbol of this authority with which we all have been endowed in order to rule supreme over the conditions of our life.

The three points of the crown represent authority in the three "realms" of human life discussed in the previous three chapters: the mind, the emotions and the physical world. This triad corresponds to the alchemical trinity of sulfur, mercury and salt. These substances represent symbolically spirit, soul and body—or mind, feelings and the power to act. As we strive to express dominion in the kingdom of our mind, soul and physical environment, we take steps on the journey to self-mastery in our lives. This is the challenge facing all human beings. The greatest enemies and obstacles are within. Only fools and tyrants seek power over others. The wise seek power over themselves.

THE PATH OF SELF MASTERY

Soul alchemy is the path of self-mastery. Those who seek to master their lives are following in the footsteps of the saints, adepts and initiates—those who have learned to govern their thoughts, emotions and actions. These are the ones who reign supreme over the fluctuations of life. It is worth noting that the "three kings" of the Christmas story were not principally ruling monarchs in the traditional sense. They were "magi," plural for "magus," the root for the word "magician." These three *magi* had authority over the elements of nature, both external nature and within their own lives. They were what the ancient Mysteries called Initiates or Adepts—bearers of the heavenly wisdom that comes from spiritual knowledge and self-mastery. Although most of us have a long way to go in realizing this ideal, acknowledging a goal or direction in life helps us take steps in that direction.

Ancient and modern metaphysics points out that the human personality consists of the three "soul forces" of thinking, feeling and physical will. The higher self—sometimes called the individuality—also has three primary attributes, often described as wisdom, love and power. The sulfur, mercury and salt of the alchemists are symbolic of, and correlate exactly to, these psychological trinities. These two "selves," or aspects of our being—the individuality and the personality—may be represented as two equilateral triangles.

Picture the triangle of the individuality pointing downward and the triangle of the personality pointing upward. The integration of these two triangles forms a six-pointed star or hexagram, often called the Seal of Solomon, which represents the fusion of these two "selves." The stellar hexagram, or Seal of Solomon, is a symbol of the alchemical marriage of the human with the divine, the personality with the higher self. It represents the journey of soul alchemy, the process of elevating our thoughts and emotions by imbuing them with the light of wisdom and the buoyancy of love. It signifies what the ancient Mysteries called *initiation*, the path that leads to higher consciousness and mastery of our lives. Alchemists sometimes called this process "the marriage of the sun and moon."

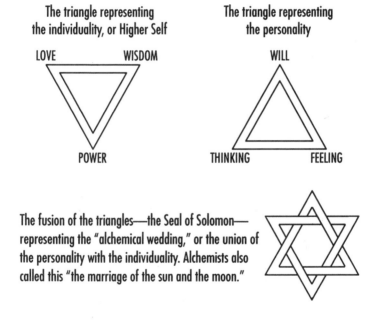

The triangle representing the individuality, or Higher Self

LOVE WISDOM

POWER

The triangle representing the personality

WILL

THINKING FEELING

The fusion of the triangles—the Seal of Solomon—representing the "alchemical wedding," or the union of the personality with the individuality. Alchemists also called this "the marriage of the sun and the moon."

OUR MAGIC WAND

All of us have been given a magic wand to help exert authority in our minds, emotions and physical life—the three fundamental "realms" of life. This magic wand is the tongue—that is, the power of the spoken word. Speech contains a tremendous power for good or for ill. The tongue's twin power, either for benefit or for bane, is seen in the capacity of speech either to bless or to curse. John Templeton tells the following African legend, which illustrates the tongue's dual power.

"...an old chief needed to test the wisdom of the young man he had chosen to be his successor as tribal head. He asked the boy to prepare two meals for him. The first meal was to contain the very best ingredients life had to offer; the second meal would contain the very worst.

On the appointed day, the chief sat down to his first meal and it was a delicious plate of sliced cow tongue with vegetables. The chief was delighted with the food and, upon finishing, asked the boy why he had chosen tongue.

'The tongue is one of the finest parts of our being,' the young man replied. 'It can speak wonderful words of truth that can help our people grow and prosper. The right words can give them courage and bolster their integrity. Tongues can speak of love and harmony and hold our village together.'

The chief was very impressed and waited for the second meal with eager anticipation. On the appointed day the chief sat down to eat his second meal and found it to be identical to the first. When he had finished, he asked the boy why he had prepared the same meal twice.

The young man answered, 'The tongue can be the best part of us, but it can also be the worst. The tongue can speak words of anger and discouragement that tear people down and rob them of hope. It can weave deceit; it can speak untruth that causes disharmony. The tongue more than any other weapon can destroy our village life.' The old chief listened closely and nodded his head. He knew he had chosen the next leader wisely."

Our words are forces that are constantly creating our personal world. When we speak, we make our thoughts and feelings audible. Ideas become sound through spoken words. Along with the face value of words—that is, the meaning or thought behind them—speech carries an additional extraordinary power, one that is only beginning to be understood. It is something within the vibratory quality of sound itself.

A Sound Education

When I lived in Europe, I had the good fortune to study at Emerson College, located in an idyllic setting among the rolling fields of southern England. Courses were offered in spiritual science, philosophy and various arts. We studied the creative and formative powers of speech—the fact that speech is an expression of our deeper soul. In the ancient temples, the study of the human being's relationship with the cosmos began with the study of speech. Speech was considered a divine gift to humanity from the angelic Hierarchies. The Creator Spirits—called in Genesis, the Elohim, or "Spirits Before the Throne"—brought the Earth into being through sound and stabilized vibration. The Gospel of St. John begins with the famous words, "In the beginning was the Word." Jesus said, "Heaven and Earth shall pass away, but my words shall not pass away." His thought is paraphrased in the English children's round that goes,

"All things must perish from under the sky.

Music alone shall live, never to die."

Sound is the underpinning to material existence. In the ancient wisdom of the temple Mysteries, every sound was recognized to have an attribute of consciousness. In other words, sounds awaken sentiments within the speaker and the listener. Philosopher and educator Rudolf Steiner reintroduced these Mysteries of the spoken word in the art of movement called *Eurythmy*. Eurythmy employs specific human movements to reflect the forms created in space by speech and music. Eurythmy is an artistic language—a kind of "modern dance"—that makes speech and music visible through movement and gesture. Through the study of the formative power of speech, one learns that each sound has unique qualities and awakens different moods and thoughts.

Consider, for example, the sound "ah." It is an expression of wonder, admiration and devotion. We might exclaim "ah" or "ah ha," when we suddenly have an inspired thought or a new idea or realization. We can see the higher qualities of the sound "ah" in the fact that the word for God in many languages contains this vowel.

In Sanskrit, the Hindu creator God is *Brahma*. In ancient Egypt, *Ra* and *Aton* were principal names for the Creator. Several Hebrew names for God contain the sacred sound "ah." These include *Jehovah*, *Yah* and *Eloha*. The word *Eloha* is especially interesting. In Aramaic, the language spoken by Jesus, the word for God was *Alaha*—derivative of *Eloha*. The very same word for God exists in Arabic; it is "Allah." The

Hawaiian or Polynesian word *aloha* may be related to *Eloha, Alaha* and *Allah.* As well as "hello" and "goodbye," the word *aloha* can mean love. The Sanskrit word *Aoum*—expressive of divinity or divine energy— starts with the "ah" sound and expands in its fullness to encompass most of the vowels. It has been said that if one pronounces the *Aoum* correctly, one sets in motion forces that cause the "etheric field," or life body, to vibrate. The etheric body is the subtle "energy matrix" or underlying vital element that gives life and animation to the physical body. The etheric body circulates the vital element called *prana* in India, *chi* in Chinese medicine, *ki* in Japanese, *mana* in Hawaiian, and the "bioplasmic" or "morphological" field by some scientists.

Not only the sound "ah," but all vowels and consonants have a specific relationship to thought, feeling and consciousness. When we become conscious of our speech, we open the door into the eternal Mysteries. With an understanding of the creative power of sound, we find new meaning in the search to find "our voice."

GOOD VIBRATIONS

While in Switzerland, I continued my studies in speech and drama. There I discovered the branch of physics called *cymatics,* which has developed in recent years in order to understand the power and influence of sound upon matter. It was pioneered by Dr. Hans Jenny, a Swiss scientist, who coined the term *cymatics* from the Greek word for *wave.* The science of cymatics has demonstrated through laboratory experiments what was known in the ancient Mystery Schools and taught by Pythagoras in his academy in Italy 2,600 years ago—that sounds change the very matrix of physical substance itself. Our words literally mold, shape, and arrange subtle physical patterns.

Hans Jenny photographed and filmed the effects that different sounds had on various mobile substances, such as powder, water and sand. His research proves conclusively that sound frequencies create forms in space and substance. Specific sounds create specific forms. These forms are geometric patterns—what might be called "lines of force." Each sound creates its own unique image in space and in substance.

The work of Hans Jenny was a continuation of the work of 18th century German physicist, Chladne. Chladne developed an experiment using a metal plate on which he placed grains of sand. Then he drew a violin bow across the edge of the plate, creating a sound not unlike a musical note. As the tone was made by the violin bow, the grains of sand formed into a pattern. In the areas of the plate with the most vibration, no sand particles settled. The areas where there was no vibration—called "null points"—were the places where sand settled, forming a distinct visual appearance. Experiments like those done by Chladne and Hans Jenny demonstrate irrefutably that sound shapes and molds substance according to the laws of vibration. Every word we speak has an effect in our lives.

Every time we speak we create vibrational patterns that affect the physical body as well as the atmosphere around us. Although subtle, these sound patterns are as real as the vibrations created by the impact of a hammer on metal or wood. The wave forms we create in space and in our bodies can be compared to the waves created when a heavy object is thrown into a still pool of water. These sound waves, vibrations, or frequencies affect not only our physical form, but also our so-called "energy bodies"—the emotional and mental field in which we live.

Our words are a major force in shaping our personal reality. Through repetition of specific patterns we create laws for ourselves. The subconscious mind is influenced by our habitual trend of speaking. As a result, we are always making suggestions to ourselves, which tend to become self-fulfilling prophecies. By our speech we decree what will come into our life.

This helps to explain the rationale and effectiveness of spoken prayers, mantras, invocations, and "decrees"—word formulas that produce a heightened awareness and cause specific results. The sound itself, through its vibrational potency, brings about a change not only in the speaker, but also in the environment.

Your words create a web of subtle energy around you that gradually crystallizes into the actual disposition of your physical body. Negative speech over time creates a slumping, hunched posture. Vibrant, positive thoughts and words make the body upright and healthy. Habitual speech, as also habitual thought, affects your physical organs and your health. Profanity, slander, and foolish speech imprison one in a kind of vibratory web. In many cases, people prone to negative speech habits create a "sound wall" between themselves and their higher consciousness. We improve our lives when we strive to utter only significant speech.

When we guard our speech, taking care not to utter negative remarks, we find that other good qualities in us become stronger. This was recognized by the Sufi woman Rabi'a, a saint of ancient Baghdad. When her followers asked her how to develop the spectrum of spiritual virtues that she herself possessed, she simply answered, "Stop complaining."

The law of the spoken word reaches its fulfillment in the practice of blessing. To bless means "to speak good"—to speak well of yourself and others. When you utter blessings, you activate beneficial forces through your speech. One who develops the habit of speaking blessings, either in word or in thought, becomes a force for good in the world. A facet of the practice of blessing is the technique of *affirmation*. "Affirmation" means saying *yes* to life. It is a positive declaration of our higher potential, the greater being we are in process of becoming. Affirmations are a means of healing and renewal. When your words are positive and life-bestowing, you will create a more beautiful future for yourself and others. When we mentally affirm truth, we create a consciousness of success and capability. When we speak these affirmations aloud we stir up forces on the physical plane, which go forth like a swarm of invisible helpers, working to produce positive results.

CHANGE YOUR SPEECH AND CHANGE YOUR DESTINY

The combination of affirmations with silent or spoken prayers is truly an awesome power. Many people have realized their goals and life ambitions by using prayer along with affirmations in a consistent and persistent manner. Jan Ross is a gifted and internationally-known intuitive, who has helped and inspired thousands of people over her long career. She owns a popular bookstore in Phoenix, Arizona, which bears her name. She told me that she established and built her impressive store through the positive power of prayer and affirmations. Like Jan Ross, many successful people have used prayer, invocations and spoken affirmations to help construct the life they desire.

For our words to regain their full magic, we must begin to master our thoughts and feelings. The origin of speech lies in our innermost thoughts, moods and reflections. Those who use the gift of speech to speak well of others are releasing constructive, healing forces into the world.

Conversation is an area of immense potential for service and personal growth. A kind, helpful word is enough to change a person's mood, or alter their day's experience. Words can change a person's life. We have a great responsibility to use words carefully and constructively. For this reason, *right speech* was one of the cornerstones of Buddha's Eightfold Path.

Conversation is an art. Few realize the power and potential of constructive conversation. Most people complain and criticize, find fault with others, or bemoan their lot in life. If we use speech and conversation consciously as a field of helpful expression, we find that we are presented with many moments through the course of a day in which to help others and make progress ourselves. It has been said that "Good words are worth much and cost little."

"There is always something beautiful to be found if we look for it," said White Eagle. A beautiful story from the early apocryphal writings illustrates this truth. The story describes Jesus walking with his disciples when they come upon a dead animal, half-rotted and partially eaten by scavengers. The disciples groan and exclaim at the stench and decay. After a moment of silence Jesus remarks to them, "What beautiful teeth the creature had!"

Our Words Can Never Be Fully Retracted

Truly, our words are magic powers that do much to determine our lives. Once they pass our lips they are gone forever. From Shakespeare's drama of *King Lear* comes a powerful example of the decisive nature of speech. The tragic king learns that his beloved daughter, Cordelia, has been sentenced to death. Lear sends a desperate command to halt the execution, but the message arrives too late. The previous order has been carried out and the devoted Cordelia is dead. Our words set in motion forces that sometimes cannot be retracted. Mikhael Aivanhov tells the following story of Mohammed to illustrate this truth.

One day a man came to Mohammed and voiced his sadness and frustration. He was miserable at himself for having argued angrily with a friend. He felt sorrow for his unkind words and asked the Prophet what he should do to make amends. Mohammed told the man to go around town placing feathers on the steps of many homes. He instructed the man to leave the feathers during the night and retrieve them in the morning, then he was to report back to Mohammed.

The next day the man returned with a look of distress on his face. "Mohammed," he cried. "I did as you told me, but when I returned this morning to gather the feathers, I could not find a single one!"

"So is it also with your words," explained the Prophet, "for they have flown from you and done their work, never to be recalled again."

The power of words, especially when they are charged with emotion, should never be underestimated. During the last century, a theater group in London was preparing a performance of Shakespeare's tragedy *Macbeth*. In the drama there is a famous curse spoken by "three hags." During rehearsals and throughout the course of the play's stage run, the cast and nearly everyone involved seemed to be plagued with a run of bad luck. Several actors had serious accidents. It was the opinion of a number of the theater troupe that it was the malicious curse itself—spoken at every performance and rehearsal—that was literally cursing the players themselves. This anecdote illustrates that it is unwise to speak potentially harmful words, even in jest. The inspired classic, *Light On the Path*, contains the following reminder for all those who aspire toward high spiritual advancement: "Before the tongue can speak in the presence of the masters, it must have lost the power to wound."

If we find we have used ill-advised words or have spoken unkindly, the best remedy is to speak good words in their place. This may heal the damage we have caused, but as the above stories illustrate, it may never be possible to completely erase the ill effect of harmful speech. "Govern your tongue above all things," advised Pythagoras. Words are a major force in shaping our destiny. Whenever we speak, the inner words of our soul "become flesh and dwell among us."

Our words are also the medium by which agreements are made. This is the basis for a healthy society based on stability and truth. In ancient times, a person's word was their oath. It was a bond, an agreement, and was considered a sacred trust. Many problems today come about because people take their word lightly and lack sincerity when they speak. Many of today's social problems could be remedied with one simple solution. Keep all agreements. If people would honor their verbal and written agreements, a host of government and legal functions could be eliminated. Keeping one's word is the foundation of a civilized society.

When we realize the extraordinary nature of speech, we can use it to our own and other people's advantage. The ancient practice of speaking to plants is rooted in this great power of sound to influence. By using affirmations, declarations and spoken prayers, we can help to bring harmony into our lives and our environment. When we employ words to bless and heal, we become a source of light in the world. The nature of our words, the type of music to which we listen and the general "audio environment" in which we live, have a tremendous influence in shaping who we are.

SPEECH AND THE "THIRD EAR"

It is now commonplace to find reference to the subtle energy system of human beings, the energy "blueprint," or matrix, that is interwoven with the physical body. Thousands of healers and physicians make constant use of a knowledge of this system in their practice. Chinese medicine and acupuncture, as well as ancient Indian ayurvedic healing—which are widely practiced now in the West—all make reference to this energy system. The effectiveness of homeopathy is based also on the underlying energy component of the human body. Despite these trends, orthodox Western science and the medical establishment are unwilling to acknowledge the existence of the energy matrix, or field of force, that bears within it the subtle pattern of our physical bodies. This state of affairs will change under the pressure of millions of people who have a working knowledge of this system.

At the core of an understanding of the human force field is a knowledge of the energy vortexes known as *chakras*. These are the principal force centers through which the currents of subtle energy flow. There are seven major chakras in the subtle field along the spinal column, along with numerous lesser centers. Vedic philosophy and medicine describe 72 billion subtle strands of life force which circulate through the energy body. This fluidic life force—often called *prana*, or *chi*—flows through the seven chakras in a manner analogous to the way blood circulates through the organs of the physical body.

Clairvoyants sometimes describe the human energy field as having "layers." One of the layers is that of *prana*, or life energy. Another layer corresponds to that of the "feeling dimension," through which emotional energy literally flows like water through a fountain system. Still another level corresponds to our thoughts, or mental energy. The chakras, also called "lotuses," are the "sense organs" of the soul. They are positioned at certain vital junctures in the energy field. In appearance, these pulsating vortices of energy are not unlike stars, or the petals of flowers, in that they are radiating centers of light and color. Each chakra has a different number of petals.

The energy center known as the throat chakra is sometimes called the "Third Ear." The throat chakra, or Third Ear, is connected to the faculty of speech and is one of the higher organs of perception that is slowly being formed as we apply the principles of soul alchemy and spiritual unfolding. The Third Ear, which has sixteen petals, bestows the power of clairaudience—the power to hear sounds not audible with our physical ears. These are not "physical" sounds, but are subtle perceptions of nuances within the inner emotional and mental states of those around us. Clairaudience includes the gift of telepathy, the ability to "hear" other people's thoughts. In the introduction to this book, I described a teacher of ancient history who gave me a beautiful, handwritten essay on ancient wisdom. This gentle and scholarly man possessed the gift of telepathy. He could literally "hear" what other people were thinking. He told me that he was stunned when he first realized he had the gift, and rarely mentioned the fact to anyone. He confided to me that it was often painful to hear other people's thoughts and implied that one needed both equanimity and a "thick skin" to avoid being embarrassed or insulted.

It is the Third Ear that enables one to hear with clarity what mystics call "the voice of God," or the "still small voice." It is akin to intuition—which means literally "inner learning," but is even more certain and direct. Clairaudience is direct perception of frequencies originating within the higher energy dimensions in which we are immersed. It is a sense faculty that perceives reality on a deeper "level."

When we strive to utter significant speech and develop the power of listening, we begin to unfold the Third Ear and other chakras. When we are able to listen without hasty, critical judgments—and when our speech is gentle, thoughtful, and kind—the sixteen petals of the Third Ear begin to unfold and revolve. Listening is the essential partner of speech. Where listening is absent or faulty, speech loses much of its value. In order for our conversations to be spiritually valuable, we need to develop the art of careful listening.

As we grow in awareness, we realize that listening and hearing are not just restricted to audible sounds, but can be extended to include the soul and spirit of the speaker. As we develop constructive speech and careful listening, we unfold the higher faculties of our soul—abilities that lead to clairaudience, the power to hear in the subtle dimensions. Perhaps this is yet another nuance of meaning in Jesus' advice to his listeners: "Those who have ears to hear, let them hear."

SOUNDING THE KEYNOTE

Because of the subtle constitution of the human energy field, all of us have an impact on our environment and other people that is the result of our inner state of mind and emotions. We are constantly broadcasting our inner life into the vast etheric sea in which we are placed. All human beings are telepathic transmitters as well as receivers, whether we are aware of it or not.

In the ancient Mystery academies, students were sometimes told that if they could say a magic password, they would be admitted into the inner, sacred precincts of the temple. This was a symbolic teaching. This password exists today, but it is not now (nor was it ever) a literal word spoken by the tongue. It is a "wave frequency" set up by one's total energy field—the vibrational impact of individual consciousness. Your thoughts, moods, feelings and gestures sound a keynote—an actual vibration—which is the sum total of your personal energy field expressed as a musical tone. If the emanations of your thoughts and feelings and the vibration of your inner soul states are profound enough, you will trigger a response from the higher dimensions. The enlightening stream of energy that will then flow into your mind and heart will bring with it a new state of consciousness. This experience is comparable to crossing a spiritual threshold, symbolized in antiquity as entering the inner sanctum of the Mystery temple.

We are all sounding a keynote that is uniquely our own. Although this may not be directly perceptible to any except the most developed clairvoyants or clairaudients, it is noticed, at least subconsciously, by everyone. We call it one's *disposition*, which is the external face of character. Your disposition is your calling card. It can be a talisman of success or a potential cause of failure. A harmonious disposition is like a password that opens doors of opportunity.

The opposite of a harmonious disposition is a state of agitation. We all go through periods of emotional and mental agitation, but through calm breathing and awareness of our inner states we can get a handle on our moods. Periods of quiet time set aside for reflection, prayer or meditation are essential in establishing a habit of inner tranquillity.

Harmonious people display an evenness of temper and a gentle disposition. They wield subtle power and influence merely by their presence. People love to be around those who have a sweet, kind temperament. The elusive, intangible element of human personality that we call *charm* is precisely a harmonious disposition. In order to acquire this psychological harmony, it is helpful to focus on thoughts of kindness, peace, and wisdom—what Plato summed up in the motto of the philosophical ideal: goodness, beauty and truth.

SOUND AS THE MANIFESTATION OF THE DIVINE

We have focused on sound primarily in its physical manifestation as the spoken word, or as music or song. This is the obvious starting point, for until we grasp the enormous creative power of speech, we cannot enter into the deeper mysteries. But speech and sound in the microcosm—the human being—reflect the divine creative "sound" or resonance of the spiritual forces that have brought the universe into existence. Essentially there are two fundamental ways to view the manifestation of divine creative power: as *light* or as *sound*. The opening chapters of Genesis describes the Creation primarily in its aspect as light: "And God said, let there be light." The opening verse of the Gospel of St. John describes the universal creative outpouring in its aspect as sound, or the creative Logos: "In the beginning was the Word, and the Word was with God, and the Word was God."

These two scriptural references are describing a sublime reality from two mutually supporting perspectives—two ways of viewing the primordial impulse that resulted in the Creation. We can view the primordial "Divine Impulse" in terms of light or as sound. Both are true, for they are two sides of the same "cosmic coin." This initial creative outpouring is called in some traditions the "divine sound current." This refers to the celestial impulse of creative projection through which a heavenly current or emanation flowed from the universal Source into the matrix of the manifested world. The vibrations of this celestial river of audible light in its higher levels has sometimes been called "the music of the spheres." Essentially, the divine creative outpouring is a stream of light—luminous divine substance—that gradually "densifies" as it reaches the outermost point of its journey, the familiar physical world. It does not remain static, but having reached its farthest distance from its point of origin, begins a return journey from the periphery to the source, forming an ongoing and continuous circuit of divine force. The universal creation is an emanation of the Godhead. The entire universe is the garment, or the body, of this Being.

In the Bhagahavad Gita, Krishna says—assuming his identity with the Godhead—"Having permeated the entire universe with a fragment of Myself, I remain." His words reveal a great mystery. Just as God is both above and beyond his creation, yet simultaneously within it, so are we present in the densities of Earth vibration, while a portion of ourselves—the individuality or higher self—remains in a pristine condition within the subtle reaches of universal space. The full glory of our higher nature pulsates "above" us in the higher or inner dimensions like a brilliant star.

Pursuing the analogy that human life reflects in miniature the cosmic life, it follows that each human individuality is also a stream of divine consciousness that can be viewed in terms of light or as sound. We are strands of loving energy that have entered deep into "matter" on a journey of cosmic importance. Each of us is a ray of light. Each of us is a divine tone, or thought, originating in the mind of God. We attune ourselves to our source by vibrating in harmony with the love and wisdom that breathed us forth. By soul alchemy—the elevation of our thoughts and emotions—we tune our instrument to the cosmic stream of light and sound of higher dimensions. As our thoughts become prayers and our words become blessings, we find our way back to the source of divine light and original sound within us. Through sacred living, we come to resonate in harmony with the pure current of heavenly consciousness and lift our awareness into regions of happiness. We can follow the stream of divine sound back to our origin. This consummates in what mystics have called the "alchemical wedding"—the union of our personality with our divine self. In knowing ourselves, we also know God. This is the path of *the word*, the mystery of sound and its progressive revelation.

The science of the spoken word is still in its infancy. As the human race evolves, we will grasp the enormous scope of the mysteries of sound. In the age to come, the study of speech and sound will be a profound science, part of the new curriculum of the sacred arts. It will be the alchemy of the future. Realization of the divine origins of the word will take us to the threshold of immortality—and beyond.

Exercises In Sacred Living:
Activating the Alchemy of the Spoken Word

Activity Number One

Be conscious of your words and your conversations. If you find yourself speaking critically of someone, make a point to say something positive about them. Never end a conversation on a negative note. Find something constructive and helpful to say.

This is not to be mistaken for flattery, which implies saying something nice in order to obtain a favor. The objective here is to transform speech into a positive, life-bestowing tool. Remember that your tongue is a magic wand with tremendous power to shape your world.

Activity Number Two

Get into the habit of speaking positive affirmations aloud, provided that you are alone, of course. When in company, mentally affirm constructive thoughts and declarations. Send forth silent or spoken blessings to those who cross your path during the day. It is possible to stop a fight just by sending the combatants a stream of silent blessings.

Activity Number Three

Here's an old technique that can be as amusing as it is effective. Stand in front of a mirror and speak positively and lovingly to yourself as you look at your image. At first this might seem comical, or even slightly ridiculous. But it can be a great way to uplift your mood and energize your feelings. If for some reason you lack confidence on a particular day, give it a try. The worst that could happen is that you have a good laugh at your own expense.

Affirmations

"My words are a magic force with which I transform my life for the better."

"May the words of my lips heal, bless, uplift and encourage."

"May all those with whom I speak be helped by my words."

CHAPTER SIX

THE ALCHEMY OF GRATITUDE

"Gratitude is the heart's memory."
– French proverb

"The pearl is the oyster's autobiography."
– Federico Fellini

The journey each of us has traveled in life is a living book containing great wisdom. We discover the essence of that wisdom when we contemplate the events of our lives with clarity and acceptance. Though we all have experiences we regret, we grow when we forgive ourselves, admitting that at least we have been led by the events of life to this point of present understanding. We can be grateful, even joyful, for the flashes of insight and jewels of wisdom we have made our own.

The alchemy of living is reflected in everyday language. We speak of "solving" a problem or finding a "solution" to a difficulty. These expressions touch on the mysterious chemistry of transformation. To solve a problem is to dissolve it—the way salt dissolves in water. The universal solvent of hardships and difficulties is the love that springs from a spiritualized heart. Gratitude is an essential element in the alchemy of love.

To be grateful is to have a divine perspective on events. Gratitude enables us to see beyond the moment, granting us a glimpse of a better future. It helps us appreciate and make the most of favorable conditions. More important, it enables us to take advantage of difficult circumstances, turning harsh situations into opportunities. We can learn a lesson in soul alchemy from the date palm tree. Surrounded by the desert's intense heat—the scorching sun and arid dryness—this master alchemist finds a way to produce one of the sweetest of all fruits, seemingly turning sand into sugar. With the help of gratitude, like the date palm we can learn to extract hidden sweetness from the dry patches in our lives. The key to a right orientation in life is found in the attitude of thankfulness. The secret to a life of blessings—to a living philosophy of life—is to express gratitude for what life brings.

All Things Can Be turned to Good Account

Challenges bring with them the opportunity for growth. It is the pressure that creates a diamond. The irritant within the oyster creates the pearl. Even in climbing a mountain, we depend on rough spots and irregularities to provide foot and handholds. It has been said that one of the traits of the enlightened mind is that it sees the good element in even the darkest of experiences. It is certainly true that if we look for the potential benefit in our disappointments, we can transform those experiences, taking some if not all of the sting out.

When I was teaching a class of fifth graders in California, we were practicing penmanship with refillable fountain pens. On every desk was a little jar of black or blue ink. The students were illustrating their history lesson books with pictures about the events. A girl named Nawana had just finished drawing a beautiful crayon illustration of a wooden ship on the sea. As she proudly showed me her work, the student in front leaned back and tipped over Nawana's black ink jar, blotting the entire page. Nawana burst into tears. I sponged up the ink and held up the notebook to dry, then set it back on Nawana's desk. The ink had not affected the wax crayon image and the colors remained vivid. Only the white portion of the paper had turned an inky black. "It's a night scene!" Nawana exclaimed with enthusiasm. Sure enough, the illustration had lost none of its beauty and in some ways was even more interesting as a "night scene." Both Nawana and I had learned a lesson in turning "negatives to positives."

Many people owe their achievements to the tremendous challenges they faced. Wolfgang Amadeus Mozart, perhaps the most beloved of all composers, is universally admired for the exuberance, grace and technical perfection of his music. He began composing as a child of five and by the time he became a teenager had written brilliant symphonies, concertos, sonatas and an operetta. Nonetheless, Mozart was misunderstood and neglected by his contemporaries. This remarkable genius had difficulty making a living. He produced his most extraordinary musical works in a period of acute hardship and misery. Despite his suffering, Mozart infused a quality of joy into his compositions that has never been surpassed. It is as if his spirit sought to transcend the misery of his circumstances by drawing upon a fountain of inspiration that lay forever beyond the reach of mortal sorrow. As a result, there is something immortal in Mozart's music.

Thankfulness is an attitude that can be cultivated so that it develops into a feature of character. This enables one to transform obstacles into stepping stones. Ordeals become the experiences that lead to enlightenment. Fear, negation and a gloomy frame of mind cannot exist in a mental atmosphere of thanksgiving.

FROM INKBLOTS TO ANGELS

Gratitude helps us to see the good in all things and to turn apparent mistakes into positive experiences. The story of Joseph Craik beautifully illustrates this point. He lived and taught in a small Scottish village and became known for his unique approach in turning his students' errors into something beautiful. In her newsletter, *Abundant Living,* Dr. Delia Sellers describes Joseph Craik as a "talented and creative penman and artist, teaching in a small village school. Often his young pupils left inkblots on their pages. Instead of chastising the students, or circling the inkblots in graphic red and taking away points for sloppy penmanship, Joseph Craik did something quite different and delightful. Beginning with the blots made by the children, he would add a line here and another line there and out of the inkblots would appear pictures of angels.

"When the papers were returned to the students, instead of criticism, they were wonderfully decorated with exquisite angels. The children were delighted and encouraged. And Joseph Craik became a legend...known far and wide as the man who turned inkblots into angels." This teacher gave his fortunate students a priceless lesson, that all things can be turned toward the good. Thankfulness is an attitude that redeems our "mistakes" and helps us to turn them into stepping stones.

The Second Birth

Many people bemoan their fate and curse their conditions. The wise know that all events occur for a deeper reason—even if that reason remains a mystery. Fortunately, life has seen to it that the periods of greatest difficulty are also those that bring about the most beautiful and remarkable developments. Difficulties, trials and hardship are often the sources of life's greatest transformations. Challenges create the very conditions that call forth our hidden splendor, the spark of greatness that might otherwise remain dormant within us. Within each difficulty lies a seed of a greater benefit. The greatest good comes out of the hardest trials. In this way the divine wisdom that governs life insures that we move in an ascending spiral of development and improvement. Life gently nudges us onto the path of sacred living, the journey of soul alchemy.

Perhaps the most remarkable of all the impressive gothic cathedrals built in Europe during the middle ages is Chartres cathedral, near Paris. The original construction of Chartres began at the dawn of the second millennium, in the year 1000. The inspired teacher who began the work was a man from northern Italy named Fulbertus. He was a man of great kindness, erudition and moral stature. Consequently, Fulbertus was beloved by his students, who numbered in the hundreds and came from all parts of Europe. They affectionately called him Socrates, after the illustrious Greek philosopher. When Fulbertus arrived at Chartres at the end of the millennium, there was a small dilapidated chapel dedicated to Mother Mary. The site had been considered sacred since pre-Christian times, when the Celts had constructed a stone monument there. According to tradition, Mary the mother of Jesus, and Joseph of Arimethea—to whom Pontius Pilate had entrusted the body of Jesus after the crucifixion—had visited Chartres in the early years of the first century. Joseph of Arimethea and Mary had taken with them the grail chalice, in which Joseph had caught the blood of Christ as it flowed from him on the cross. The old church Fulbertus first saw dated from the first century.

Conceiving a large cathedral dedicated to the Madonna, Fulbertus enlisted help from all over Europe and the work began with great zeal. Four years later tragedy struck when a fire swept though the cathedral, which was constructed mostly of wood. Undaunted, Fulbertus immediately began the reconstruction, this time in stone with a still grander design. The work went on for decades and resulted in one of the most eloquent monuments to the spirit ever constructed. Millions of people visit Chartes each year to admire one of the world's most sacred and beautiful edifices. Fulbertus and the people who built Chartres used the disaster of the fire as an opportunity to create a yet more beautiful cathedral. One of the great lessons of alchemy is that adversity contains within it the seeds of our greatest accomplishments.

A grateful attitude enables us to look for and discover the gems that lie buried beneath the turmoil of life. There is something of value hidden within every difficult experience. When we can accept with gratitude even the harsh experiences in life and train ourselves to look for the potential good that comes to us from these experiences, we extract a mysterious essence that transforms us. Our disappointments often teach us our most valuable lessons. This compensatory feature in life offers us a jewel beneath the jagged surface of difficulties—sweet fruit beyond the thorns. The highest attitude is to be grateful for everything—to see everything as a blessing, a stepping stone to greater self-knowledge and ultimately to better circumstances.

It is natural to go through periods of sorrow and suffering. Even Jesus and Buddha wept on occasion. Sadness and trials are teachers on the path of inner unfolding. All the harsh experiences of life come in order to break the shell of selfishness and open the heart to the realities of a larger universe. "The deeper that sorrow carves into your heart," said Kahlil Gibran, "the more joy you can contain." We can lessen our suffering if we seek to discover the pearl within the painful conditions of life. By reflecting without resentment on experience, searching for the jewels of wisdom, we elevate our consciousness. This releases us from suffering. If we can accept that all events tend ultimately toward good for all involved, we will experience an inner awakening and a gradual understanding of the universal laws.

When we make errors in judgment that hurt ourselves and others, we are faced with a double heartache—the knowledge of the suffering we have caused and the challenge of forgiving ourselves. Perhaps the soul's greatest task is to learn to move beyond failure, loss and sorrow. Doing so is the essence of soul alchemy—the ability to transmute experiences and extract from them the elements that help us evolve spiritually. Prayer is a divine gift and a great power in this renewal of the soul. Prayer is an activity that links us to the divine. Simply being thankful is one of the most powerful of prayers. The state of thanksgiving, like true prayer, uplifts the consciousness and attunes one to the deeper self.

If we hold on to the light of gratitude, even if the flame in the heart flickers, it will not vanish. When we face the greatest difficulties, we have a choice. We can become bitter and start to die in our souls, followed inevitably by physical deterioration—or we can respond with a reaffirmation of the beauty and bounty of life. If we can rise above our pains and challenges, our sorrows and despair, we experience what is sometimes called the second birth, the emergence of our spirit from the tomb of soul darkness. If we can learn to take our difficulties and make them into pearls, the dark night of the soul will be followed by the bright day of spiritual illumination.

GRATITUDE IS A GATEWAY THROUGH GRIEF

Linda Bergh is a woman of inspiring courage. Several years ago, Linda's husband, Paul, died suddenly of a cardiac arrest. She and her teenage daughter, Kirsten, bolstered by loving friends and their own spiritual life, learned to cope and move on. Then, barely more than a year after Paul's death, Linda and Kirsten were involved in a terrible car crash. Kirsten, who was seventeen, died instantly, along with her best friend, Nina. Linda was severely injured, and her face disfigured. Less than two years after her husband's sudden passing, she was faced with her own difficult physical recovery, while dealing at the same time with the grief and anguish of the loss of her only child.

As she slowly recovered from her injuries and learned to talk again, she set about publishing some of Kirsten's writings. Her efforts resulted in a book entitled *She Would Draw Flowers*, which contains many of Kirsten's poems and drawings. They reveal the depth and wisdom of Kirsten's heart, her love of life and sensitivity to beautiful things. Forty days after her father's sudden passing, Kirsten wrote in her diary, "Sometimes I wish I could've remained back there—back then. But I have to move on. I will be happy no matter what happens. My tears of grief will mix with those of joy." A poem she wrote reflects her ability to move beyond her grief by finding beauty in the world:

Open your eyes!

Can you not see the pale green leaves,

That cling, like a gentle mist,

To the black branches of the trees?

Will you not smile at the purple violets

Who nod cheerfully as you pass?

Do they not bring you happiness?

The creamy blossoms dancing, floating

like fragrant snowflakes on the breeze,

Do they not fill your heart with gladness?

Look! Can you not see the sunlight,

Shimmering and flashing on the water?

The blue sky fluffed with lazy clouds?

Can you not see their joy?

Can you not share it?

The air is filled with song:

The wind whispers in the trees,

Blackbirds warble out their melodies,

The water chuckles happily to itself,

Distant thunder grumbles harmlessly,

Will you shut your ears to their gentle voices?

Will you shut your eyes to their compassionate smiles?

Do not close your heart to the joy and beauty around you,

Rather, embrace it.

For if you cannot love the world, you cannot love yourself.

And without love,

There is nothing.

Although Linda Bergh published Kirsten's art and poems as a tribute to her daughter, it was also an essential part of her own healing. This creative work was Linda's way of affirming that it is possible to embrace life, even when faced with nearly unimaginable sorrow. In Linda's presence today, many people feel almost a sense of awe, knowing all that she has had to go through. Despite her suffering, Linda has remained open to the wisdom and beauty of life. She is living testimony that when we can open our hearts and our eyes to see with gratitude, a power enters into us that can restore the goodness of the world. Through us, *something that surpasses us* is able to walk, and speak, and act on Earth. We come to embody the eternal love and wisdom of the soul, whose vision for our lives was captured by Kirsten Bergh in her letter to her best friend, Nina, the day before their young lives abruptly ended. "The world will be a little better because of us, even if our names are forgotten...."

GRATITUDE HELPS US FORGIVE

In order to make progress in our lives, both materially and spiritually, our souls must open to the lessons of forgiveness. So long as we are unable to forgive others and ourselves of past mistakes and perceived wrongs—either those we have inflicted or those that have been inflicted on us—we remain trapped in a web of blame, resentment and anger. Forgiveness is not easy, especially considering the pain, difficulty and hardship that unwise and unloving actions create. No person alive has been spared some form of ill treatment or acts of cruelty at the hands of others. Consciousness of one's own failings can be an even greater burden to bear. Forgiveness implies releasing ourselves from the torments of the past. Forgiveness doesn't mean we have to "become friends" with those who have injured us. It only means that we let go of our bitterness, anger and resentment. This enables soul healing to occur and lifts us back into the light.

It is easier to forgive if we make a habit of expressing gratitude for all the circumstances and experiences of life, no matter how difficult or seemingly unjust. Often, acceptance and gratitude for a small good will open the way for a still greater benefit to come into our life. Everything comes to teach us something. The wise acknowledge this fact and ask themselves what they can learn from difficulties and hardship. Gratitude makes us gentle and gentleness is one of the most powerful of attitudes. Gentleness removes obstacles on our path and awakens higher faculties in our souls. Gentleness is the antidote to anger, one of the most destructive of emotions.

The story of the crucifixion can be seen as a metaphor of our inner life. In the familiar historical drama, Christ is crucified on a hill between two thieves. The first thief derides him, saying, "If you are the Christ, why don't you free yourself, and the two of us as well?" The second thief reproaches the first, saying, "Why do you speak to him in this manner? We are guilty and deserve our punishment. This man is innocent." Then he turns and says to Christ, "Remember me when you enter your kingdom." Christ answers him and says, "This day you shall be with me in Paradise." The two thieves symbolize two elements of our soul life. The first thief represents the intellect unillumined by the light of wisdom. It is arrogant and at the same time, angry at its circumstances. It feels no remorse for its crimes, but can only deride the divine principle—the divine spark represented by Christ. The second thief symbolizes the feelings, or the heart. It too is guilty of anger, greed and jealousy, but because it is capable of love, it knows that it has done wrong and asks forgiveness.

Through gentleness, the heart is able to rise above anger and pride. The higher self—"Christ in us"—forgives, and through the power of forgiveness and love, we enter the state of consciousness referred to as "Paradise," or the kingdom of heaven. Pride, anger and a lack of forgiveness—characteristics of an intellect unwilling to acknowledge the higher laws—prevent the soul from knowing truth and peace. When we can forgive ourselves and others we make contact with the divine principle within us. The gateway to heaven—to a higher state of consciousness—immediately opens.

For the intellect to overcome anger, resentment and hatred, it must come to accept that higher laws operate through human events. The way of wisdom is to ask ourselves what we can learn from a challenging event. In the words of Confucius, "It is better to light a candle then to curse the darkness." When we open our hearts to forgiveness and gratitude, we light our inner lamps—higher energy centers within our minds that are the portals into the Christ consciousness, the kingdom of heaven. Through forgiveness and gratitude we can turn our pain into power, our wounds into wisdom, and our losses into love.

THE ELIXIR OF LIFE

Gratitude is indispensable to finding joy. Joy is a deep state of consciousness, related to happiness but beyond it. Most people experience a measure of happiness when things are going well in their personal lives and they are "getting what they want." As we grow spiritually and develop our inner powers, those elements that make for personal happiness become more subtle. Material acquisition becomes less important. Our esthetic sense and appreciation of beauty mature and become increasingly the basis for personal happiness. We discover that happiness arises from a loving, grateful heart.

Joy is not contingent on external satisfactions. Joy is the experience of our deeper soul. It is a pure state of consciousness. As we come into contact with our deeper self, we touch that mysterious, elevated state of consciousness characterized by inner joyousness. The natural condition of our deeper self is a state of perpetual joy.

Joy is an essential element in the Elixir of Life, sought by the alchemists. We build a bridge to that higher state of awareness by cultivating gratitude. Those who express gratitude come under the influence of the deeper self. Emotions of happiness, inner peace and love are indispensable to creating the inner state of consciousness represented metaphorically by the alchemists as the Elixir of Life. Gratitude is necessary to experience happiness, peace and love. As we express gratitude and allow ourselves to forgive, we make a joyous state of mind possible.

It is probable that some of the alchemists did, in fact, distill a special fluid from the elements that contained a condensation of pure life force, and that this conferred tremendous vitality and longevity. Yet the Elixir of Life is not primarily a physical substance. It is a distillate of *consciousness.* In other words, it is a perfect blend or extract of the spiritual elements that bring about perpetual new life in our souls and our physical organisms. Gratitude is essential to the creation of this soul elixir, for thankfulness prevents negativity from taking root in our thoughts and attitudes. Gratitude keeps the "waters of life" flowing within us.

The alchemists often said that "The seeds of gold are contained in all substances." Though they may well have meant this literally, it may be most useful for us to see this expression as a metaphor. A grain of "spiritual gold" is contained in every experience. In other words, every event in our lives contributes precious elements for our growth and developing. We "mine" this inner wealth as we seek for the positive and beneficial elements in all events. Soul alchemy is the process of elevating our experiences and uplifting our emotional states—turning the "base metal" of ordinary happenings into the "gold" of happiness and inner illumination. Gratitude is indispensable to this sacred activity— what the alchemist's called the "great work." Gratitude is a leaven that causes our soul states to rise beyond the ordinary and commonplace.

Gratitude releases a light in our minds that chases the darkness. Like an inner sun, its bright beams dry up the gloomy swamps of anxiety and depression. Its presence within our consciousness stirs and awakens forces that lead to constructive actions and courageous efforts. We ignite the spark of happiness in our hearts when we express an inner attitude of thanksgiving. Constant gratitude fans this tiny spark into a flame of joy.

The thankful attitude is an elixir drawn from the deep reservoir of the soul. Like a divine tonic, it produces contentment and a sense of well-being. Thankfulness is a healing balm that dissolves the toxins produced by a bitter and resentful state of mind. Gratitude grants strength and enthusiasm for living.

Thankfulness is one of the soul's most beautiful qualities. People who express gratitude emanate an intangible quality of magnanimity—literally "greatness of soul." Gratitude expands the radiance of the heart and triggers a response from the larger life of which we are a part. It is the indispensable element in our soul life that enables us to transform the irritants of life into pearls of understanding. The grateful state of mind puts one in touch with a universe of immeasurable power.

GRATITUDE CONTAINS THE GIFTS OF THE SPIRIT

An important characteristic of gratitude is that it not only enhances the quality of life, but it increases our ability to achieve our goals and expand our prosperity. When we express gratitude for the good we have, we open up hidden channels of supply. We prepare the way for the reception of even greater good. Gratitude has an almost magical power to create opportunities and release the flow of abundance.

In the estimate of many, money is the most desirable commodity on Earth. We all know that money is essential in modern life, but there is so much that is of far greater value. How much money would you give in trade for your eyes? Would you part with your thumb for a million dollars? Is any tangible value of equal worth to the happiness that comes through the birth of a child? Can you put a price tag on the natural wonders of the world? It is precisely through our earthly experiences that we extract a quintessence, an extract bought at the price of our struggles, mistakes, triumphs and tragedies. We can't place an economic value on the wisdom we gain from our life experience.

The universe has bestowed upon us many extraordinary gifts. The stars, the seas, the forests and the natural wonders of the world are an awe-inspiring treasury—an infinite storehouse—of magnificence and mystery. So much comes to us each day that is the result of the labors of others, most of whom we do not know. All of this is cause for gratitude.

The grateful state of mind releases a force from within. Like a breath of the divine, this power brushes aside negativity from one's life. Gratitude brings inner peace, serenity and tranquillity of spirit—

the precursors of true wisdom. Gratitude counters arrogance and false pride, negative qualities that turn people away.

Gratitude is an inexhaustible source of renewal, growth and rejuvenation. When we express thankfulness by our inner attitude, we release a mysterious power from our minds and hearts that has a healing, beneficial influence. We begin to emanate an indefinable quality that others feel or perceive and which attracts them to us.

Gratitude smoothes out countless difficulties and unlocks a portal into nature's treasure house of safeguarded secrets—a portal that remains forever sealed to the ungrateful. These secrets were referred to allegorically by the alchemists as the Philosopher's Stone and the Elixir of Life. Gratitude helps us distill an essence from experience that transforms our consciousness and elevates us from the ordinary to the exceptional. Thankfulness is indispensable in our efforts to make life sacred.

Those who experience gratitude become emissaries of a more luminous culture. Thankfulness enables us to discover the secrets of our deeper self. Our higher self is linked to the transcendent dimensions of life. Through the divine spark within our hearts we contact the universal fountainhead of existence. Those who give thanks for life's blessings come under the influence of angels and higher beings. If we live in accordance with the sacred laws that govern life, living becomes an ever-unfolding miracle.

Gratitude is the alchemy that leads to a sacred life.

Exercises In Sacred Living:
Activating the Alchemy of Gratitude

Activity Number One

Think of someone who has done you a favor or helped you in some way for which you never expressed gratitude. Perhaps a friend or relative will come to mind, possibly one or both of your parents. Write that person or those persons a card or letter thanking them for their help or inspiration. Or, if you prefer, pick up the telephone and call them.

Activity Number Two

Make a list of all the benefits and blessing of your life. Reflect deeply on all of the good things that have come your way and all the beautiful experiences you have had. Practice saying "thank you" mentally as often as you can during the day. It has been said that the highest prayer, the most effective mantra, is composed of the two simple words: "thank you."

Affirmations

"I give thanks this day for my wonderful life and the opportunities for growth and happiness."

I live forever in a beautiful, marvelous creation. I give thanks to the countless beings who have made my existence possible."

"I know that as I create an attitude of thanksgiving in my mind, I increase my ability to draw all good into my life."

"All things are working together for good in my life."

CHAPTER SEVEN

THE ALCHEMY OF FAITH

"The dice of God are always loaded."

– Emerson

"Trust in God, but tie up your camel."

– Unknown

A simple image of alchemy comes from the art of bread-making. By adding a small measure of yeast, or leaven, to the dough, the bread rises and its consistency changes. The substance of the loaf is altered—made finer and lighter—by the presence of the yeast. The leaven that raises the bread may be likened to the presence of faith in our minds and hearts. The inner attitude we call belief, or faith, has a tremendous power to uplift our lives. Faith elevates the mind and infuses the emotions with the spirit's presence. Faith is like a leaven in our soul life. It raises our consciousness and makes us buoyant and light.

Many people today misunderstand the essential meaning of faith. Faith does not mean a blind belief in a dogmatic position of a scientific or ecclesiastical authority. It is a conviction that comes with life experience and spiritual maturity—as one begins to make contact with the radiant inner source of wisdom and power. Little is possible in life without faith.

Mikhael Aivanhov tells the story of an illustrious sage named Nathan, who lived in Jerusalem centuries ago. When Saladin, the great Sultan of Damascus, recaptured the holy city from the Christians following the first Crusade, he sent for the sage and asked him the following question. "Of all the religions of the world: Christian, Jewish, Moslem, Hindu and Buddhist, which is the best?" Nathan replied by telling him a story. "Once there was a king," he narrated, "who possessed a magical ring that gave him every power. Because of the ring, the kingdom was free of wars, hardship and pestilence. When the king became old, he could not decide on which of his three sons to bestow the ring, as he loved them all equally. So he had two other rings made that looked identical to the first one, but lacked the magic power. He then summoned the three sons one after the other and gave them each one of the rings along with a third of the kingdom. The king himself did not know to which son he had given the authentic ring and each of the sons believed that he had received the treasured talisman.

"Some time passed and the old king went to visit his eldest son. He found that his kingdom was plagued with continual wars and hardship and he knew he did not possess the true ring. He then visited his second son and found that his kingdom was also beset with illness, misery and want. He had not received the ring of power. At last he visited his youngest son and found that his people lived in happiness, prosperity, peace and health. He knew that he had given the magic ring to his third son. "This is how you will know the true religion," explained Nathan, "for it brings peace, goodness, abundance, health and happiness."

One can rightly interpret Nathan's story as a scathing critique of the orthodoxy of the time. His critique applies to this very day. But the "true religion"—that of "peace, goodness, abundance, health and happiness"—has always existed on the Earth. And its adherents may be found both within and outside of all of the world's great religious establishments. This enduring wisdom was taught in the ancient temples—sometimes called Mystery schools—of both East and West. It is the eternal philosophy imparted throughout the ages by the world's illumined teachers—the prophets, saints, masters, adepts and initiates of all times and places. Spiritual alchemy is an expression of these truths.

The "true religion" that brings every blessing is the ability to live in harmony with the sacred laws that govern life. Faith is an essential element in this art of sacred living. Though faith has always been associated with religion, and many great saints have developed a high degree of this quality, essentially it has nothing to do with external doctrines. Faith means an unwavering assurance in the infallibility of divine laws and in the essential goodness of life. It is a deep certainty, an unswerving conviction, that the laws and principles that govern life always work. It is an evolving awareness that the universe is permeated with a divine principle that is present both in nature and in the souls of human beings. Faith becomes a dynamic power when we realize we are linked to the great chain of universal life. With this recognition of our connection with all living things, the energy and inspiration of more highly evolved beings—angels and archangels—may flow into us.

Those who doubt that absolute law governs life become unsure of themselves. To those unschooled in the eternal wisdom, life seems uncertain, arbitrary, even whimsical. Faith is the opposite of doubt and uncertainty. It is a deep-seated conviction that the laws governing life are good, wise, just and true—and that these divine principles govern all manifestations of life. External social codes and customs change often, and nowadays most societies are not based upon a perception of these higher truths. But the eternal laws devised by universal intelligence are unchanging. We may discover these laws, but we cannot alter them.

These laws of life—the cornerstones of the universe—are active always and everywhere. When we act, we may rest assured that the universe will react. The universal laws will bring justice. These laws are not human inventions. They operate with or without human belief, just as gravity is in operation whether you believe in it or not. In this sense these laws are entirely impersonal; they aren't swayed by personality or by externals. Money, power and prestige cannot corrupt them. For this reason, Justice is depicted with a blindfold. She is not influenced by outer appearance, but looks at the motives of the heart. She is not swayed by social position or worldly eminence, but perceives objectively our actions.

Although the laws of life are just, they are not cruel. The celestial Spirits that designed this universe and set the stars and planets on their courses are the authors of the sacred laws. The Hierarchies of angels who work with the Creator have designed the universe with infinite love as well as a fathomless wisdom. Divine justice is tempered with mercy and grace. Heaven does not want to crush us under the weight of our difficulties. It wants us to grow and become wise and luminous, loving and strong. Faith means that we know and trust that the universe has a heart.

The events of life follow an inscrutable divine plan of ever-increasing wisdom and growth toward perfection. The sacred laws have been constructed so that if we work with goodness and love in our motives, goodness and love will flow back to us. Paraphrasing the words of Jesus, "In the measure that we give to others, so will life give to us." If we approach life with a loving, trusting attitude and give our best, our needs will be met. Faith means that we trust that all things are working together for good in our lives.

FAITH CREATES MIRACLES

Certain remarkable people have developed the faculty of faith to an unusual degree, causing seeming miracles to occur around them and in their lives. Faith, or belief, becomes a power that triggers a response from the hidden dimensions—a response that can at times seem almost magical or supernatural. The lives of saints and deeply religious people are full of such incidents. A wonderful example comes from the life of St. Francis of Assisi.

In his travels through the Italian countryside, Francis lingered some days in a forest with the loyal brother monks who later became the nucleus of the Franciscan order. Word of St. Francis' whereabouts spread among the nearby villages and people journeyed by the hundreds to catch a glimpse of the beloved saint. More arrived by the hour and the gathering soon swelled to a large crowd.

The brothers became nervous, for they had no food of their own and the people had brought little with them. It grew late in the day and the brothers feared that the people, many of whom were ill and elderly, would begin to suffer.

Again and again Francis told them that all would be well and that they would be amply cared for by Providence. The brothers remained unconvinced. Then in the late afternoon, several wagonloads arrived, heavily laden with food, blankets and provisions. A wealthy merchant had heard of the gathering and wanted to send a gift to Francis and the people. As they passed out the food and provisions, the brothers rejoiced at the "miracle" and marveled at the faith of their leader.

Events like these—which might be termed "miracles of faith"—are still within the province of universal law. It in no way demeans the greatness of St. Francis if we see a miracle like this in the light of the law of affinity. Francis was able to set in motion certain currents by the qualities of his inner life that produced a response—a sympathetic resonance—from the "universal mind," or from the spiritual beings who act as the agents of these universal principles. The law of affinity draws to us what is in accordance with the conditions of our inner soul world.

Walter Russell, of whom I will speak of again in Chapter Ten, displayed a great faith in the unseen universal power. An extraordinary incident in his youth demonstrates this faith. In 1886, as a boy of fifteen working himself through art school, he promised his girlfriend he would take her to a whole series of operas that cost almost eighty dollars—more money than he had ever held in his hand. The day the box office opened, he stood in line to get tickets behind a long row of people. Despite having only six dollars in his pocket, he believed absolutely in his heart that by the time he reached the window he would have the full amount. Then a stranger approached him with a request that Walter Russell recognized as an opportunity. In his marvelous little book entitled *The Man Who Tapped the Secrets of the Universe,* Glenn Clark describes the incident as follows:

"In the morning a man said to him, 'Sonny, would you like to make $5.00?'

'Yes, sir, how?'

'By selling me your place in line so I can get to my office by nine.'

Quick as a flash he replied. 'I'll do better for you than that. Give me the money and I will deliver the tickets to you.' Without even asking his name, the man gave him the money and his address, and he put it down in a notebook. Holding the money between his fingers and with notebook and pencil in hand, looking like a bookmaker at the races, he became a magnet drawing scores of people to him. By the time he reached the box office he had the amount necessary for the entire series.... and $110.00 in excess, enough to carry him through months of school. The strange thing was that no one even asked him his name and address!"

This remarkable anecdote shows that seeming miracles are truly possible when one acts out of deep trust—knowing that the universe has a heart.

From the Brothers Grimm comes a simple story illustrating the transforming power of faith and a giving heart. A young orphan girl with nothing but a crust of bread and the clothes she is wearing, sets forth into the open country, "trusting in the good God." When she meets a poor man who asks her for some bread, she hands him the whole piece. Further along she comes upon a child who begs for some clothing to keep her warm. The good-hearted little girl gives the child her hood. Still further on she finds two more shivering children. To the first she gives her jacket and to the second she gives her frock. At last as evening falls she enters a forest. There she comes upon yet another child who begs the girl for her shirt. As it was fast becoming dark, and thinking that no one could see her, she gave away the very last of her possessions. As she stood there, alone and bereft, "suddenly some stars from heaven fell down." When she picked them up she saw that they had become shining pieces of gold. And though she had given away her shirt, yet another one appeared, made of the finest linen. The story concludes with the words, "And she was rich all the days of her life." This enchanting tale reminds us that when we give fully of ourselves, trusting in the beneficent laws, we elicit a response from the universal life of which we are a part.

THE POWER OF PRAYER

Prayer is a most effective tool in accomplishing our goals and achieving results in our lives, both spiritually and practically. But prayer without belief has little power. Jesus said, "Whatsoever you ask in prayer, *believing*, you shall receive." If we short-circuit our prayers with doubts and negativity, we cancel much of their effectiveness.

Prayer is an attitude of mind and heart that attunes us to our higher consciousness. Many people beg for handouts in their prayers, but this is not true prayer. It is fine to ask for things, but we must back our requests with action. True prayer will result in opportunities for us to attain what we seek through our own efforts. This doesn't mean we shouldn't accept gifts. But prayers that weaken our own will-to-act are really self-defeating. The best approach is to work with the divine power by living in accordance with the laws that govern life. Then our right desires become powers that realize themselves as if by magic. When we live harmoniously, our deeds themselves become our prayers.

Soul alchemy means working with all our powers, all the elements woven into the fabric of our nature. Sincere prayer is one of our soul's inner powers. There may be times when it appears all other resources are exhausted and we have no recourse but to rely on prayer itself, backed by faith, to accomplish the desired result. At times, this can result in true miracles of the spirit. An incredible story of the miraculous power of prayer backed by faith comes from the life of Kaye and Edwarda O'Bara. Wayne Dyer tells their unusual story in his book, *A Promise is A Promise.*

The O'Bara's live in Miami, Florida. As a child, Kaye's daughter, Edwarda, was unusually compassionate and thoughtful. She went out of her way to make friends with handicapped children at school. Throughout her school years she made a point to see that they were included in all activities. Edwarda baby-sat for neighboring children and refused to accept money. She was described as incapable of telling a lie, or of even exaggerating the truth. She displayed remarkable generosity, always giving any change she had to beggars, even carrying an extra sweater around in cold weather in case she saw a homeless person who might need it.

When she was 16 years, Edwarda fell into a diabetic coma, which has continued for more than 27 years. Her family, especially her mother, Kaye, has had to care for her at home, without insurance support. During this time she has had to be fed intravenously every two hours around the clock. Despite a medical prognosis that Edwarda will not regain consciousness, Kaye has rendered incredible, ongoing devotion. She has given up personal needs and has spent all her love and time caring for her comatose daughter in her home.

There are many miracles that are a part of this story. Edwarda is hooked up to life support systems and needs steady attention—at intervals never less than two hours. Kaye has had very little money to pay for medical bills and cannot work due to her daughter's constant need for care. After her husband died, Kaye accumulated a number of debts. She describes one particular debt that she paid off through the course of several years, a loan which amounted to thousands. One day a man appeared at her door demanding 600 dollars as final payment for the loan. Kaye had thought she had paid off the debt years before. The man insisted that Kaye pay him the money in cash that day. His eyes kept falling on a pair of scissors and he hinted that there could be dire consequences if she did not come up with the cash. Fearful of what might happen if she did not meet his demands, Kaye promised to have the cash by six o'clock. The man told her he would return that evening and left the house. It was a holiday and Kaye had no way to raise the money. She spent the afternoon praying for a miracle. She describes in her own words what occurred that day:

"I thought someone might just call me on the phone five minutes before six, but nothing was happening. Then I heard the doorbell ring and figured the guy was back a few minutes early and wondered what I was going to do. There was a little man at the door, a little Spanish man, and he said, "This is for you," as he handed me an envelope. I invited him to come in, but he said he couldn't, that he was just delivering the envelope.... I went back and sat in the brown chair again and decided to look in the envelope expecting fifty or so, and maybe the collector would accept it as partial payment. When I looked, there were six new $100 bills, exactly the amount I needed.

"I jumped up and ran across the street to (my neighbor) Anne's house. She was standing at the door and I asked her to quick, tell me which way the man who was just at my door went. But she insisted there had been no man at my door. She said she saw me at the door, and Abe (her husband) was about to come over and see if there was something the matter.

"She described me standing at the door, holding my hand out, but there was no one there, and there was no car in front of the house. According to Anne there hadn't been a car in front of my house for about three hours when that man (the collector) left earlier. They had seen the collector and no one else. There had been no one and no car."

Prayer backed by faith can work miracles. When we live harmoniously with higher law, we can win the assistance of compassionate beings from higher dimensions. Such assistance may be a facet of the mystery of divine grace. Although we have no certain explanation for this miracle, Kaye O'Bara's remarkable experience appears to involve intervention by angels. She herself says, "God has given me the strength to care for Edwarda by sending me angels in many forms—friends, family, strangers who became friends, and many others."

Our prayers become most effective when we work with divine law, doing all we can out of our own resources and capabilities. When we first do all within our own human power, then prayer becomes an added "miraculous" ingredient in the alchemy of sacred living. Prayer gives us an infusion of luminous consciousness. It attunes us to the dimensions in which miracles are natural occurrences—harmonious manifestations of light. When we attune ourselves to the light by harmonious living, the emanations of our hearts and minds become prayers which invoke blessings.

THE AMAZING HILDA CHARTON

One of the really remarkable individuals of the twentieth century was a woman named Hilda Charlton. Hilda trained as a dancer in the San Francisco Bay area and spent three years from 1947–1950 touring India and Ceylon with her small dance troupe. She stayed in India for an additional fifteen years, traveling and studying with spiritual masters. Hilda became well-known toward the end of her life, after her return to America, when she began to teach classes in meditation in a tiny apartment in New York City. From two students at her first meeting, her weekly classes grew to as many as a thousand. Eventually they were held at the Cathedral Church of St. John the Divine, the second largest church in the world. Hilda's inspired lessons on meditation, prayer, service and the inner life were laced with humor and highlighted by moving anecdotes of her personal life journey. She changed the lives of thousands of people. Many were cured of illness and disease, drug addicts and alcoholics outgrew their addictions, and prostitutes left the streets. Hilda saved hundreds from despair and hopelessness and guided them on the path of spiritual awakening and life renewal. She demonstrated that the power of the spirit is living alchemy.

In her autobiography, *Hell Bent for Heaven*, Hilda describes how she learned to apply the power of faith and prayer to perform seeming miracles. On a number of occasions she used prayers to heal, even to bring people back from the brink of death. She describes one incident that took place in her New York City meditation group. A man came to Hilda after the meeting and thrust a photograph in front of her, saying, "This is a picture of my wife. She is only thirty-one and the doctors say they cannot keep her at the hospital. We have driven across country so she can be healed, but the hospital says they can't help her." Hilda was impressed with the young man's faith and persistence. She and the others in her group meditated and prayed for a healing. The young man returned the following week and announced that his wife had been declared completely healed the day after the group healing service. He and his wife both came to the next meeting to thank Hilda before they journeyed back across country to their home.

Because true prayer creates an intensely positive vibratory field, it can reverse dark patterns and discharge accumulated negativity from our cells. When backed by faith, prayer becomes an instrument by which miracles may be accomplished. In accordance with all true healers, Hilda acknowledged that the healing power emanates from the divine world and operates through the life force streaming through our energy fields. By faith, positivity and a loving heart, we can become instruments of this healing force.

Faith can open a doorway into the unseen dimensions, allowing higher beings to assist us on the Earth. Hilda Charlton tells a charming story of a young French girl who prayed incessantly to St. Therese of Lisieux that she might get a particular job. (St. Therese, known as Little Flower, had died in 1897, pledging to "spend her Heaven doing good on Earth.") The employer called to tell the young girl they had no opening. Then he called again several days later saying that they had decided to hire her. On the girl's first day at work, her employer confided that they had made the decision to hire her after "her friend the nun" came in and recommended her.

As this anecdote suggests, there are many instances of miraculous intervention from the unseen dimensions, and of assistance from angels and spirit helpers. But the healthy cultivation of faith relies on developing the attitude of mind that propels us as individuals to do everything within our power to achieve our goals. We would diminish ourselves to think that possessing faith means we should wait passively for some external power or a force outside ourselves to come to our aid. Faith works best when we combine it with practical efforts and ordinary common sense.

This was a lesson Hilda Charlton had to learn. When just starting out on the spiritual path, she drove her old "jalopy" for months, never refilling the gas tank, constantly repeating the affirmation "the gas tank is full." One day the car stalled and she asked a man who stopped to help her if the car was out of gas. The man answered that the tank was full but that the line connecting the gas tank to the carburetor was clogged. Hilda's prayers and faith had worked; the gas tank was full. Still, the car didn't run due to other causes. Hilda was learning that faith doesn't mean we should be above the commonplace requirements of living on the Earth. Prayer and faith need to be balanced with down-to-earth common sense. Although prayer can heal, we can often avoid illness by a healthy lifestyle coupled with good nutrition and exercise. One can beseech Heaven all day for food to appear on the table, or simply go to the store and buy some food. Similarly, we can pray for a bountiful home harvest, but the prayers aren't likely to do much good if we don't also weed and water our garden. We can try through mental concentration to make a pencil levitate, but it makes a lot more sense and expends far less energy simply to pick up the pencil with our hands. Prayers are most effective when backed by knowledge and persistent action.

Like many others who focus on spiritual matters, the youthful Hilda Charlton had to learn some hard lessons regarding combining faith with practical awareness. Once when she was walking in a poor part of Oakland, she felt herself swaying back and forth and thought that the big earthquakes predicted for California had begun. When she came to her senses she realized someone was cutting off her purse from its handles. She turned in time to see a man running off with the purse. She was left with the handles. Angry at God, she complained saying, "I completely trusted in You, why didn't You protect me?" Instantly she heard an inner voice declare: "How dare you walk in a poor part of town swinging a large shiny purse, putting temptation in the way of the needy? You harm others with your carelessness.... Your feet must always be firmly planted on the Earth. Don't float through life."

Rightly understood, prayer and faith are means to align ourselves with the divine life in which we live and move and have our being. Then our actions themselves become the means of fulfilling our prayers. In Hilda Charlton's words, "With the positivity of faith, you align yourself with those of faith and prayer who have gone before and trampled down the weeds of failure and despair, the positive doers, the saints—and you tune into the vortex of positive power which manifests all sincere and right desires." True prayer is alchemy, for it attunes us to the heavenly dimensions through which we change ourselves from within.

OPTIMISM AND INNER RADIANCE CREATE SERENDIPITY

A Persian folk tale describes three brothers from Serendip for whom things always seem to fall into place, as if by magic. From this story we get the word *serendipity*, which describes the knack of being in the right place at the right time and of having situations in life work out smoothly and gracefully. Although it does seem that some people are especially blessed with this quality, it is no accident. They have created their good fortune by their actions and emanations. We can all increase our serendipity by releasing constructive forces through our words, thoughts, gestures, feelings and actions. If you vibrate at a high level inwardly, you trigger a beneficial response from the heart of the cosmic life in which we live. It is as simple as acknowledging and applying the principle of the echo. If we shout "I love you" against a canyon wall, the canyon returns the blessing. So it is in our lives. The experience of serendipity is largely a creation of one's mental attitude.

When we act with faith and conviction, little "miracles" of serendipity will often come about. When Mia and I returned from Mexico one summer, we spent the last of our money buying gifts, saving only enough for the hotel in San Francisco the night of our return. We forgot about the Mexican airport tax. After paying the tax, we arrived in San Francisco at midnight with no checks or credit cards and only enough cash for transportation to the hotel. We calmly told ourselves that we had done all we could and that we could trust in the universal supply of abundance to come to our aid.

When the taxi arrived at the hotel, we paid the driver ten dollars, literally the last of our money, and calmly stepped out into the street. There on the sidewalk was a five dollar bill, which Mia deftly scooped up. We persuaded the hotel to take that as a deposit on the room until we could go to the bank the next day, smiling to each other at our little "miracle."

OUR TRIALS MAKE US STRONGER

Although it is human nature to want events to always flow smoothly, without problems or difficulties, life sometimes refuses to oblige us with an easy path. The fact is, without challenges we simply wouldn't grow. By acting consciously and seeking to learn from our experiences, we can reduce our difficulties and extract the most from events. When I was a student in England, I had a somewhat grueling test of my patience and my faith, which proved ultimately to be both valuable and memorable.

Some friends and I decided to escape the winter by going to the beaches of North Africa during Christmas break. Hoping to save money, we decided to camp out on the beach in sleeping bags. At the last minute my friends backed out, but I was undeterred. I journeyed alone by train through Europe, then flew from Rome to Tunis, site of the ancient city of Carthage and home of the legendary conqueror, Hannibal the Great.

All went well for a few sunny days, but then one morning I rather absentmindedly left my backpack and sleeping bag in a lemon grove and returned to find them gone. I had no credit cards and was forced to spend my limited money in hotels. Cutting short my holiday, I decided to return to England. Even then, I was so short on funds that I had to sell my coat to a merchant to scrape up a bit more cash. I had my plane ticket to Palermo, Sicily, and enough money to buy a train ticket from there to the French Riviera. That was it.

I arrived in Palermo in the evening and bought my train ticket, but the train left the next day and I hadn't money for even the cheapest hotel. So I walked for several hours in downtown Palermo, wondering what to do. Years later I would live in Rome, but at the time I couldn't speak a word of Italian. I had thought I might sleep in a park, but all the parks were fenced in and the gates were locked at night. Finally, at midnight, I paused on a downtown thoroughfare and leaned against a tree, exhausted and out of ideas. Glancing up, I realized what to do. Making sure no one was watching, I climbed the tree, cradled myself in its branches and went to sleep!

The train ride through Sicily and Italy was picturesque but interminably slow. Spending the last of my money on stale croissants, I finally arrived in Monte Carlo two days later, literally penniless. Figuring to hitch through France to the port of Calais and then by ferry on to Dover, I stood for two days in Monte Carlo without getting a ride. (With its fabulous beaches and famous gambling casinos, I began to see why Monte Carlo was known as a sunny place with a lot of shady characters.) At night I slept in a park. In desperation, I remembered I had the name of a friend of a friend—Nicole—who lived down the road from Monte Carlo. I called her and she came to meet me. She gave me the address of an American acquaintance in Paris, then bought me a train ticket to Lyons, France. I was speechless with gratitude.

Lyons was still a long way from Paris and the weather had turned bitterly cold. There was nothing to do but stick out my thumb again and hope for the best. As I stood by the freeway, shivering without my jacket, it began to snow. Fortunately, this time it was only a few hours before I got a ride to Paris with a jovial German businessman. I looked up my "friend's friend's acquaintance," a man named Patrick, and he let me stay at his place. On top of it all, he gave me a royal tour of Paris. Then he gave me about fifty dollars, enough money for a bus ticket to Calais and a ferry ride to Dover. (Though I later sent money to repay both Patrick and Nicole, they each were insistent that I not feel obligated by their helpfulness.) I arrived in Dover relieved, but once more penniless. A Belgian businessman gave me a ride to Sussex and I was soon back at my school in the cozy town of Forest Row, a little worn, but wiser by far. In addition to learning about the value of making contingency plans, I learned a bundle about the importance of faith and patience, and volumes about gratitude. Adversity sometimes teaches us what nothing else can.

The little incidents that test our faith are often the most telling. Soon after Mia and I opened our bookstore in San Rafael, we were experiencing the tightest financial squeeze of our lives. We knew the very existence of our business hung in the balance. One day a denim-clad stranger barged into the store and strode up to the counter, looked me hard in the eyes and said he needed eight dollars right away. I hesitated a moment, opened the cash drawer and handed him eight dollars. In a flash he was out the door and I never saw him again. Within a week of that strange incident, a woman pulled up in her flashy new car and parked beside me as I was getting out of mine. She seemed about thirty-five, was dressed in a blue and white dress, and appeared to be a self-possessed businesswoman. As if there to meet me, she blurted out that she was having financial troubles and needed twenty dollars at once. I barely had that much in my wallet, but something told me to give her the money. She thanked me, got into her car and drove off. Several other incidents like these two happened over a three- or four-week period. Although feeling in part like a simpleton for giving sorely needed cash to complete strangers, a deeper part of me felt it was the right thing to do. In retrospect, I felt that those were tests given by the spiritual world to probe my sincerity and trust.

Following these peculiar incidents—which seemed almost to have been staged—a scruffy woman came into our store with her two children. Although she appeared only slightly better off than some of the local bag ladies, Mia and I were friendly and courteous and tried our best to answer her questions. Soon she began to pile mounds of merchandise up on the counter—toys, books, sacred art, jewelry, cards—items by the fistful. I thought she was either crazy or playing a joke. It finally dawned on me that she was making a purchase. It turned out she spent more money in that single transaction than we had ever made in a full week prior to that time. It seemed to us almost a "cosmic vindication" of our faith. In the months that followed, our business took off and we prospered financially as never before. When we live by the laws of generosity and faith, the universe bestows its bounty.

When Mia and I made the decision to leave California, we figured it would not be easy. We would have to sell two stores—each with less than two years remaining on the lease—as well as our home. We made a trip to Arizona to see if we liked it. We did, and decided to act boldly and swiftly. As we drove out of the charming town of Prescott three days later, we placed non-refundable deposits to purchase a store that was going out of business, and a beautiful home nearby that we had driven up to "by accident." Having made an absolutely firm commitment to our goals, we acted instantly with a degree of confidence and "audacity" that almost surprised us.

That night we wrote down specific affirmations to fit our goals of selling our home and two stores in California smoothly and easily, "under grace and in perfect ways." We affirmed our intentions both together and individually almost constantly during the next three months. Within a week of our return to California we had placed our home on the market. But we knew nothing about selling our businesses. We made some calls and were fortunate to find an attorney whose "hobby" was helping people sell their businesses. With his assistance, we put our two stores up for sale. At the same time, we did everything we could think of to make our home attractive, including painting it inside and out. On Easter Sunday, five weeks after we put the house on the market, we received our first offer on our home. A week later we received our first phone call about the business. Before eight weeks had passed, the sale of our home and both businesses had gone into escrow. Less than four months after making the decision to move, we had completed the deals on our home and businesses and were living in Arizona.

THE ALCHEMY OF FAITH

The alchemists spoke of a mysterious "fifth element," or *quintessence*, which was an essential part of their work of transmutation. The quintessence is the life force that pervades all of nature, including our own organism. We attune ourselves to the dynamic power of the life force by our knowledge of its existence and by living in harmonious attunement to the higher laws. Faith links our minds and our hearts to the life force. Faith is a dynamic knowing that the divine laws that govern life always work. When we believe wholeheartedly in the goodness of life, the universe becomes our friend. When we have faith, we become agents for a culture of light—a culture that the divine Hierarchies of angels are working to bring to life on Earth.

Nothing can stop the emergence of the new culture, for it has been ordained since the dawn of time when the seed of the sacred self was planted in our hearts by the celestial Hierarchies. Human error and foolishness may delay it, but eventually the divine seeds within our souls must come to fruition. The old culture based on violence and exploitation will fall away, becoming fertilizer—compost—for the new era of light. Those who tread the way of sacred living become emissaries of the coming civilization of light and peace. A new and better world is inexorably coming to birth, and with it, more abundant life for you and your loved ones. Believe that your highest good is coming to you, set to work to make it so, and watch the miracle of your life unfold.

Exercises In Sacred Living:
Activating the Alchemy of Faith

Affirm the fact that the universe will give you exactly what you want, provided that you work with persistence, and on the condition that your goals do not infringe on the well-being and freedom of others. Develop the attitude of mind—the unbending conviction—that universal law never fails. The universe will most certainly do its work, if you will first do yours. Just as spring follows winter in accordance with natural laws, so will a better future come to you as you live a constructive life.

Affirmations

"The universe is a place of goodness, justice and grace. As I give forth out of the abundance of my heart, all good will flow to me."

"I am the source of my experience. I am the master of my life and the creator of my future. My world constantly gets better and more beautiful."

"I live in a world of magic and miracles."

CHAPTER EIGHT

THE ALCHEMY OF MANIFESTING

*"We must attune and harmonize ourselves with
Cosmic Intelligence by vibrating on the same wavelength
and creating true beauty."*

– Mikhael Aivanhov

*"The stream of knowledge is heading towards a
non-mechanical reality; the universe begins to look more like
a great thought than a great machine."*

– Sir James Jeans

Every human being is naturally creative. We are constantly creating each moment of our lives—by virtue of our thoughts and feelings, as well as by our actions. It may be that the creations of most people do not amount to very much, for they have never tapped the inexhaustible powers at their disposal. But the truth is that we are creative spirits by nature. Not only do we have the power to fashion our lives, but the circumstances in which we currently find ourselves have been created by prior actions and by the thoughts and emotions we have previously entertained, albeit often unconsciously.

It has been said that "The entire universe rearranges itself to fit your picture of reality." This has a nice ring to it, but is not completely true. Our opinion of the law of gravity, for instance, does not change the operation of this law. We may think that the sun moves around the Earth, but our misperception will not influence these heavenly bodies.

The fact is that the larger universe in which we find ourselves—the macrocosm, or "greater whole"—is the creation of higher beings. Our personal opinions—our "picture of reality"—will not alter the universal laws. What *is* true is that we fashion our *personal universe* in the image of our own minds and hearts. It is a truth of great significance that we are the artisans of our individual destiny. We can accurately say that our personal world arranges itself to fit our picture of reality.

THE ANCIENT MYSTERY SCHOOLS

In the ancient world, the deeper truths of life were taught in the Mystery schools or temples. Eleusis, a small town just outside of Athens, was a principal center of culture in the Mediterranean for nearly 1000 years. A temple to Demeter, the goddess of the harvest and of nature, was erected there, and it became the center for what were called the Eleusinian Mysteries. Cicero wrote that the Mysteries enabled one to "live with joy and to die with hope." The teachings of the great philosophers, Socrates, Plato and Aristotle, were extracts of the teachings of the Mystery schools. According to the Greek writer, Plutarch, the Mysteries taught that the higher soul was "incorruptible and immortal." In the Eleusinian Mysteries, sacred dramas were enacted to illustrate the laws of life. Candidates for initiation were shown a vision of Hades, or the "underworld." This was a ghastly place, where unfortunate souls were tormented by a host of frightening creatures and circumstances. Following this scene, the participants in the Mysteries were shown a vision of the Elysian Fields, a heavenly state of splendor, beauty and ceaseless happiness.

The initiates were made to understand that they created their own future conditions, both on Earth and in the afterlife, by the quality of their thoughts, feelings and actions. Destructive thoughts, words, emotions and deeds would lead to conditions represented by the vision of Hades. Conversely, luminous thinking and activities would lead to circumstances represented by the grandeur of Elysium. The participants' current environment and position in life was not the result of an arbitrary decision made by a whimsical deity, nor was it due to "chance." The conditions in which each person found him or herself was the result of processes they themselves had previously set in motion, either in this life or an earlier one. According to the luminous wisdom of the ancient Mysteries, each man and woman holds the key to the future in his or her own hands.

Coping With Karma

The principle of karma—the law of sowing and reaping—exists in some form in all of the major world religions. In the Sermon on the Mount, Christ is precise about the law of karma when he states that "With the judgment you make you will be judged. And with what measure you give, so shall it be given back to you." He also says that "Not one jot or tittle shall pass away until the law be fulfilled." The "jot and tittle" refers to the balanced measure or reciprocity of the law of karma. Perhaps his most succinct reference to karma is "As a man sows, so shall he also reap."

The law of karma dictates that your current circumstances did not happen by accident. You caused them by the manner in which you have lived all the years of your existence. If one accepts the primordial fact of causation as the law that determines our life circumstances, it is only natural to consider the causes we may have initiated prior to this lifetime. Our circumstances beg this question, for few things are more obvious in life than the gigantic disparity in the conditions humans find themselves in at birth. As one ponders life from an existential perspective, it is natural to wonder about the possibility of repeated Earth lives, a fundamental doctrine of the ancient Mystery schools of Europe as well as of the Eastern religions.

Many Biblical references also imply a belief in the law of rebirth. It is plausible that the term *generations,* found in the Old Testament, may refer to successive incarnations of the same individuality. A belief in reincarnation is prevalent among Hasidic Jews, and most students of the Kabalah—the mystical doctrine of early Judaism—adhere to the Kabalistic philosophy of repeated Earth lives. In her book *Reincarnation, the Missing Link in Christianity*, Elizabeth Clare Prophet quotes the following dialogue from Aryeh Kaplan's translation of the *Bahir*, the earliest medieval Kabalistic work:

Q. Why are there evildoers who are well off and righteous who suffer evil?

A. Because the righteous man was ... an evildoer in the past and is now being punished.

Q. Is one then punished for his childhood deeds?

A. I am not speaking of his present lifetime; I am speaking of what he has already been, previously.

There are other Biblical references to reincarnation. Jesus speaks to his disciples on several occasions about the identity of John the Baptist as the old Testament Prophet, Elijah. Elijah lived six hundred years before Christ. It was commonly taught that Elijah would return (reincarnate) before the coming of the Messiah. After "the transfiguration"—during which Peter, James, and John see Jesus in his glorious celestial body, or Body of Glory—he and his disciples are walking down the mountain. The disciples ask him "Why do the scribes say that Elijah must come first?" He replies that "I tell you Elijah has come again and they treated him as they pleased." (John the Baptist was largely ignored by the religious orthodoxy, and Herod Antipas had him beheaded at the request of his wife Salome.) The Mark gospel version states subsequently that "Then the disciples understood that he was talking about John the Baptist."

Perhaps the most interesting scriptural statement that implies reincarnation is Christ's admonition to "Be perfect, as your Father in heaven is perfect." It is obvious that perfection is impossible in the course of one life. If Christ were serious about his commandment, (and why else would he have given the injunction if he did not mean it seriously?) it implies the need for multiple Earth lives.

It is the opinion of many scholars that the more obvious references to the doctrine of the law of rebirth were stricken from scripture and orthodox belief during the famous Church councils held in the fourth and fifth centuries, many of them in Nicea, in what is present day Turkey.

Then as now, Christianity was divided into many thought streams, and the Church Fathers sought to codify these diverse beliefs into a comprehensive system. They hammered out theological points in a manner comparable to the way modern-day Boards of Directors of large corporations might hammer out a uniform system of policies and procedures.

Giving the Church fathers the benefit of the doubt regarding motive, one might allow that they hoped humans would evolve more readily if the emphasis were placed on just one lifetime. But it is difficult not to concede that a major motive was simply the exercise of power over the masses through the threat of eternal damnation. The historical record is sadly eloquent regarding the intolerance of the official Church toward "unbelievers" and "heretics"—in other words, people who dared to have a mind of their own. Despite the danger of horrible punishments at the hands of the Inquisition, the belief in reincarnation persisted throughout the centuries in Europe.

Unless one believes in a capricious universe ruled by chance and random occurrences, one is led to accept causation as the inner law of one's being. The necessary extension of this truth is multiple Earth lives, in that it often takes long periods of time for the full effects of our deeds to manifest. We do not reap all the consequences of our activity in the short span of one life. Arguably, it doesn't much matter from a practical standpoint whether or not you accept the idea of successive embodiments of the human spirit. Your circumstances in the moment won't instantly change contingent on your beliefs. What *does* matter is that you accept the fact that your future will be what you make it now. Wisely applying the law of the seed will lead to a golden future.

I believe it is helpful, though not indispensable, to believe in reincarnation. An understanding of repeated Earth lives can shed light on many of the riddles of existence, including providing an explanation for the apparent injustice in the extraordinarily wide range of people's varied destinies. Knowledge of the sacred laws helps us unravel the knots in which we presently find ourselves. If understood correctly, the law of rebirth tends to give one a tolerant, philosophical trend of mind. It can also grant hope in a better future—one that we ourselves create by how we live today. Human beings tend to be acutely shortsighted from the standpoint of eternity. As the saying from the sixties goes, "We want the world and we want it now." But the cosmos frowns on such arrogance. Without patience in the outworking of celestial law, the soul cannot unfold the perceptions that bring wisdom.

There is a story told of Alexander the Great that after he began his conquests at the age of twenty-three, he came to a town in Asia where there was a famous knot made of thick rope called the Gordian Knot. The legend was that whoever could untie the Gordian knot would conquer the world. The impetuous Alexander drew his sword and with one blow severed the knot. He went on to conquer most of the ancient world from Greece to India.

The Gordian Knot is an apt metaphor for the circumstances each of us face. All of us must untangle the knot of our personal destiny. Initially, we are faced with unraveling our twisted thoughts and emotions. The sword we use has two edges, representing *discernment* and *vigilance.* Discernment enables us to perceive in advance the consequences of our deeds. Vigilance is required in guarding our inner life. The world we conquer will not be an external kingdom. It will be that of our own life and relationships. Self-mastery begins as we learn to govern our own unruly thoughts, emotions and responses to events.

Rudolf Steiner once described karma by comparing it to the situation of an individual who has decided to build a house. After the plans have been drawn up and the building is constructed and paid for, there is little choice but to live in it. (We'll imagine that selling the house is not an option.) Our karma, or destiny, is like a house that we have built. In its physical dimensions we have to accept it essentially as it is. But exactly how we live in our house is entirely our own choosing. Regarding the external features of karmic circumstances, the basic outlines have been shaped by us in previous lives. There are limits to what we can change. There will be people we cannot avoid meeting and some circumstances and incidents that are inevitable. Yet within the parameters that are "given," or predetermined by earlier actions, we have great mobility and choice. How we respond to circumstances is entirely open. Our inner resources are essentially limitless. In other words, it is entirely up to us how we choose to live in our "house."

Perhaps the real mystery is not how we come to be born on Earth many times, but rather how we come to be born on Earth at all! From the standpoint of our immortal selves, there is really only one life—a continuous stream of development and experience through countless ages. In the words of the saintly teacher Hilda Charlton, "There is a continuity of experience making up eternity." Whether we are on Earth or in the spirit dimensions, it is still the same life—*our life*. Though we may enter physical embodiment hundreds or even thousands of times, we have one life that flows from the "dawn of existence" into infinite eternity. We identify with the changing costumes and scenery, forgetting our true identity. We are the authors of the play. All of our incarnations are "here now" in the present moment. We come to realize our identity and manifest the fullness of our being as we live a sacred life in harmony with divine laws.

WE CAN PREDICT OUR OWN FUTURE

In ancient Greece, the Oracle of Delphi was famed for its accuracy in forecasting the future. The priestess in the temple of Apollo was admired throughout the world for her pithy utterances of events to come. In fact, the word *pithy* comes from the Delphic Oracle. The temple priestesses were known as "pythonesses"—or *pythia*—and this term became synonymous with a brief, astute remark. We work our own oracle in daily life when we use the powers of mind, emotion, imagination and will in a consistent effort to achieve our goals. Results follow when we work with determination and persistence.

Feelings and desires are essential ingredients in the process of manifestation. Desire is emotion that is filled with the yearnings of the heart. The more powerful the feeling within a desire, the more rapidly it tends to be realized. Emotion is a mighty force—life's dynamic principle—which always leads to action. Feelings and desires are the bridge by which thoughts become physical realities. They are the gateways to experience.

The law of manifestation is the synthesis of all the chapters presented so far. The fruits of the law of the seed, the collective impact of our thoughts, emotions, actions, and speech—along with faith and an attitude of thankfulness—are the magic forces by which we fashion our lives and our circumstances. When we use all these together, we become our own oracle. Not only do we consciously create our future, but we can begin to predict it.

THE PROPHECY OF TOMORROW

The world today is full of predictions about the future, running the gamut from "doom and gloom" to instant paradise on Earth. It is likely that the reality of what is to come will be somewhere in between these two extremes. Though millions of people are waking up to the reality of the sacred laws, historically humanity has all too often sown seeds of violence and destruction. We have entered a time of planetary harvest, a season in which we will reap the consequences of human actions over many centuries. It is possible we will pass through a time of great ordeals. This period has been called "the chastisement," or "the tribulation," indicating that it will be a time when ancient karma "comes home to roost." Native American elders call it the time of the Great Purification, the convulsive end of an age. The prophecies of Nostradamus, Edgar Cayce, Gordon Michael Scallion, Sean David Morton, Native American teachers, and a host of others, point to a time of upheaval in human affairs. Old Testament prophets, particularly Daniel, gave what appear to be explicit warnings of this era. There are many New Testament prophecies, including the words of Jesus and much of the Book of Revelation. The Mayan calendar ends strangely on December 31, 2012, suggesting both a conclusion of a grand cycle as well as a new beginning.

We are facing the greatest crisis the world has ever known. Through the monumental challenges of our self-made ecological, moral and spiritual dilemmas, we have the opportunity to transform ourselves into something greater and better. This is the alchemical moment when out of the cauldron of current events can emerge a new type of human being. The great saints and masters of the human race are the prototypes. We ourselves are the saints and masters of the future. Only by evolving into more compassionate and loving people can we avoid potential cataclysms. The purpose of prophecy is to serve as a catalyst for change. An effective prophecy is one that stimulates us to awaken to our true nature. The prophecies are not cast in concrete. To the extent that we act out of love, we can transform the future. Dire predictions can be nullified if enough people become agents for a sacred culture. When we change ourselves, we change the world.

In the years of the new millennium, the human race will have the opportunity to create a new civilization. An image for the era to come is the phoenix. According to legend, this mythical bird flies into a flaming tree. As the feathers of the winged creature go up in flames, a new phoenix emerges out of the ashes and smoldering cinders. The phoenix is an image of the alchemy of transmutation. Death is a catharsis. Out of seeming annihilation comes new life. Those who sow the seeds of a new culture will find that their seeds will spring to life in the years following the beginning of the new millennium. Out of the ashes of the old will come a new culture of light and beauty. The task of soul alchemists in the years ahead will be to stay in consciousness above the external upheavals. Those who remain poised within their higher consciousness will be focal points of harmony and stability.

The result of the coming tribulations may well be a worldwide spiritual awakening unprecedented in its magnitude. Though changes are likely to be swift and massive, these can be times of joyous renewal. Millennium changes are the alchemical crucible in which we can forge a new consciousness. Upheavals in human affairs will be the testing ground for us to express the light and courage of our spiritual selves. We are passing through a global initiation of the human race, "the initiation of the world," as some have called it. External upheavals give us the opportunity to find our true selves—the anchor of pure consciousness within us. Contact with the spirit enables us to establish equanimity in our feelings and helps stabilize the frequencies of our consciousness at a high level. This stability of thought and feeling allows the higher self to express through us. Equanimity is the emotional composure that comes from remaining poised within the "I"— the point of consciousness at the center of the soul. Remaining centered, we can live "above the fray." Regardless of externals, we come to realize that our spirit lives beyond the flux of karma and destiny. We can remain active and creative at the still point of pure spiritual awareness, which is our "I"—our true self.

Regardless of the events that affect nations and humanity as a whole, it is well to keep in mind that our individual future will be the result of the seeds we're currently sowing in our lives. Regardless of what the next highly publicized "prophetic event" might be, it is well to remember that your world of tomorrow will be determined by how you live today.

CONCENTRATION CREATES CIRCUMSTANCES

When we are faced with difficulties in our destiny, we can employ a toolbox of powers and faculties with which to transform events and circumstances. Regardless of external conditions, we can release forces from within ourselves that gradually cause darkness and obscurity to vanish.

An essential means by which we can harness our inner forces for maximum benefit is through concentration. Concentration is the focusing of mental attention on a specific topic. It may be compared to the power of a magnifying glass to focus the rays of the sun. Just as a magnifying glass can burn a hole through wood or ignite a flame, so can the focused mind penetrate to the solution of a problem, or spark new ideas and insights. Concentration is indispensable to any creative mental work. Control of thinking makes possible the high state of linking ourselves with the divine consciousness. This state of higher awareness, cosmic consciousness, or "absorption in God,"—called *samadhi* in Sanskrit—is only possible when we can focus the mind at will. Only through mental concentration can we sustain the frequencies of a higher level of consciousness.

Concentration is like a laser, which amplifies light into a single beam of incredible power. Essentially, a laser is a ruby rod surrounded by a spiral lamp. When the lamp is on, the chromium atoms of the ruby are stimulated. When the stimulation is sufficiently great, a narrow beam of intensely powerful light extends from the ruby crystal.

The spiral lamp, which stimulates or "excites" the chromium atoms in the ruby rod, may be compared to our emotions. When we are sufficiently interested in something, our enthusiasm stimulates the "molecules of our mind," represented by the ruby rod. By focusing the light of our intentions and our dreams through mental concentration, we can achieve remarkable results very rapidly.

Not only is concentration induced more easily when we feel enthusiastic about something, the act of mental focusing will itself awaken interest and enthusiasm in any area of study. A person who learns to concentrate need never be bored again.

The power of concentration is a magical tool that can create or destroy, depending upon the subject of our attention and the nature of our thoughts. Hence the saying of the Buddha: "Suffering follows an evil thought as the wheels of a cart follow the oxen that draws it. Joy follows a good thought like a shadow that never leaves." Buddha's words are the foundation of all metaphysics. The formative principle that shapes substance is mind. When you focus your mind on a visual scenario, you are forcing into your field of experience the very scenes you visualize. For every mental cause there follows a physical result. Positive thoughts will produce like effects. Constructive thoughts build a bridge to a better life. Destructive thoughts harden into chains that enslave us. When we refrain from discordant thinking, our circumstances improve. What the mind conceives, it eventually receives, so long as the intention is strong enough.

THE LAW OF MIRACLES

The law of manifestation is the law of miracles. Said Yogananda, the great Hindu saint and yogi, "The law of miracles is operable by any man who has realized that the essence of creation is light." Quantum physicists state that the material world is really variable fields or frequencies of energy. All energy is ultimately reducible to light. In other words, our universe is a light-wave universe. A miracle is a manifestation of light energy, an amplification of the light in our minds beyond its habitual intensity. Thoughts imbued with the light of wisdom produce miracles. When we aspire to truth, we enter the dimension of the miraculous.

What this means to us practically is that we can create our own miracles and manifestations at will, providing we understand the process. Our mind—that is our thoughts and emotions—conditions the oscillating fields of light, and our inner states of consciousness are projected onto the landscape of experience through a process of time. The metaphor of the cinema projector is helpful to picture the creative process. The divine spirit within us is the light of consciousness, of which the light of the projector is the symbol. The screen on which the projector throws the images is analogous to our environment. Just as the movie projector casts images onto the screen, so are our mind images projected onto the "screen" of our reality by the light of spiritual consciousness that lies behind our thought and emotional life. In truth, we see and experience everything through our own field of awareness. Put another way, our personal energy field, or aura, is the template of our experience. We create our personal reality with the universal substance given to us by the divine beings. Our lives are self-created and our experiences are self-bestowed. Self responsibility is the beginning of personal life mastery.

A YOGI'S MIRACLE

A friend of mine named Lloyd recently passed away at the age of ninety. Half a century ago Lloyd was the beneficiary of a miracle performed by India's yogi-saint Paramahansa Yogananda. Lloyd once described the remarkable incident to Mia and me, remarking that during the late 1940s he often went to Sunday services at Yogananda's temple, which overlooked the Pacific in Encinitas. One day after the worship, he and several friends were getting into their car to drive away. The long-haired swami in orange robes hurried over to them and in a serious voice told them each precisely where to sit in the car. They were surprised by Yogananda's unusual request and his emphatic manner, but they did as he told them. Minutes later they were driving along Route One, high above the Pacific cliffs, when an approaching car skidded into their lane. The driver of Lloyd's car swerved to miss the oncoming car. In that perilous moment, Lloyd and his traveling companions *saw* Yogananda seated on the front of their car, a serious expression on his face. The driver was able to stabilize the vehicle and avoid a collision, whereupon the vision of Yogananda immediately vanished.

Lloyd and his grateful comrades were amazed at the miracle. They agreed that Yogananda must have clairvoyantly perceived the accident coming and intervened, probably saving their lives. Though the mechanics of the miracle elude us in their details, the great Yogi undoubtedly had them sit according to his instructions so that he could better visualize them in their car. He was then able to project himself into the situation and avert a disaster. Lloyd and his friends had apparently seen Yogananda in his partially materialized subtle body. Applying the law of miracles, Yogananda used his knowledge of our light-wave universe to influence material substance with the power of his God-attuned spirit.

THE MAGIC MAN

One of the most remarkable individuals I've ever had the privilege to meet is the American spiritual teacher, Peter Rosen. Seeing him for the first time was a truly memorable moment in my life. I realized I was standing face-to-face with an enlightened man—someone who lives and breathes the deeper truths of life. Peter exemplifies in his life an extraordinary knowledge and mastery of the laws of manifestation. In the wonderful little book entitled *The Magic Man* by "Friends of Peter," a number of people whose lives he has touched have compiled some notable examples of his creative and enlightened approach to life.

When Peter decided to move from Fort Lauderdale to Gatlinburg, Tennessee, he told his friends that there was a thirteen-acre parcel adjoining the National Forest that they would be able to buy. However, the Realtors assured them that no such parcel existed. (Gatlinburg is a resort town and developers would have long ago snatched up such an available piece of land.) Peter insisted that the land was there and they would be able to build their home and teaching center on it. So he, Ann, and a few close friends packed up their belongings and made the long move.

Three months cooped up in a rental home with near-constant rain was trying for virtually everyone—everyone except Peter. He was always happy and brimming with optimism. Sure enough, at the end of three months the "non-existent" parcel was "found"—bordered on three sides by the National Forest. At the same time the rain stopped, and they began to build the Center known today as Mystic Mountain.

Peter has a remarkable relationship to animals. There are usually a number of wild bears sleeping on the deck of his forest home. Once, while walking in the woods, Peter encountered a female bear that was soon to give birth. He spoke gently to the bear and lay down in the forest, letting her sniff his face and beard. Weeks later the mother bear came bounding to Peter's house with the little cub trailing behind. It's not unusual for ten to twelve bears to sleep at night on Peter's wooden deck. The bears respond to Peter's words—and those of his partner, Ann—in the manner of gentle house pets. Wild deer and bear are often seen in close proximity to each other near Peter's house, coexisting amicably.

Peter's world is interwoven with the magical and the miraculous. People have witnessed him raise his hands and make heavy clouds disperse, letting sunlight stream through. One day when he and his friends were building his home in Tennessee, it was raining hard all around them. Although the roof was not yet built, Peter insisted they continue despite the rain, saying, "It's not going to rain on us; keep working." Sure enough, it showered constantly for hours all around them, yet no rain fell on the house.

There have been many seemingly "miraculous" healings around Peter. Once he lay his hands on a young boy's broken foot. Minutes later the boy stood up and walked without his crutches. Peter seems to have the uncanny knack of knowing what's going on in other people's minds, even from a distance. He loves to play little "tricks" and games, like pouring wine from his finger or making it snow. But the greatest manifestations are the changes wrought in people's lives by Peter's loving and enlightened example. As he would be the first to say, all of us have in ourselves the extraordinary power of our deeper self, waiting to blossom into full creative expression. Individuals like Peter Rosen remind us of the awesome creative might within each of us.

We are here to learn eternal truths and apply them in our lives. The result will be self-mastery. Nothing matters essentially except our ability to control our own lives. Gaining this personal mastery is the heart of soul alchemy. We may have an encyclopedic knowledge, but if we do not have the power to transform our circumstances and our environment, we have missed the point.

Many people entering upon a spiritual path have a tendency to become dependent on a "guru" or "master"—often surrendering basic life decisions to that person. They risk giving away their own power of spiritual discernment and personal authority, thus setting back their spiritual development. Peter Rosen suggests the following for people inclined to look outside themselves for authority figures: Stand in front of the mirror each morning and say, "I'm responsible for my life; what am I going to do about it?" That is a healthy approach.

CHARACTER BECOMES VISIBLE IN OUR FEATURES

As stated previously, all things in the physical world have been created from mind. Our thoughts, feelings, desires and decisions are the building blocks of life. For every mental cause there is a physical result. When you fashion an idea, it gives birth to a form. Because all physical creations or manifestations are the results of thoughts, it follows that by working with these ideas we can create the kind of life we want. Even our facial features and bodily characteristics reflect the influence of our habitual thought and feeling. A story from Abraham Lincoln's life illustrates this truth.

As President, Lincoln often met with private citizens. For several days a man kept trying to see him, but each time he tried to make an appointment, the President declined. Lincoln remarked to an aide that he could tell by the man's face that he had nothing constructive to say and that meeting with him would only be a waste of time. The aide expressed dismay that Lincoln would judge the man on the basis of his external features. Lincoln replied that it would indeed be wrong to judge a young person on facial characteristics, but that after age forty, a person's face begins to take on the cast of their dominant thoughts and emotions. Lincoln himself is an example of this truth.

Lincoln's face was not beautiful by any conventional standard. It was plain and homely. Yet upon his features were sculpted the qualities of patience, compassion, sacrifice, and deep spiritual insight. This great soul mirrored the suffering and trials of a nation during its severest spiritual crisis. Lincoln's immortal spirit etched its genius and love into his rough countenance and as a result will always have the power to awaken admiration in the hearts and minds of those who contemplate his features. Few individuals have ever been as universally loved as Abraham Lincoln.

The dynamics of soul alchemy assert that thought waves gradually densify or crystallize into the "stuff" we call matter. This holds true also for our physical bodies. We create our bodies according to our mental images. The frequencies of thought create the geometry of the body. In other words, the soul is the template of the body—or more accurately—the soul creates a multidimensional template through which our three-dimensional physical bodies crystallize. We are liquid light poured into a geometric chrysalis.

THE LAW OF AFFINITY

The metaphysical basis for the law of manifestation is the law of affinity, or the fact that "like attracts like." This principle of affinity is called in physics the law of acoustic resonance. This law is known to all musicians. If you pluck the string of a violin, the same string of a second, identically-tuned violin will begin to vibrate in sympathetic attunement. The same experiment can be done with tuning forks of the same pitch. In like manner, our inner life of moods and feelings, ideas and sentiments, stirs up a response or resonance from the universal life in which we are imbedded.

In the ancient Mystery schools and temples, this truth was expressed in the famous Hermetic Axiom. According to one legend, when Alexander the Great was on his journey of conquest, he visited the grave of Hermes Trismegistus in the town of Hebron, located in present-day Palestine. Hermes Trismegistus was the legendary Egyptian teacher credited with the invention of writing, the creation of paper (papyrus) and the development of alchemy. Knowing Hermes' reputation, and hoping to discover something of importance for the world, Alexander unearthed the antique grave and found a plaque made of polished emerald, which became known as the Emerald Tablet.

Inscribed in several languages on the Emerald Tablet, Alexander and his entourage of scholars discovered what has become one of the world's most famous proverbs, appropriately called the "Hermetic Axiom," in honor of its presumed author, Hermes Trismegistus. The gist of this formula is usually translated as, "That which is below is as that which is above, and that which is without is as that which is within, for the working of the one law." This saying has multiple interpretations. It cryptically informs us of the intimate relationship between the spiritual dimension and the material world. These two aspects of universal reality—spirit and matter—are inseparably united as one. Jesus elaborated on the Hermetic Axiom when he spoke of the Kingdom of Heaven (above) becoming a reality on Earth (below) in the words "Thy Kingdom come...on Earth as it is in Heaven." The notion of creating Heaven on Earth is the highest and most profound meaning of the alchemy of manifestation. Those who live to bring about a sacred culture are uniting the "above" with the "below." As we create a culture of light, we are engaging in divine alchemy—replacing the "lead" of materialism and selfishness with the "gold" of an enlightened consciousness.

Another essential meaning of the Hermetic Axiom—"as above so below"—is that one's inner world of thought and feeling creates one's outer world of circumstance. Our material circumstances will in time reflect our inner or spiritual activity. We magnetize to ourselves people, circumstances and conditions that correspond in nature to what we emanate from our inner life of thoughts, feelings and attitudes. Our inner world is the prototype of our outer world.

This fundamental natural law, sometimes called the law of affinity, is a more subtle explanation of the alchemy of the seed. The consequences we experience as a result of our actions occur in a two-fold manner. On the finer levels of energy and vibration, our emanations at any given moment set up an immediate response from the universal life in which we find ourselves. In the world of thought or consciousness there is an instantaneous effect. On the "physical plane," which is governed by the experience of time, there is a secondary effect that will bear fruit in the future.

The twofold operation of the law of affinity can be understood through the analogy of planting actual seeds in a literal garden. You know that the seeds you plant, say pumpkin seeds, will only bear fruit after several months. But the activity of planting gives you immediate experiences as well. These are the bodily and emotional sensations that accompany the gardening activity—the benefits of exercise and fresh air, for instance. The same is true for all actions, even the most subtle activities of consciousness. Every thought and feeling that we emanate sets up an immediate response from the cosmos that reflects the nature of these thoughts and feelings. In this way the universe at all moments reflects back to us—mirror-like—exactly who we are. In addition, we will experience an effect later in time that is also the fruit of our deeds.

The immediate response from the universal "ocean of existence" elicited by the law of affinity helps explain the mysterious "coincidences" and synchronicities that occur in life. There is a correspondence between what is going on in our minds at a specific moment with what is going on in our environment. The inner connection between external events and what goes on in our minds may be linked in this way and may have more of a causal basis than many psychologists believe. The law of affinity also helps us understand the wonderful, serendipitous feeling of being "in the flow" of life. This state of attunement is a result of an inner harmony that links us to the deep underlying harmony of the universe.

By comprehending this truth we can begin to shape our lives as we wish by becoming conscious of what goes on in our minds. Thoughts, feelings and desires are the stallions that lead one's chariot through life. Each of us is the charioteer, who must guide and direct these powerful forces so that they take us where we want to go. We create better external conditions when we improve the quality of our habitual states of feeling and mind.

This idea of affinity is closely related to the notion that those with whom we associate have tremendous influence upon us. An ancient spiritual maxim holds that those who would advance toward enlightenment should be careful in selecting their associates. The type of "crowd" one draws into one's sphere of activity will have great impact on the directions one takes in life. The cliché is true that "birds of a feather flock together." Change your "feathers"—that is, your thoughts, feelings, interests and habitual moods—and you will attract a different kind of "bird." Those who wish to associate with angels learn to think the thoughts which the angels think.

BUILDING YOUR FIELD OF DREAMS

The movie *Field of Dreams*, starring Kevin Costner, has created an appealing modern metaphor in its slogan, "If you build it they will come." The movie involves the creation of a baseball field, which may be seen as a metaphor for the field of consciousness we create by our thoughts, emotions and intentions. Our energy field can become the instrument by which we manifest our fondest dreams, enabling us to live a fulfilling life.

Valerie Hunt has spent many years studying the human energy system using empirical methods of scientific research. In her fascinating book, *Infinite Mind*, she describes meeting a young woman who called herself a shaman. Valerie Hunt observed the woman give an incredibly energetic dance performance for several minutes while seeming hardly to exert. She was not winded by the strenuous display, and showed almost no sign of her rigorous effort, not even a trace of perspiration. Amazed, Valerie Hunt asked her how she did it. The young shaman dancer explained her method by saying, "I build a field of energy and then I ride it."

This anecdote captures an essential principle of manifesting personal accomplishment. Our energy field is the most powerful instrument in creating our lives. We have around us a literal field of energy that constantly radiates and projects streams of thought and feeling into the world. Not only does our field emanate, but it is also magnetic and receptive. Consequently we draw to ourselves ideas, images and forces that are in accordance with the contents of our "field." In our field of consciousness we are always planting seeds. The harvest comes to us in the form of events, opportunities and circumstances. When we sow sacred seeds, we reap in time a golden harvest.

We Create Our Souls

Our field of consciousness is perhaps most easily comprehended through the concept of the human aura. Each of us is wrapped in an energy envelope composed of our psychic and thought emanations. Our aura may be a nasty collection of colors, particles, and residues, or a place of beauty and light. Our auric field may act as a protective shield or as a festering swamp that attracts all manner of undesirable creatures. It depends on the materials—our thoughts and feelings—that go to create it.

Although our inner life of mind, heart and soul is responsible for the external world we inhabit, it is well to recognize that the ultimate creation of each of us is the soul itself. John Keats, the great English romantic poet, said that we are on Earth to forge our souls. Like a spider weaving its web, we spin the strands of our inner life, creating a shining tapestry or a dark web that entraps us. We choose the elements that go to form our inner world, and in so doing we fashion who we are. We are the artisans of our future and the weavers of our souls.

In the future, there will be a return to sacred living. The eternal values of spiritual unfolding will take precedence over purely material ambitions. People will consider how their lives affect others. We will examine ourselves in the light of our impact and influence on the world around us. The humanity of the future will readily acknowledge that as we make our inner soul world a place of beauty, harmony and goodness, we will make the Earth a better place as well. Reciprocally, in our efforts to spread a sacred culture, our personal environment will also become a "field of dreams"—a sacred place of light and happiness. In time, we may even find ourselves invited to the heavenly banquets—the communion of the angels and saintly masters. At least we can prepare to become worthy. Ultimately, the light and love in our souls will be our calling card. The lines from Henley's poem *Invictus* are eternally true: "I am the master of my fate, I am the captain of my soul."

Exercises In Sacred Living:
Activating the Alchemy of Manifesting

Think of something you want or desire. It could be an intangible quality or a virtue, but for this exercise a material object is best. It should be a "stretch," that is, something requiring effort—perhaps a new computer, a car, a bicycle, a fine piece of jewelry or a new living situation. It could be a gift you want to give someone. Give yourself from 2-4 weeks in which to obtain the item. Write down what you want. Visualize it clearly, in minute detail. Then devise a plan for acquiring it. Think about your objective every day.

Remarkable events often happen with conscious manifesting. Sometimes the item you seek will be given to you. It's perfectly all right just to go out and purchase it, but it should be something requiring effort, not something you ordinarily might buy. Unless it is a major acquisition, try not going into debt. If you use "credit," be sure you are in a position to make timely payments so as not to hurt yourself financially.

The purpose of this exercise is to gain confidence in the laws that underlie the process. We draw to ourselves that upon which we focus our attention and for which we exert effort. Of course, material gains are of far less importance than the ability to change character and acquire new habits of thought and feeling. The ultimate "manifestations" are developing the virtues of a more enlightened consciousness. Use this exercise as a stepping stone to the acquisition of qualities of enduring value—determination, the light of understanding, and a loving heart.

Affirmations

"I am the source of my experience. I am the author of my life. I am creating a more beautiful future for myself by improving the quality of my inner world."

"All that I need and more is coming my way. I live in a world of abundance and beauty."

"I am transforming myself into a being of light, love, wisdom and ability."

CHAPTER NINE

THE ALCHEMY OF PROSPERITY

"Success is a journey, not a destination."

– Wayne Dyer

*"Seek and you shall find. Ask and you shall receive.
Knock and it shall be opened unto you."*

– Jesus

Abasic premise of this book is that living a sacred life is a result of a conscious quest for spiritual understanding. Alchemy gives us vivid images of this quest. As we have seen, the alchemists desired to transmute ordinary metal into gold. Although alchemists certainly worked with actual metals in their search for the secrets of transmutation, their activities are essentially metaphorical. The alchemists sought the secrets of a more abundant life. Their pursuit of these secrets is an image of the process of increasing the light in the soul and illuminating all of life with this inner brilliance. Alchemy, in its most vital meaning, is the power to elevate and transform every aspect of life.

Because alchemists started with only a small amount of gold, and as a result of their efforts procured quantities of the precious yellow metal, their work was sometimes referred to as the "multiplication of gold." In soul alchemy we start where we are. By focusing on the best within our minds and hearts, we magnify the good in ourselves and the world. We multiply our "inner gold." In time we will see that our quest enhances and vivifies every part of our lives. We might define the alchemy of sacred living as the "multiplication of good." This includes expanding our material well-being as well as developing our spiritual qualities. Alchemy represents increase—the art of becoming prosperous.

To those who understand the principles of soul alchemy, the universe is a place of unlimited bounty. Alchemists asserted that "The seeds of gold are contained in all substances." Because all substance is infused with the light and goodness of the spirit, the potential for plenitude is everywhere. There exists in the universe a limitless source of all good things. Life is an inexhaustible cornucopia of energy, substance and variety. Limitations do not exist in the universal mind that underlies creation.

The truths that lead to abundance are not carefully guarded mysteries. They are open secrets. All human beings have the capacity to become prosperous—to multiply good—through the right use of their faculties. A simple bar magnet is useful to illustrate one of the essential principles of prosperity. If a magnet is struck a heavy blow with a hammer, the tiny iron atoms are shaken out of alignment and the magnet loses its drawing power. By stroking the iron again with the end of another magnet, the microscopic iron crystals will realign and the full force of the magnet returns.

All of us have a "prosperity magnet" within ourselves. With many people it has become "demagnetized" due to the heavy blows of life—or as a result of the destructive impact of discordant thinking and emotion. A sure way to weaken one's prosperity magnet is through fear and negative thinking. Fortunately, regardless of the condition of our "magnet," we can restore its full attractive power. When our thoughts become positive, we align the "crystal atoms" of our mental magnet in one direction. Automatically we will begin to pull to ourselves the resources we require. Not only is it necessary to overcome habitual negativity in order to improve as a person, but one's ability to prosper is also largely dependent on replacing a negative trend of thought and feeling with enthusiasm and hope.

To Change Your Finances, Change Your Mind

In order to grow financially it is necessary to grow as a person. This may mean learning new skills, or simply changing our attitude from one of pessimism to optimism and expectation. The flow of our income is directly proportional to the positive and constructive energy we emanate. The greater our outpouring of energy, in the form of constructive activities that have a beneficial influence, the greater our receiving. All that we receive into our lives is equated to the forces we release into the world.

The basis of economic life lies in supplying needed goods and in providing beneficial services. By opening up a channel of helpfulness we make it possible to receive benefits. Here again we come to the conclusion that the fundamental economic law is the law of the seed. As you sow, you shall reap. If you sow radishes, you won't reap roses.

Just as you cannot harvest what you have not planted, you can only extract from your life what you have put into it. The fruits of our labors are in direct proportion to the seeds invested through our activities. The law is always just. As we act, the universe responds. What we draw into our lives is inseparably connected to the forces we have triggered in motion by the manner in which we have lived from the dawn of our existence. Regardless of where we are now financially, our conditions will improve if we make it a matter of personal life policy to serve constructively.

The remarkable American teacher, Peter Rosen, demonstrates a seemingly effortless mastery of the laws of prosperity. In the inspiring book by John Roberts entitled *The Fruit of Your Thoughts*, the author paraphrases Peter as follows: "Give what you have in complete faith that if you contribute to life then life will return the bounty... You only attain wealth in the long run by enriching the lives of others first. This is the law of enrichment. The universe rewards when you are a faithful steward. It is a spiritual law that when you serve and enrich others by bringing beauty, joy and comfort into their lives, an abundance of time, money, health and prosperity will seek you out."

When I was teaching at a small private school in northern California, I was on the "tuition assistance committee," which worked with parents who could not afford the school's full tuition. The school had a fund to help these families. In return for the assistance, the parents were expected to "volunteer" their services by performing tasks such as classroom cleanup and grounds maintenance, which would help the school by reducing costs. There was one woman, a parent, who was always complaining about how tough her life was and how difficult things were financially. Yet she almost never showed up to perform the tasks that were her responsibility as part of the tuition-assistance agreement. It seemed to a couple of us that she could benefit from a dose of prosperity thinking. So we decided to send her a copy of Catherine Ponder's book, *The Dynamic Laws of Prosperity*. Inside the cover we placed a crisp new twenty dollar bill, then mailed the book to her anonymously. The change was gradual but dramatic. She was quiet for a few weeks, but the complaints stopped. Soon she was performing her tasks cheerfully, even offering advice to other parents receiving tuition assistance. This little incident also demonstrates the power of anonymous giving to change people's lives.

Prosperity begins in the workshop of our minds, where the architect within us draws up the master plan. The blueprint of your personal economic conditions is created in your thinking process. Positive mind-images create positive circumstances. Many people have small goals and limited expectations. Life provides for them in accordance with what they expect and request. If we want more out of life, we can increase our expectations, and be prepared to back up our demands with personal effort. Life will give us what we ask of it, provided that we perform useful service to back up our desires.

When we release energy in service, we establish a cause that will result in a definite effect. This effect is first felt in the lives of those whom our service benefits. But the eventual result will be a return of energy as a reciprocal force that impacts us and our living circumstances. In other words, when you give of yourself, you are making deposits in the "vaults of heaven"—your divine bank account. In times of need you will have something on which to draw. The act of giving results in receiving. In the long run, your income and the status of your personal economy, rests entirely in your own hands and in your own mind.

In a sense, we all perform alchemy—transforming "base metal to gold"—whenever we perform constructive work. I was reminded of this fact when I visited my local printer. I saw him laboring beside his giant printing machine, working cleverly with piles of paper and ink. Off the press rolled attractive newsletters, for which he would be paid by his clients. Here was an image of alchemy. The printer was literally transforming paper and ink—along with "the sweat of his brow"—into the wealth he would receive in payment for his labors. We all do this in whatever kind of service we perform, turning the materials and "tools of our trade" into the medium of exchange we receive as recompense. Like the little old man in the folk tale *Rumpelstiltskin*, when we act constructively we turn "straw into gold."

Treasures On Earth, Treasures in Heaven

Jesus advised his followers to "Build up treasures in heaven, where moth and rust will not corrupt and thieves will not break in and steal." Fortunately, we may follow his advice, seeking to develop the virtues of our higher nature, while also prospering in our material lives. Jesus was warning of the futility of seeking material gain *only*, while ignoring the inner life of the soul. The wise individual recognizes that earthly life, in the scale of cosmic time, is a mere flicker, and so cultivates virtue while on Earth. As such, we may enhance our material affluence even while making deposits in our "heavenly bank account."

The "heavenly bank account" is that invisible repository in the higher dimensions that stores all the jewels of truth and wisdom that we make our own. It also contains the results of our good efforts, which live on in our higher consciousness in the form of light, beauty, wisdom, energy and virtue. If we give more than we take, and if our giving truly benefits those around us, we will store up "credits" in our divine "bank ledger." These heavenly credits comprise our good karma. It is this "cosmic credit" that enables us to live a prosperous and bountiful life on Earth. It also creates beautiful conditions for us in the spiritual dimensions after physical transition. A constructive service will benefit our personal economy on Earth, while also building up "treasures in heaven,"—that is, it will increase the virtue and brilliance of our spiritual *light body,* the celestial garment which it is our task to develop during earthly life. Our light body is the transformed field of our thoughts, emotions and vital energy. When we "turn base metal into gold" by transmuting our inner life into a field of radiant emanations, we build our light body. In so doing we discover the Elixir of Life—that stream of divine energy that pours from our divine self into the energy centers in our vital, or etheric, body. The light body will become our "garment" in the higher worlds—the vehicle that transports us through all the regions and dimensions of universal space. By acting with kindness and light, we develop the virtues and radiance of our light body while also improving our material environment. In this way, we may live a sacred life that is also an affluent one.

The sun is constantly demonstrating an essential law of prosperity. This "day star" may be described as a repository of cosmic treasures in the form of light, warmth and radiant substance. The sun is blessed with all these treasures because it gives ceaselessly of itself. If the sun produced only enough light and warmth for itself alone, our very Earth could not exist. This radiant orb is an image of a basic truth of life—that those who give, prosper. Like the sun, successful people learn to produce a shining surplus. They open up a channel of helpfulness that transcends purely personal needs. When we become like the sun, a source of abundance and blessing, our lives becomes enriched.

The surest way to improve the conditions of your celestial bank account is to give. You get out of the red by giving more than you take, and by giving only that which is good, beneficial, helpful and kind. No giving can go unrewarded. In time, you will reap a bountiful harvest, for giving opens the floodgates of receiving.

YES, THERE IS A SANTA CLAUS

Many people have used religion as a justification for a "poverty equals spirituality" mindset. But poverty in itself has nothing to do with authentic spirituality. In fact, Jesus' "parable of the ten talents" indicates the desirability of making the most of our abilities and our wealth, material as well as spiritual. In the parable, the steward who buried his wealth—his ten talents—out of fear, doing nothing with his resources, was scolded severely by his master and he lost even the little that he had. Jesus used the parable to reprimand those inclined to lethargy or apathy. This parable reminds us that those who engage in constructive efforts, using wisely the substance and resources at hand, inevitably prosper.

From the early Christian era comes another example of a healthy approach to balancing spiritual and material values. The modern figure of Santa Claus—the jolly old elf of Christmas gifts and cheer—has his origin in the historical character Saint Nicholas, who was a bishop of the early Christian church. Bishop Nicholas was tall, austere and dignified, and was respected by everyone in his native land of Myra, located in what is now Turkey. He was deeply devout and given to long periods of prayer. He has been credited with numerous miracles. On one occasion during his travels, Bishop Nicholas came to a small village where a peasant woman was bathing her infant child in a kettle on the hearth. When she heard of his arrival, the woman rushed out to catch a glimpse of the saintly bishop, leaving her baby in the kettle above the flames. She became so engrossed in the excitement of the moment that many minutes passed before she suddenly remembered her baby. Shrieking, she cried to St. Nicholas to save her child. St. Nicholas told her not to worry, all would be well. The woman hurried back and found her infant relaxing in the boiling water, happily playing with the bubbles.

St. Nicholas was also extremely wealthy. Notwithstanding his fame as a wonder worker, the saint's reputation was created as much by his generosity as by his miracles. He often walked the streets at night, stopping unseen at the homes of poor families. The good bishop would throw gold and silver coins into the windows and hasten off in order to avoid being recognized. He gave freely of his wealth, often leaving gifts of food and money on the doorsteps of the poor. Saint Nicholas—the true Santa Claus—used his wealth in a sacred manner. He combined saintliness with affluence and used both material and spiritual means to make the world a better place. "Good Saint Nick" demonstrated that material means and spiritual attainment need not be mutually exclusive. Poverty does not equal spirituality, and one may safely be both wealthy and wise.

LET'S MAKE WAVES

My friend, Ricardo, and I were once talking about the laws of prosperity. One of his favorite words is *abundance.* He told me that it came from the Latin root *abundare,* which can be translated as meaning, "to make waves." This is enlightening when we consider the modern view of quantum physics that sees the material universe as an ocean of light-wave frequencies of varying modulations and "densities." Becoming prosperous and abundant means "to make waves"—the right kind of waves. The right kind of "waves" are the emanations we set in motion by thoughts, feelings and actions that benefit, help, assist and prosper. The universe is a gigantic sounding board that will send back to us what we send out into the world, often enhanced and multiplied many times. I knew a man who had a great expression for this truth. His advice—paraphrasing scripture—was to "Throw your bread upon the waters and it will come back fruitcake."

Many spiritual leaders and saints demonstrate that the concept of a "struggle for existence" is an illusion. Thousands of people have witnessed Sai Baba, the great Indian spiritual leader, materialize rings, food and many other things seemingly "out of the air." Although few of us have reached a point where we can directly manifest from the ethers with a wave of our hands, many people who have made spiritual goals a priority find that material things come to them more easily. If we express good in all that we do, the universe provides for us. This is one of the meanings of Christ's words, "Seek first the Kingdom of Heaven and all these things will be added unto you." "All these things" refers to the normal wishes and aspirations of most people: material security, fulfilling work, friendship, a successful intimate relationship. When seeking spiritual enlightenment—"treasures in Heaven"—becomes a priority, other areas of life start to fall into place as if by magic. Once your life has an influence that spreads beyond purely personal gain, the floodgates of universal supply are flung open. This means creating an avenue of service that goes beyond the satisfaction of purely selfish interests.

Many individuals short-circuit the good effects of their constructive efforts by mixing them with many negative, destructive seeds. Some people live a lifestyle far exceeding their income. They pile up debts which become a mountain they have to surmount in order to reach stable prosperity. Those who receive benefits without reciprocating for what they receive build up a debt in their cosmic treasury account. The backlash effect of the causation principle insures that even what they appear to have will eventually be taken from them. Cosmic law demands that the piper be paid.

It is wise to consider the moral and ethical implications of your economic activities in the light of the law of reciprocal exchange. What kind of future are you creating for yourself? Are your professional activities truly constructive and life-affirming? If your current employment is destructive or less than ethical, ask yourself why you are there. If your work truly provides benefits to others, do it with enthusiasm and excellence.

Many people, particularly if they are an "employee," work with a listless attitude, holding back their best, as if they are really meant for better things than the work currently before them. Such an approach is self-defeating. In reality, everyone is self-employed, no matter who signs their paycheck. New and better possibilities will only open up if we give our best in our present work. Paraphrasing scripture, we must learn to be faithful in small things before we can be faithful in large things. One of the best gifts we can offer others is simply to do our work with excellence. No matter what our current employment or financial circumstances, if we work with energy, kindness and enthusiasm—performing service to the best of our ability—we will prosper.

ECONOMICS AS IF PEOPLE MATTERED

Years ago, when I was a student at Emerson College in England, I had the good fortune to meet E. F. Schumacher, one of the most original economic thinkers of the twentieth century. By a stroke of serendipity, after his morning lecture I found myself seated beside him at a small table in the lunch room. Only later would I read the book that had made him famous, *Small Is Beautiful*. But I was impressed with his unassuming manner, especially considering that he was currently being wined and dined by international heads of state (and had just returned from a visit to the Carter White House.) Schumacher's ideas appealed to my youthful idealism. He valued beauty as much as utility, and deplored the trend toward huge, multinational corporate monopolies. He encouraged small, community-based enterprises that preserved the beauty of nature and environment. He was influential in spreading the ideas of cottage industry and self-sufficient communities. He was a student of Mahatma Gandhi and admired Gandhi's efforts to spread the use of the spinning wheel in India. He himself baked his own bread each day. Schumacher said that if you want to make the world a better place, "Work to put your inner house in order." When someone once asked him for political advice based on his economic insights, he answered, "I can't speak for others, but my own suggestion would be to plant a tree." He believed we would solve the world's economic problems by developing virtue—and overcoming a "small, mean, calculating attitude to life." E. F. Schumacher deplored greed and believed a healthy economic approach should support the sacredness of life.

Someone once said that "A bowl made of greed can never be filled." Greedy people never appreciate what they have. To them the glass is always half empty, never half full. Miserly people tend to lose what they have. Their constant worry and fear make them miserable and ruin their health. The root of the word "misery" is the same as the word "miser," meaning one who chokes off the flow of supply by refusing to give. The wisdom of language reveals that greed—the absence of generosity—is one of the root causes of suffering. Human misery has its origins in selfishness and the unwillingness to give. Generosity cancels out miserliness. To give is to plug into the eternal storehouse of divine life. The new culture of light belongs only those who will give of themselves and their talents. Giving is the origin of receiving. When we give of ourselves, we triumph over the inner poverty of miserliness that knows only how to take.

Happiness and prosperity result from a generous approach to life. Jesus said, "To those who have, still more shall be given." This means that when we use what we have to benefit the greater life of which we are a part, we prosper. As we employ what we have to make the world a more beautiful place, we are richly rewarded.

MONEY WON'T MAKE YOU RICH

In most people's minds, money is equated with prosperity. The reason for this is obvious, for money is needed to purchase goods and services and is the central means of financial power in today's world. However, many people make money the primary focus and objective of their career efforts, which is a fundamental error in approach. Money is not the *source* of affluence and prosperity, it is a *result* of services performed and benefits created. "Money," said the Roman philosopher Seneca, "has never yet made anyone rich."

Strictly speaking, money is not wealth—nor is it the source of wealth. Real *wealth*—as distinguished from money—implies generosity of mind, heart and character. When one is inwardly wealthy—in terms of character, attitude and soul qualities—external abundance will also appear. If one creates the right inner conditions, material wealth will manifest. Among the most important of these inner characteristics are a positive attitude, gratefulness for life experiences, a harmonious disposition, and the ability to enjoy both solitude and the company of other people.

The true function of money is as a medium of exchange. Money *represents value* that has been created by goods produced or services performed. Essentially, money is a symbol of the universal life force that permeates all things and which is, for all practical purposes, limitless and infinite. When we live a constructive life, money—representing the life force—automatically flows in our direction, so long as we do not obstruct this flow by selfishness and by negative thinking and action. We tap the cosmic treasury of universal abundance by the attitude that realizes there is no lack in the spiritual or material universe. To this opulent attitude of consciousness must be added a constructive lifestyle. A basic criterion of prosperity is to work positively in whatever field of service one chooses. Abundance lies in constructive employment of talents and abilities. When you give your best in service, benefits will accrue in direct proportion to your helpful efforts. Money always tends to flow in the direction of activity and energy, so long as these are positive. Enterprise and initiative designed to provide assistance to others will always lead to financial rewards.

Unfortunately, our modern economic life is burdened by a tremendous distortion, which is the result of our currency being created out of nothing, and issued as debt. Since going off the gold standard, there is nothing tangible to back up the "money"—that is, the debt—that is issued by our central bank and the large commercial banks. This leads to inflation and the centralization of financial power in the hands of a few.

Compound interest, when applied to personal indebtedness, becomes an all-consuming monster that can bring about financial ruin. Many psychological and health problems—as well as tensions in relationships—are related to the trauma and difficulty of getting out of debt. I saw a bumper sticker that reflected this fact. It read: "I don't need therapy. I need money!" The debt system is insidious because *everyone* is made to over-exert just to keep up with payments. It has been estimated that as much as fifty percent of all bills paid—including those paid by individuals who have no debt of their own—goes to the service of corporate debt. (Not to mention the federal government debt.) The commercial propaganda of the corporate and financial institutions has influenced an entire culture to embrace a lifestyle of living beyond one's means. In the future, this system will be reformed, which will lead to universal prosperity and abundance on a scale never before experienced on Earth.

Even with the current distortions in our economy, we can build the foundation for an abundant life right now. We can prosper despite the present flaws in our system. Two keys are essential. First, plug into the limitless universal storehouse of all good things by a positive life outlook and an unwavering faith in the overwhelming goodness of the universal laws. Secondly, live a positive and constructive life, in thought and gesture, remembering to stay out of debt insofar as is possible.

Pay Yourself First

In order to experience financial gain over time, it is essential that you pay yourself first. This means putting yourself at the top of your financial list. To develop prosperously, it is essential to establish a long-term account dedicated to your future. This account is your "financial independence fund" and should not be touched until you have reached your goal of "financial independence," however you define it. Add money to it regularly—weekly, monthly or annually. Allow it to accrue. This is your long-term "nest egg" for a financially secure future. Even if complete financial independence seems an unrealistic proposition, we benefit by paying ourselves first.

In addition to your long-term "financial independence fund," you should, ideally, have at least two other accounts. One is your "emergency fund" which has two to three months income set aside. The other is your normal checking account, to which you make deposits and from which you make payments for day-to-day living expenses. By having an emergency fund, you can pay for unexpected expenses that come up—such as an unanticipated medical bill or car repair—without touching your financial independence fund.

Still another account you may wish to establish is one designated for your future "world service." When Mia and I decided to start a bookstore, we did not have the money to do so, but we opened a mutual fund account with five hundred dollars and designated it as our "Project Omega Fund." This money, along with some initial copies of my favorite books, became the "starting capital" for what eventually became our bookstore four years later. If you sincerely dedicate a portion of your life capital for purposes that benefit the world, adding to it as you can, opportunities will mysteriously come your way.

Anyone who has ever owned a business knows that if you can't operate at a profit your business is doomed. Long-term financial prosperity is always reduced to this simple equation for success: your income must be greater than your expenses. It appears that this elementary financial concept is entirely ignored or forgotten by many people today. It seems frugality is not valued any longer. In the era of credit cards, many people believe they can have everything they want instantly. The result has been the creation of a consumer debt of more than ten billion dollars, with more than a million people declaring bankruptcy each year. There are many current economic distortions contributing to these trends, including growth in white collar crime and an expanding mania for litigation. Nevertheless, the problem is caused mainly by people spending money they don't have. A person with a small income who saves and invests a portion routinely is building on a more stable foundation than one who earns a great deal but spends more than he or she earns, thus growing gradually into debt. It's not what you earn, but *what you keep*, that counts. As far as possible, keep any long-term debts to major investments such as your home and car. For everything else, pay as you go. Use credit cards like charge cards and pay off the balance each month.

As Good as Gold

There is much talk today of creating a single global or "one world" currency. There can be little doubt that the financial institutions that seek a monopoly on the creation of money would love to have a universal currency, preferably an electronic one. It is highly questionable if this would be good for the world, however, for monopolies always tend toward economic distortions and exploitation.

But the idea of a world currency is nothing new. In fact, the world has always had a universal currency. That currency is gold. Gold has been valued in every developed society since the dawn of history. Gold is a beautiful metal with unfading luster. It will not tarnish. Gold has always been a symbol of the spirit, the immortal divine spark, the true source of all wealth. It represents the immortal virtues of our higher nature. It is only natural that alchemists would use gold as the symbol of their quest.

According to the wisdom of ancient sacred teachings, gold is condensed sunlight. The Earth is a master alchemist. Not only does she turn plants into diamonds in her hidden laboratories, but she also renders sunlight into gold. Gold represents the source of all wealth and abundance on Earth, which is the sun itself. Alchemists referred to gold as *sol,* meaning the sun. The alchemists believed, as did the ancient metaphysicians, that gold was a metallic form of solar radiance. The alchemical quest of turning base metals to gold gives us an image of the laws of prosperity. We become prosperous as we transform our dark thoughts and emotions into golden ones. This is soul alchemy—the magic of turning darkness into light. As we do this, we prosper.

In 1964, coinage in the U.S. was altered. Silver was taken out of the coins minted by the Treasury and replaced with common metals. This is known as "debasing the currency." Within a matter of months, almost all the silver coins disappeared from circulation. This phenomenon is sometimes called "Gresham's law," which states that when two currencies circulate side by side, the one that has the inherently greater value, due to the type of metal used, will be removed from circulation by the people.

Gold and silver are honest forms of money because a currency tied to the precious metals makes it difficult for the banking system to loan money it does not have. When U.S currency was backed by gold, the United States became the most prosperous country the world has ever known. Since the federal government went off the gold standard, the U.S. has become the world's largest debtor nation. A dollar today buys what two cents bought in 1900. The quickest way to reverse this trend is to write off the national debt and return to the gold standard.

Central banks and governments still think it prudent to accumulate gold and silver when they can afford to buy them. It's not for nothing that gold and silver are called "precious metals." You may wish to put aside gold or silver coins as security for your financial future and that of your loved ones.

THE MAGIC OF TITHING

Another ancient prosperity principle that contributes to sacred living is that of proportional giving, known as *tithing*. When you give a portion of your income to organizations that work to make the world a better place, you align yourself with the advancing momentum of life itself. Your efforts become linked with the divine force that is drawing all things toward a higher state of being. By pledging a proportion of all your earnings to further the objectives of the divine world order, you build your life on a firm foundation.

The word "tithe" comes from the Anglo-Saxon word *tethoa*, which means "a tenth." The tithe is traditionally ten percent of earned income, though you can start with a smaller percent and work up to that. Some individuals give even more than ten percent. The important thing to consider in tithing is that a portion of the fruits of your labor flows to organizations that are truly worthy. These can be any spiritual or charitable institutions that are uplifting humanity, relieving the suffering in the world, and whose philosophy is in accordance with the beneficent laws of the universe.

John Templeton is a man of humble origins, who grew up on a poor Tennessee farm. As a result of living in accordance with the deeper laws, he has become one of the world's wealthiest men and a noted philanthropist. The famous family of mutual funds that bears his name is one of the most successful and respected of all investment companies. In his inspiring book entitled *Discovering the Laws of Life*, he notes that, "In my lifetime of observing many hundreds of families, almost without exception, the family which tithes for more than ten years becomes both prosperous and happy. This is the one investment suitable for all persons." Tithing is an investment in your future which will help you to establish financial security in your life. Tithing is an indispensable ingredient in living a sacred life.

YOU ARE THE SOURCE OF YOUR FINANCES

During the past several decades there has been a tremendous expansion of the "lottery mentality." Governments have promoted this way of thinking in order to expand their revenue base; most states now have a lottery. More and more people are staking their future prosperity on buying the winning ticket, or getting rich with a "lucky strike" in the casinos. This is an unhealthy trend, for it indicates a lack of understanding of the fundamental law of life, the law of the seed. The law of causation decrees that you can't get something for nothing. Only service produces affluence. Only *your* service can increase *your* personal affluence. People could begin to expand their personal prosperity by diverting the money they might throw away in the mad chase for the elusive lottery jackpot and invested it in their own or another worthy business. Or they might give this money to charitable organizations or to people in financial need. When you give, you invest in your own future. Gambling is not an investment; it's a form of taxation.

We can only depend on ourselves for our long-term financial security. Each one's life is self-created. In order to improve your finances and increase your prosperity, begin now to more effectively serve those with whom you come in contact. Initiate a method of constructive activity that goes beyond your personal needs only. Every helpful act, every beneficial deed, carries the seed of its own return. Your financial condition and the environment in which you live are the result of all that you have ever thought, felt, said and done. You will draw to yourself the very conditions you focus on mentally, for "like attracts like."

We may have whatever we desire if we are willing to pay the price in energy expended through effort and service. We reach the place in life where we begin to receive what we desire when we can picture ourselves having what we want, but we must first set the necessary energy in motion that will bring us what we have earned. We have to "make waves." These "waves" are created through frequencies of inspired thought and loving feelings, and by engaging in constructive actions. Keep in mind that "service" can be anything of a helpful, beneficial nature. It is well to remember that we can't give what we don't have, and we only have what we have earned through meaningful use of talents.

Alchemy in the realm of finances is the process of turning the light of loving and wisdom-filled actions into the gold of spiritual and material well-being. The sacred culture of the future will be built on the impulse of giving. Exploitation will give way to commitment. We will become custodians of Beauty and caretakers of Wonder. We will learn the secret of turning darkness into light.

As humanity learns the wisdom of living in harmony with the universal laws, we will move beyond the violence and greed of the present world. With our commitment to inner peace, gradually peace will come to the nations of the world. The current economic order based on destruction and exploitation will give way to the new economic order of sacred living and kinship with life. Our luminous thoughts and good actions will create a level of prosperity never experienced on Earth before. Humanity will discover the final secrets of alchemy—the secrets of how to transform darkness, violence and greed into the light of a sacred culture.

When we work with a feeling of love and gratitude—out of a desire to benefit the world—we may be sure the rewards will take care of themselves. Each of us holds in our hands the keys to a more prosperous life.

Exercises in Sacred Living:
Activating the Alchemy of Prosperity

Activity Number One

An excellent means of enhancing your level of prosperity and increasing your success consciousness is by keeping a diary for this purpose. Divide each page in half down the middle, creating two columns. Title the left column "gifts and services," the right column "miracles and manifestations." At the end of each day note down in the left column all your kind, helpful actions and gifts. This could be almost any constructive act: giving flowers, sending a greeting card, donating money or clothing to a homeless person or volunteering your time. The possibilities are endless. The other column is for the miracles and benefits that begin to flow into your life. The left hand column is outflow, the right hand column is inflow. Make an entry each day. If you persist with positive efforts and seek to expand your givingness, you will be amazed and delighted at the increasing abundance and "miracles" that begin to flow to you. When you combine this with affirmations and visualizing the achievement of your goals, you can transform your life. To be truly effective you must work this plan for at least ninety days. You may want to keep this little "book of miracles" as a permanent part of your inner and outer work.

Activity Number Two

Many people block the circulation of abundance into their lives by accumulating vast amounts of material things that they no longer need or use. Make a thorough inventory of all your material possessions. Decide which ones are just taking up space, or no longer serve you. Resolve to move them out of your life! Have a garage sale of these items. If you can't sell them, give them away. There is a saying in India that, "What isn't given is lost." Remember that giving opens the way for receiving.

Activity Number Three

Sit down in your favorite chair with a pad of paper and a pen in your hands. Reflect on your long-term life goals. What would you most like to do with your life? Ask yourself if your work or career is really helping to make the world a better place. If not, why not? In the light of the law of the seed, consider the long term implications of engaging in your present vocation.

Many people would like to change their work or their profession, but are not able to do so, for numerous valid reasons. Even if your work is not your ideal, think of activities you can engage in that will help create a better world.

Affirmations

"I hold the key to limitless abundance by the constructive use of my mind and all my faculties."

"As I benefit others through service, I open a channel of abundance to flow into my life."

"There are no limitations in the Universal Mind. I affirm abundance and prosperity for myself and others."

"All that I need and more is coming my way."

CHAPTER TEN

THE ALCHEMY OF HARMONY
AND HEALTH

"Don't cry, mother," he would answer. *"Life is paradise,*
and we are all in paradise, but we won't see it; if we would,
we should have heaven on earth the next day."

– Dostoyevsky, *The Brothers Karamazov*

"We want a road map, but God hands us a musical score instead."

– Woodene Koenig-Bricker, *365 Saints*

The essence of alchemy can be expressed by the word *harmony*. Harmony is the balanced interrelationship of all parts within the whole. Soul alchemy is the process of harmonizing all the elements within the soul in order to arrive at a state of beauty and illumination. The Philosopher's Stone is a symbol of the dynamic power produced by a sustained level of inner harmony and soul radiance. A stone is something that is relatively fixed, unlike a gas, liquid or vapor. The alchemists referred to the goal of their quest as a *stone* because they sought a harmony that was sustained. The frequencies of the enlightened consciousness are stabilized. As we are able to maintain inner equilibrium and sustain loving, harmonious feelings, we are approaching that inner state of being the alchemists referred to metaphorically as the Philosopher's Stone.

Underlying all seeming disturbance, imbalance and irregularity, there exists a world of profound harmony. For some mystics this universal harmony has become audible to their soul's inner ear as "the music of the spheres." The ancients called this equilibrium of living things by the name *cosmos*. The absence of order—of cosmos—was *chaos*. As we grow toward wholeness in our inner selves and balance in our outer lives, we will readily grasp and express the underlying laws of the universe, for they are expressions of exquisite harmony.

This deep underlying harmony of life was perceived by Admiral Richard E. Byrd when he spent five months alone in Antarctica, near the South Pole. In his journal he described an experience that came to him one bleak and frozen night:

"I paused to listen to the silence. My breath crystallized as it passed my cheeks, drifted on a breeze gentler than a whisper. The wind vane pointed toward the South Pole. Presently the wind cups ceased their gentle turning as the cold killed the breeze. My frozen breath hung like a cloud overhead.

The day was dying, the night was being born—but with great peace. Here were the imponderable processes and forces of the cosmos, harmonious and soundless. Harmony, that was it! That was what came out of the silence—a gentle rhythm, the strain of a perfect chord, the music of the spheres, perhaps.

It was enough to catch that rhythm, momentarily to be myself a part of it. In that instant I could feel no doubt of man's oneness with the universe."

Many mystics have described the great peace and concord that lie at the center of all apparent motion and restlessness in nature. Beyond all seeming agitation there exists an overwhelming harmony that unites and organizes all created things. Jesus called the awareness of this state "the peace that passes understanding." Harmony is the keynote of the universe.

The four elements of the ancients—fire, air, water, and earth—were understood by them to correspond to the fundamental principles within each human being. *Earth* represents the physical body and the material world. It also stands for practicality, the capacity to get things done in physical life. *Water* represents the feelings and the reflective qualities of imagination. *Air* represents thinking, or intellect, and the ability to communicate. *Fire* represents the enthusiasm of our spirit and the ardor and intensity of love. The foundation of success in life is establishing harmony among these "elements" of personality, which leads to light in the mind, warmth in the feelings and vitality in the body.

It was this meaning of the elements applied to human psychology that Shakespeare had in mind when he has Antony say of Brutus, "His life was gentle, and the elements so mixed in him that Nature might stand up and say to all the world 'This was a man!'"

Harmony Means Finding a Healthy Life Rhythm

Everywhere in nature we can see reciprocity or balanced exchange— what might simply be called *breathing*. It is evident in the alternation of day and night and in the rhythmic flux of the seasons. We see it in the rhythm of the tides, in the inbreath and outbreath of our lungs in respiration, and in the cycle of sleep and waking. Even the constant exchange of carbon and oxygen that exists between plants and animals is an image of this law.

Whatever our natural temperament or inclination, we will live more balanced and healthy lives if we find time for activities that develop all areas of our potential. Rhythmic alternation and harmony need to exist in our activities if we are to maintain harmony in our bodies, minds, and our deeper selves. Some people tend to live mostly in their "heads," expressing an excessive intellectualism. Others lean toward feelings and imagination, often favoring religious or artistic pursuits. Still others live almost entirely in their bodies—in physical, sensory experience—remaining unawakened mentally and spiritually.

When we can develop a daily and weekly rhythm of living that gives balanced expression to all these areas—thinking, feeling, and physical action—we will find that we become more harmonious as individuals. We then develop "comprehensive" personalities and are less prone to illness and fatigue. We will also find that as we become more harmonious, we attune our minds more easily to our spiritual selves. This is due to the fact that harmony is a master key that unlocks the portals of higher understanding.

Two Who Discovered the Secrets of the Universe

Lao and Walter Russell were two individuals who lived in near perfect harmony and accord with the great laws of life. Their life together seems almost the stuff of fairy tales and dreams. They demonstrated a level of mastery and artistry in living that is truly rare.

Walter Russell, whose faith in the universal laws was described in Chapter Seven, was a true modern "Renaissance man." He was an accomplished musician, architect, philosopher and scientist. He is also one of the few individuals to demonstrate virtuosity in both painting and sculpture. Not until after his fiftieth birthday did he take up the study of science, yet through his extraordinary penetration into the nature of matter and the spiritual laws behind the visible universe, he was able to discover two new elements—neptunium and plutonium—before the rest of the scientific world acknowledged their existence. Yet he never studied physics, had almost no formal schooling, and read only a few books in his entire life. Walter Russell's knowledge came through direct experience and what we might call "revelation." His scientific masterpiece, *The Universal One,* was known to sell for thousands of dollars after it had gone out of print.

He and Lao Russell first "met" when they spoke by phone. They recognized instantly the depth of their connection. Walter Russell caught an immediate flight to meet the woman who was to become his wife. Their life together was a demonstration of harmony and creative endeavor. As they eloquently expressed in words—and lived even more eloquently—happiness in a relationship can only come when each partner seeks first to give happiness to the other. The "art of relationship" is mastered when giving and receiving—or as they would say, giving and regiving—becomes a balanced interplay of loving exchanges on all levels: physical, emotional, mental and spiritual. In their own words, "What you do to your neighbor is the most important event of every moment."

In 1948 they acquired a marble Renaissance palace on a Virginia mountaintop. Today their beautiful home, named Swannanoa, is often open to the public. It is graced with many of Mr. Russell's world-renowned paintings and sculptures. They founded a correspondence school called the University of Science and Philosophy. Together they wrote a year-long study course on the principles of universal law. This course has been sent to students throughout the world and has changed the lives of thousands of people. They themselves said that each sentence of this lengthy course was written by both of them together.

I had the good fortune of meeting Lao Russell at Swannanoa briefly on two visits to their beautiful home. Once in her presence, I knew that I was meeting a living saint. Although quite elderly at the time, she was vital and energetic. Her voice had a remarkable resonant quality and she emanated extraordinary gentleness and love. She is one of the few people around whom I have seen a brilliant field of light. She expressed words to me that I will never forget. "In awareness of your God-light is your greatest happiness and the fulfillment of your purpose on Earth."

The University of Relationships

One of the great challenges facing every human being is to establish harmony in their relationships. Intimate relationships are a primary "testing ground" for the law of harmony. The experiences of family and partnerships are "basic training"—the "boot camp" everybody has to pass through. Earth is a school of relationships. One might truly call it a reform school! Everyone has lessons to learn and tests to pass. Few there are who haven't flunked at least a few exams in "Relationship U." It isn't surprising that relationships have been called the "last frontier." To achieve harmony in an intimate relationship, each partner must be able to express their individuality and be free individuals within the partnership. At the same time, freedom in a relationship needs the framework provided by mutual concern for each other's well-being and happiness. This finds expression through acts of kindness, assistance and generosity.

Social harmony among people produces a healthy circulation of "life force" in a group, whether it be a family, a business, or a larger institution. This implies that the gifts of all individuals find expression in the community and that the well-being of the community is considered by every individual. This doesn't mean there aren't problems, but that there is an attitude of goodwill that promotes resolution of conflicts and misunderstandings. Lines of communication stay open and feelings are expressed constructively. The attitude that leads to harmony includes an active interest in the well-being of others, along with respect for the rights and liberties of individuals.

As all musicians and music lovers know, rhythm is a feature of harmony. For harmony to exist in a relationship, there needs to be a rhythm—a balanced interplay—to the interactions between partners. Put simply, each partner must learn to give, receive, and then give back. Attentive listening is vital to this process. By living in accordance with this principle of harmonious giving and receiving, tensions and resentments do not build to the breaking point. If one partner does most of the giving, the relationship is out of balance and unhealthy.

Successful relationships are built on the foundation of reciprocity—of rhythmic balanced interchange between partners. Without kindness, harmony in relationships cannot exist. In order to experience love, one must give love. When partners apply the principle of reciprocal giving and receiving, there is a flow of harmonious exchanges in the relationship.

RELATIONSHIPS ARE ALCHEMY

Relationships are a kind of "soul chemistry" between people. One might say relationship is alchemy, for we change and grow as we improve our relationships. The desire for a loving relationship is one of the most powerful drives in the human soul. A relationship between two people creates a new being, the entity that is formed by the union of forces of two distinctive personalities. When two people combine their unique emotional, mental and spiritual qualities in a harmonious fusion, the blend of their forces can create a soul elixir of happiness. Love is the alchemical spark that ignites two hearts with the same inner fire.

There are three attitudes in particular that can help immensely in establishing and maintaining healthy relationships. Although the alchemical trinity of sulfur, mercury and salt were never linked to these qualities by alchemists in the past, these attitudes can nonetheless be instrumental in producing the living elixir that makes a relationship thrive. One might call them "the three A's of harmonious relationships." They are *acknowledgment*, *appreciation*, and *admiration*.

Acknowledgment is perhaps the easiest to experience and express, although we often forget to put it into practice. To acknowledge someone is to make them aware that *you are aware* of their contribution. It can be as simple as expressing thanks or greeting someone when they come or when they go. A heartfelt smile is one of the highest forms of acknowledgment. When we acknowledge another, we affirm their best qualities.

Appreciation is a step above acknowledgment. To appreciate someone is to recognize the value of their work and their efforts—and to let them know our feelings. Appreciation has to be expressed in order for its full power to manifest. When we appreciate someone, we draw out the best in them. Appreciation is an essential method of the good educator. To show appreciation to children is an act that contributes enormously to their self-esteem. The word *educate* comes from the Latin root *educare*, which means "to draw out." We help draw out the higher potential of an individual when we show appreciation.

Admiration is the highest attitude of all these three. It may not always be possible to admire someone—sometimes because we don't know them very well and other times because we may know them only too well! We might have to look very deep to find qualities to admire in some of our associates, particularly those who have done us ill. Realistically, it is not always possible to admire everyone. Perhaps this has its good side, because if everyone were worthy of admiration, its value would be cheapened. Admiration is precious precisely because it is rarer than acknowledgment or appreciation. We grow through the example of individuals whose lives and inner qualities we admire. The very qualities we admire in others begin to blossom in ourselves. This is a secret of the alchemy of inner developing. By focusing on qualities and virtues we admire in others, we unfold them in ourselves.

When partners can express admiration for each other's best qualities, their relationship becomes fruitful and harmonious. They help each other to grow, for admiration is a magical tonic that releases the best in people. Admiration is just short of adoration, an emotion most often reserved to mystical or devotional fervor, or to the first blush of young romance. Even adoration is possible at times, when we see the divine spark in another. The Eastern science of Tantra Yoga is an effort to perceive the divine in one's partner. By seeing our life partner as a manifestation of the divine mother or heavenly father, we can transform ourselves and our relationships. The way to lift relationships on to a higher plane is to be able to see the deeper self in the one we love. In this way can we lift our perceptions from the commonplace to the poetic—the dimension of wonder and admiration. Raising the perceptions of our soul is the essence of alchemy.

The secret magic of these three attitudes—acknowledgment, appreciation, and admiration—is that they can cause a great transformation in those who express them. We benefit ourselves and release a flow of constructive energy in our affairs by practicing acknowledgment, appreciation, and admiration. Expressing these qualities is like tapping into a fountain of enthusiasm and healing light that spreads goodwill and harmony.

THE VALUE OF HUMOR

An intimate relationship is not a business agreement or a bargaining process, nor is it a field of negotiation where each side tries to get the upper hand. First and foremost, it is a friendship. Only friendship can give long-term staying power to a relationship. Emerson said that a friend is the highest product of evolution. The foundation for friendship is a sharing of values—a harmony of viewpoint. In addition, we sweeten the chemistry of a relationship by expressing humor. In relationships of all kinds, a sense of humor can do wonders in maintaining harmony.

A story from the Brothers Grimm illustrates the power of laughter. A young simpleton is given a golden goose by a little gray man with whom he has shared his lunch. A young woman, thinking to steal a golden feather from the goose, becomes stuck fast to the bird as soon as she touches it. Her sisters in turn become latched on to her, and soon there is a whole row of people stuck one to the other in a line, following behind the simpleton. The zany procession arrives at the castle of a princess so somber she has never laughed in her life. The king has promised his daughter in marriage to the first man who can make her laugh. When the princess sees the parade of people stuck fast to the simpleton's golden goose, she breaks out in hilarious laughter, as if she would never stop. The simpleton marries the princess and becomes heir to the kingdom; they live together happily for many years.

The princess represents the soul. Humor introduces the lightness and joy that free the soul from the heaviness of material concerns. When the soul achieves freedom, it can rise to a higher state and become fused with the eternal spirit. This fusion is often called the mystical or alchemical marriage, the harmonious union of our soul with our higher self. As a result of this inner harmony—this marriage of our mind, emotions and will—we inherit the kingdom of happiness. Through laughter, we open ourselves to the lightness of life. Humor dispels darkness. Laughter is a universal language of the heart that everyone understands. There is a wisdom in laughter that goes beyond words.

Laughter plays a harmonizing role in the healing of body and soul as well as relationships. Even the four temperaments of medieval medicine—based on the ancient Greek practices codified by Hippocrates— were linked to four particular body fluids, called *humors*. The predominance of a specific fluid, or *humor*, resulted in a person's essential temperament, or disposition. This indicates that the origin of the word *humor* is itself related to the idea of health, which implies a harmonious balance among all bodily and psychological functions. When we laugh, we open ourselves to the influence of harmony. Laughter heals the soul as well as the body.

HARMONY CREATES HEALTH

Another area where harmony is crucial is that of health. Disease is a symptom of imbalance in the organism and the personality. Health is a sign of harmony. Many people think of illness as the cause of their problems. In fact, illness and disease are the organism's effort to heal itself of disharmony. What we call illness is actually a cure. Pain is the body's way of warning us something is wrong. Pain is not the source of the problem, neither are symptoms the problem. The cause lies elsewhere, often in the realm of erroneous thoughts, misplaced beliefs or hardened emotions. It does no good to blame—either ourselves or anyone else. Healing begins with acceptance.

There are many mysteries to illness that we do not fully understand. There are cases where the person seems to be doing everything "right," and yet they still suffer. They are living a constructive life, eating healthy foods and expanding themselves spiritually. Despite this, they cannot seem to eliminate their illness. The causes of illness often are deeply hidden. The very last thing we should do is to stand in judgment—of ourselves or of others. Illness often teaches us what nothing else can. Poor health or a bout with illness can often dramatically change one's life, opening the doors to a larger reality. Health difficulties teach important life lessons and can challenge us to unlock the deeper powers of the self. Our power to heal ourselves is closely linked to the spiritual strength of our higher nature—a power that can perform miracles in every area of life. The inner exertion and effort of the soul that is often required to overcome or live with an illness may be likened to a spiritual transformation or "conversion" that leaves one permanently changed. The life-altering power of illness can have a redemptive quality and be liberating if one is open to the lessons that come through the healing process. Illness is one of life's greatest teachers; disease can be a potent, albeit drastic, medicine of the soul. By overcoming an illness, we strengthen ourselves and can even transform character. More than one person has said, "My illness saved my life."

An example of the power of illness to trigger a life-changing transformation comes from the remarkable experience of Greg Anderson. In 1984 he was diagnosed with lung cancer and told that he had thirty days to live. Not only did he respond to this "death sentence" by healing himself without the aid of conventional medicine, but through his bestselling books he has taught thousands of people the laws of healing and wellness that he discovered in the process. Greg says healing and wellness begin with developing a love affair with life—"shifting our awareness to look for the joys that come in small, precious packages."

Illness can be a stimulus to growth. It is a call for harmony. If any part of the body is ill, one must seek the cure in the health and harmony of the whole organism, the whole human being. Poor health is a call for the restoring of order and harmony in one's thoughts, feelings, words and deeds. The cure for illness can be found in the way one lives.

A woman I knew in California applied these truths of healing and became a "walking miracle" as a result. She was legally blind and confined to a wheelchair due to a partial paralysis of her legs. A year and a half later she was fit and active, licensed to drive a car, an avid outdoorswoman and a book enthusiast. The only sign of her former paralysis was a slight limp. She still wore thick glasses and had to wear sunglasses outdoors, but in most respects she was completely healthy and "normal." What accounted for the "miracle"? To begin with, she had an intense desire to heal herself. She enrolled in many personal growth classes and applied the principles of right thinking, forgiveness of self and others, positive affirmation and faith in the beneficent laws of life. She radically altered her diet, became a vegetarian, ate pure and wholesome "living foods," and surrounded herself with loving and supportive friends. She herself said often, "If I can do this, anyone can." When we approach life with the right consciousness and a constructive attitude, miracles of healing are possible.

THE ALCHEMY OF NUTRITION

Alchemy is the process of transforming substances into more subtle or refined states. One of the spiritual axioms of the Emerald Tablet of Hermes advises us to "separate the subtle from the gross with great diligence." Separating the "subtle from the gross" is a process of refinement and purification. It is the basis of alchemy and the starting point of sacred living. When we work to elevate our inner lives, selecting thoughts and activities that improve us, we are separating the subtle from the gross. A key to this process is *discernment*. The exercise of discernment requires that we extract essential elements and release unwanted elements. Every time we let go of dark, discordant thoughts and replace them with constructive reflections, we exercise discernment. In digestion, also, our bodies separate the "subtle from the gross." The alchemy of nutrition begins even before we eat, when we select and prepare our foods.

There are thousands of books on dieting and nutrition. Despite the fact that Americans are acutely health-conscious, disease treatment is one of the nation's largest industries. We are either ignoring good advice or not receiving it in the first place. The medical establishment, with its nexus of giant pharmaceuticals, insurance companies, hospitals and HMO's, has become a multi-trillion dollar business. As it is in the fiscal interests of a large market sector for Americans to continue to spend huge sums on "disease management," rather than disease elimination, there is obviously strong motivation to keep the status quo. The basic solution to a wide spectrum of illnesses receives little publicity in the health literature. Perhaps this is because it is such a simple approach and costs so little, that the medical establishment chooses to ignore it.

The origin of health, or the lack of it, is in the mind, soul or emotional field. We build a strong foundation for a healthy life when our thoughts, feelings, attitudes and beliefs are harmonious and free of the discordant frequencies of negativity. But many of the factors relating to health are entirely related to physical factors and causes. Disease is often a result of toxicity in the body—the accumulation of metabolic waste, which the body does not fully eliminate. Health is the result of the elimination of all or most toxins. Many toxins are produced by a poor diet. Good health begins with good nutrition. Tens of millions of people are addicted to junk foods. A diet high in processed, "denatured" foods creates a buildup of metabolic wastes in the body. The kidneys and other organs of elimination are overly taxed and do not adequately rid the body of accumulated waste products. These wastes build up in the tissues and cells. The blood becomes filled with toxins that are never removed. The body never completes the process of "separating the subtle from the gross." This leads to a variety of illnesses.

Eventually, if the body does not rid itself of accumulated toxins caused by the build up of metabolic wastes, the tissues succumb to what might be called "cellular asphyxiation." Illness is always systemic. We must treat the body as a whole. When we purify the blood and tissue of waste buildup, we remove the physical source for most illness. One of the simplest ways to assist in the elimination of toxins and metabolic wastes from the system is to drink plentiful amounts of pure water daily.

Nutrition is alchemy. When we eat, substances are broken down, refined and transformed chemically into the unique pattern of our own bodily make-up. The transmutation of substance is perhaps never so obvious as in ordinary nutrition and respiration. Our bodies turn chlorophyll into blood, and carbohydrates, proteins and fats into bone, muscle, skin and hair. The ancient physician, Hippocrates, said "Let your food be your medicine.... your medicine be your food." If we give the body pure, wholesome food, we prolong its life and health. When we are careful in selecting what we eat, we are following the ancient advice of Hermes to separate the subtle from the gross with great diligence.

BODY MIRRORS THE MIND, MIND MIRRORS THE BODY

It is becoming more widely accepted today that inner states of feeling and thought are reflected in the outer disposition of the body. It is also true that we can change our moods and our health by altering our posture and bodily gestures. You can change your mood for the better by "acting as if" you are in a happy, healthy frame of mind. Simply by smiling we can improve our psychological state. William James, one of America's greatest philosophers and psychologists, said that "It is physically impossible to remain blue and depressed while acting out symptoms of being radiantly happy."

Sorrow and fear cause the blood vessels to contract. This restriction of the arteries leads to loss of energy and to physical apathy. Because our cells and organs do not receive the blood they need, we become tired and listless. In the long run, this leads to poor health. The antidote is not drugs or medication, but an inner change in attitude. When we restore harmony to our feelings and thoughts, we increase the flow of vital energy to our physical organs.

Two of the chief sources of bodily illness are anger and irritability, which create a harmful substance in our emotional field. This substance has been called "imperil." Clairvoyants can see imperil as a dark, grayish haze that dampens the vibrancy and radiance of our aura. Over time, imperil enters our vital organism—the subtle field of prana and life force that sustains and vivifies the physical body. When it reaches the densest layer of the life body, or etheric field—which interpenetrates the physical body—our immune function is inhibited and we easily succumb to illness. The practice of equanimity or emotional composure is one of the most effective ways to maintain long-term health and youth. The feelings of happiness, equanimity and love are to the emotional field what pure water is to the physical body. They are vital in creating the alchemical "elixir of life"—the emanation of the soul that bestows well-being and longevity.

Self-acceptance plays an important role in health and harmonious living, but the idea can be ambiguous. Self-acceptance doesn't mean becoming lazy in the face of personal shortcomings, or "throwing in the towel" when it comes to making life changes. Virtually everyone has areas in which they can improve. We are "diamonds in the rough" that need polishing and refinement to enhance our inner beauty. Passive acceptance of personal weakness is self-defeating. Paraphrasing the old adage, wisdom implies knowing the difference between what we can change and what we can't.

The other side of the coin is that people have a tendency to be needlessly self-critical and unhappy with themselves. This can undermine one's self-image and health. A haircutter once told me that nearly all of her customers with straight hair wished they had curly or wavy hair. Virtually all of her customers with wavy or curly hair wished their hair was straight. Similarly, anorexic girls see themselves as "overweight" regardless of how thin they become. We seem to have an inherent dissatisfaction about our appearance. Much of this comes from the commercial culture's immature obsession with external beauty.

Personal dissatisfaction on the "soul level"—the level of attitudes and emotions—becomes constructive when it spurs us to become wiser, stronger and more loving. A "divine discontent" that urges us toward self-improvement is a good thing. Self-acceptance means recognition and acceptance of our true essence. In the best sense, self-acceptance implies embracing the light, love and goodness of our deeper self. When we can love ourselves for the beauty of our "hidden splendor," not egotistically but out of joyous acceptance of our intrinsic nature, we open the "windows of our soul." That's why it's been said that "Enlightenment is falling in love with yourself for the first time."

HARMONY CANCELS OUT HARM

We cannot achieve harmony in ourselves if we continue to cause suffering to other beings. It is of great consequence how we treat the animals as well as fellow human beings. If our thoughts and behavior cause distress, we will feel the backlash. One day in the near future, the elimination of suffering—insofar as it is humanly possible—and the cruelty that leads to suffering, will become a central motivation in the lives of a significant portion of humankind. Through the study of the laws implicit in nature, one inevitably arrives at the following basic maxim: in order to eliminate harm from one's own life, cause no harm to others.

We can only create a sacred culture based on the principles of wisdom, love and truth, if we realize that all of life is interrelated. We cannot harm one area of nature without causing repercussions that damage ourselves. Years ago, when I made the decision to search in Peru for the ancient sacred retreat near Lake Titicaca, one of the things that captivated me about the description of the hidden valley was that it was a place where blood had never been shed. The history of the human race is a history of bloodshed—of "man's inhumanity to man" and to the animal kingdom as well. Mankind has been afflicted historically by an almost ceaseless cycle of wars and violence, and disease has always been a scourge on the human race. This inevitably raises the issue of our treatment of the animals. One is forced to consider if our slaughter of the higher mammals does not bring about wars and disease in human beings. The fabric of life is a finely integrated web of harmonious exchanges. If we cause the animals to suffer, by the principle of the backlash—of reciprocity—we unleash suffering on ourselves. As humanity evolves, it is likely that people will gradually adopt a vegetarian lifestyle. Those who have already made the shift know of the advantages in health and well-being. In the world of the future, humanity will seek to create a civilization where the blood of innocents need no longer be shed. Only then will we have a truly sacred culture.

Today, many experience a feeling of being isolated and cut off from the rest of life. Yet all creatures and beings in the complex web of life are interconnected. We are linked by invisible cords of light, not only to the animal, plant and mineral kingdoms, but also to the higher angelic "kingdoms"—traditionally known as the Hierarchies of divine life. From these higher levels of existence flow continuous streams of light, love, joy and inspiration. Only when we live in harmony with life can the beautiful stream of light and love that originates with the higher beings find its way into our souls.

At times in our lives we may feel emotionally exalted and uplifted by a beautiful feeling. It is possible that this feeling originated as an inspiration from an angel. If we are not able to maintain these feelings, it is because of our tendency to indulge in negative and critical thoughts, or because of harmful actions that hurt other beings. Our destructive thoughts and emotions cut us off from the divine circulatory flow that originates among the heavenly beings. In order to maintain health and to find the serenity that leads to happiness, we must live in harmony with the kingdoms of nature and the Earth itself.

THE EARTH AND NATURE ARE ALIVE

Although it may be difficult for many people to accept, we will not ultimately remedy our environmental problems until we see the connection between "psychic pollution" and pollution of the air and water. The "environmental crisis" will not be solved until humanity begins to clean out the "psychic smog" in the thought and feeling life of the planetary organism. Polluted air is the result of toxic thinking. Polluted water represents a destructive, contaminated feeling life. When we "clean up our act" on the inner levels of mind and emotion, we will begin to a see that external pollution of the Earth begins to disappear.

Most people today have barely an inkling of the intelligence with which nature is imbued. Our civilization has lost most of the awareness earlier cultures had of the consciousness within the natural world. A legend of the Southwest Indians illustrates the interrelatedness of life.

The Indians of New Mexico value salt highly, as it is necessary for life. According to their legends, they would gather slabs of salt for their clans from the salt lake south of Zuni. According to one legend, the Laguna Indians taught the Zuni and the Hopi how to obtain salt from the lake. The Salt Mother would not give up her precious substance unless the clans first made preparations and purification. Prayer sticks were carefully prepared. Ritual pilgrimages were then made to the lake. Solemn prayers were offered to the Salt Mother. Without prayer and purification, the salt would remain in solution and could not be gathered. Only after sincere prayer and proper observances did the salt harden in large sheets for harvest by the grateful Indians.

This story, related as history by tribes of the Southwest, can help us better understand the following astonishing incident. As a young man,

Mikhael Aivanhov would often go with students of the saintly Peter Deunov to the High Lakes above Rila in Bulgaria. One evening, he and a friend observed some tourists stopping by a particular lake. Several of the chattering tourists took off their shoes and socks and amused themselves by wading at the water's edge. The next morning Mikhael Aivanhov and his companion went to meditate by the lake. They were stunned to find that it had vanished! The entire lake had disappeared, leaving not a trace where the evening before had glistened a large body of water. The astonished youths reflected on the matter and concluded that the lake was inhabited by an intelligent being of the angelic kingdom—a nature spirit, or *deva*. Apparently the spirit of the lake was disturbed by the crassness of the tourists, as if the sanctity and purity of the waters had been violated. Through mysterious processes and laws of nature not yet revealed to science, the lake simply relocated to another spot. Although admittedly this seems unbelievable to the materialistic bias of the modern mind, we would do well to humble ourselves before nature's mysteries, admitting that our civilization is still in its infancy in understanding these matters. As we refine our sense of the sacred, we will gradually comprehend many secrets of nature.

Despite destructive trends in modern civilization, there are millions of people living to create a better world. The seeds of a new culture of harmony continue to be planted. The old systems—predicated on exploitation and the use of force—will become fertilizer for the seeds of the new era of light. One group that has worked for nearly sixty years to promote spiritual healing and the end of violence is the White Eagle Lodge. It was begun in England in the 1930's by Grace and Ivan Cooke and has since expanded to dozens of countries. There are more than twenty White Eagle books in print, spreading a gentle message of wisdom and spiritual unfolding.

The White Eagle Center in the Americas is located in a lovely forested part of Texas, and features a newly-built, non-denominational chapel, with colorful and inspiring stained-glass windows. They have made their beautiful land a nature preserve and wildlife haven. Sick or wounded animals are brought to them from many miles away and are cared for lovingly. Many make a full recovery and are returned to the wild or to their owners. Jean LeFevre, the director of the Center, points out that their philosophy is to live by the principle of harmony and kinship with all of life. The animals must sense this, especially the birds, for they come from all over, as if knowing that here they have a safe haven from harm. Groups such as the White Eagle Center foreshadow the time when all humanity will live in a sacred manner, in harmony and communion with the natural kingdoms.

EACH OF US IS A UNIQUE STRAND IN THE FABRIC OF LIFE

Harmony is the blending of all elements in sympathetic accord. Harmony dissolves contradictions and integrates all virtues and powers. It implies equanimity in the life of feelings, positivity in the mind, and happiness of heart that can only spring from a loving attitude.

To live in harmony means to live at peace with ourselves and the world. Living in peace requires accepting the differences of all people in the world. Every human being expresses a unique pattern that is a necessary part of the whole texture of life. Each of us is a strand in the universal tapestry. All human beings weave a singular thread in the universal pattern.

The Sanskrit expression *namaste*, which means "I honor the light within you," is a refreshing reminder of the fact that the divine principle lives in every human being. This celestial spark may be covered over with layers of darkness, but it pulsates within the heart of us all. We search for God in vain if we cannot see the divine in those around us. The more we see light in others, the more we will perceive it in ourselves and the more active it will be in our affairs. Seeing the light of the soul in ourselves and others is the cornerstone to sacred living.

A world of infinite peace surrounds the Earth and all creation. We allow this peace to enter us as we embrace the path of harmony. When we apply the sacred laws of balance, reverence and reciprocity, we begin to create harmony in our lives, our health and our relationships. Through our inner attitude of love and goodwill, we activate the magic of soul alchemy and raise ourselves into the light of the divine self. Peace in the soul begins when we can embrace the world with love in our hearts.

Activities for a Sacred Life:
Activating the Alchemy of Harmony and Health

Activity Number One

Upon waking in the morning laugh loudly and heartily. Then say aloud and with conviction, "I feel great!" It may take practice to really be able to laugh and affirm these words with enthusiasm and with feeling. Keep trying! Do this every day for at least a month and you may never want to stop.

Sacred living implies seeing ourselves in the light of our higher nature—the divine spark that illumines our inner soul world. We link ourselves to our sacred self when we strive to begin each day on a positive note. Stretch and speak affirmations aloud. Tell the world you love it. Affirm your unity with life. Laugh out loud and tell yourself what a wonderful being you are. In order to establish a connection with the universal life, you have to feel it.

Activity Number Two

Picture a triangle with sides of equal length—an equilateral triangle. Draw this triangle on paper. Write your name in the center of the triangle. Then write the words "thinking" at one corner, "feeling" at another corner and "action" at the third corner. Realize that the triangle represents your own threefold personality. Each angle represents one of the three dominant "soul forces" that energize all human beings. Most likely, one of the three will be dominant in your personality, and one will be less developed than the other two. You will tend to emphasize either thinking, feeling or action.

Think of activities and devise a weekly plan to help you balance your triangle. For instance, if you are less developed in the area of emotions or feeling, you might want to enhance your artistic sense and your appreciation of beauty and esthetics. Perhaps you could visit local art galleries, or see some live theater. Or you might want to explore the music of some of the great composers. Best of all, take up an artistic pursuit, such as learning to play a musical instrument, or taking classes in painting or drawing. If you are very active in your mind, but tend to be physically sedentary, make a point to take regular walks (in nature, if possible), work out at the gym, ride a bicycle, or become active in a movement or dance group. If you are predominately a feeling person—or if you are "short on words, but long on deeds"—you may want to exercise your intellect. In this case, begin to read some of the classics of literature or the works of great philosophers. The reading list at the end of this book would also be a good starting point. Reading the world's finest poetry is an excellent way to enhance both the feeling and the thinking points of your triangle. Astonish your friends with your newly ripened wisdom!

Recognize that these three forces of thought, feeling and will are reflections of the attributes traditionally associated with divinity: wisdom, love and strength. As we introduce harmony and balance into our lives, we will become more capable of expressing these higher qualities. They make their appearance in our personalities as intelligence and light in our thinking, warmth and kindness in our feelings, and in the ability to act swiftly, effectively and decisively.

When you make the effort to develop yourself as a balanced, harmonious individual, you stir unseen forces that come to your aid. Who knows? Perhaps one day the angels themselves will begin to whisper to you their secrets.

Activity Number Three

Drinking hot boiled water or herbal tea every day is one of the best ways to eliminate harmful substances and deposits from the body. You can transform your health in a fairly short time with pure water that has been boiled, then taken in small sips. If the water is purified or distilled to begin with, it needs only to be brought to the boiling point. If you use tap water, you should boil it for about five to ten seconds. Over time, drinking hot water in this manner will dislodge accumulated wastes and toxins. It is especially helpful if this practice is accompanied by physical activity that induces sweating. Pure, boiled water also acts as a stimulating tonic—a veritable elixir of life—for the blood, organs, glands and vital centers. Hydrogen and oxygen are living elements, building blocks of life. Infused in pure water is *prana*, or the life element. Those who find that drinking hot water by itself is too bland for the taste buds, can substitute herbal tea instead. But it must be high quality herbal tea, without caffeine. If you drink two to four cups of hot water per day for forty days, you may be astonished at the transformation in your health. (Many healers assert that the body needs at least eight cups of pure water daily) To be really effective, the practice of detoxification by drinking pure hot water must become a long-term, daily habit. This low-cost remedy can truly work wonders.

Affirmations

"I live in a world of perfect harmony. My mind and heart are at peace."

"I develop a harmonious disposition by holding luminous and loving thoughts in my mind."

"All events and all people are working together harmoniously to help me achieve my goals."

"May the light of wisdom stream through my thinking, may warmth and kindness flow through my feelings, and may strength of will characterize my every deed."

CHAPTER ELEVEN

THE ALCHEMY OF INNER UNFOLDING

*"I shall endeavor now to make the divine in me arise
and meet the divine in the universe."*

– Plotinus

*"At the still-point in the center of the circle one can see
the infinite in all things."*

– Chuang Tsu

S oul alchemy teaches us that all of life is a development, a pro-
gression, an unfolding. Our life on Earth is a series of lessons that
lead to maturity—the growth of our soul and spirit. The Earth is a
school—an institution for wayward souls, one might argue—and all
individuals will find themselves drawn to the classroom appropriate
for the lessons they need. We always attract the exact combination of
elements that help us take the next step in our growth. Our teachers
are everywhere. We find them in the challenges and opportunities life
brings us, the people we meet and the discoveries we make.

Our souls are unfolding in the manner of a flower, each petal
revealing a different facet of our nature. The lotus is an ancient symbol

of the soul's growth because it is an emblem that reflects the human condition. Out of the mud the shoot extends upward, pushing through murky water until it reaches the clear water near the top of the pond. Finally it bursts forth into the pure air and blossoms radiantly beneath the brilliant beams of the sun. The lotus is a picture of the soul that must grow through experiences of earth (physical experience), water (the emotional life) and air (intellectual experience)—finally blossoming into maturity under the influence of the divine spirit, represented by the fire of the sun.

We all live in the universal ocean of life—a complex field of energies, elements and forces. By the law of affinity, we draw to ourselves the elements that exactly correspond to the nature of our thoughts, feelings and deeds. Just as a fish absorbs from the water precisely the minerals and particles that correspond to its nature, so does each human being attract what it needs from the great etheric ocean of life. If we change our "nature," that is, the qualities of our inner world of thought, feeling, moods and imagination, we change the flow of materials that we attract. Every impulse toward a better life instantly releases the elements one needs from the universal mind. When we send out a thought of love—a vibration from our heart—the heart of the universe responds.

The alchemy of spiritual unfolding is a process of transformation and enlightenment. We grow from darkness toward light, from ignorance to wisdom, from frustration to fulfillment. The American spiritual teacher Gangaji gently reminds us that we are already free. Who we are, essentially, has always been awake and enlightened. But we must discover this essence—the truth of our being. We must have that experience of illumination, that blazing self-recognition that transforms us.

Why is it that so few people have this experience, even among experienced meditators and those who have spent years on the spiritual path? Perhaps it is because we have not created the appropriate conditions for enlightenment to occur. Illumination itself takes place in an instant of serene self-remembrance, but we must create the conditions for this to happen. Creating those conditions is a process that evolves through time in the manner of a plant unfolding. A newly planted rose seed does not blossom into a fully formed rose overnight.

THE ANCIENT MYSTERIES AND THE NEW MYSTERIES

In the ancient Greek myth of Demeter, the goddess of nature and the harvest, she told the people to build a temple in her honor so that she might come and dwell on Earth. According to the myth, the temple was built in the little town of Eleusis, just outside Athens, and the goddess did indeed take up her abode there. The temple at Athens was a "Mystery school," one of many in the ancient world. In these Mystery temples—located also at Stonehenge, the great Pyramid, Ephesus and elsewhere—students were instructed in the science of initiation, the mysterious process by which human beings completely transform themselves. The goal of initiation was a spiritual metamorphosis. In the Mystery schools or temples, under the guidance of advanced mentors and evolved souls, those who were ready were guided through the training, tests and ordeals that led to rebirth on a higher plane of consciousness. The candidates unfolded their divine nature and discovered the immortal essence of their souls. Centuries later, Saint Paul called this essence "Christ in us, the hope of glory." The initiate emerged with new faculties and abilities. Through initiation in the sacred temples, men and women learned the secret of their own immortality—becoming conscious of their eternal spiritual core—and literally triumphed over death.

Nowadays the scenario has changed. No longer do we experience the great transformation of our inner and outer selves in the Mystery temples, as of old. Today we find ourselves in the temple of initiation wherever we go. We pass through our tests and ordeals in daily life. We take our initiations in the world. In the words of the Austrian educator and scientist Rudolf Steiner—himself a great initiate—the temple of initiation is our ordinary daily life. Steiner said: "In the new Mysteries the whole earth becomes a temple. The hidden tragedy and triumph of the pupil begins to become external fact. Our friends begin to become—though we may know little of it—the terrible and wonderful actors in the ceremony of our initiation."

When we awaken to this profound truth, life takes on a completely new meaning. The harsh and difficult experiences of life are the means to our transformation. Anyone who has passed through an experience of hardship—one that demands effort and the practice of virtue—knows how these moments can temper and strengthen the soul. The greater the test that we face, the greater will be our joy as we grow through the experience. If we will accept it, we can open ourselves to the ever-new joy of spiritual becoming—the radiant celebration of expanding life. Says White Eagle: "Every new affirmation of your divine being is the starting point of an eternity of happiness."

The new Mysteries declare that the Earth is to become a sacred planet. The task of the future is to make the whole Earth a sanctuary. The Earth itself will become a temple. We will transform our own bodies into temples of light. Just as Demeter, the goddess of nature, needed a temple in which to manifest her divinity on Earth, so does our higher divine nature need a "temple" in which to live. The spirit is mighty, beautiful, joyous and free. It is stifled if instead of a temple it has only a "dusty hovel or a ramshackle ruin." We build the temple of our enlightenment by transforming our personalities—that is, our thoughts, feelings and our power to act. The tools we use are light, love and truth. In the age to come, each of us will be our own priest or priestess. Wherever we go we will be in the temple of the Mysteries. All will realize that life is sacred and we will unfold the full potential of our divine selves. Everywhere, humanity will affirm the sanctity and beauty of life.

Sacred Time

We spoke in Chapter Four about the importance of creating sacred space. The same holds true regarding time. When we can make sacred our experience of time, we elevate our experience of life. To the Greeks, the god of time was Chronos, whom the Romans called Saturn. So powerful was Chronos that he overthrew his father, the sky god, Uranus, and became ruler of the world. It was Chronos' son, Zeus, who became father of the Olympians.

The divine Olympians, led by Zeus, eventually eclipsed Chronos in greatness, suggesting that the Heavens are not governed by time. Nevertheless, it can be argued that time governs all manifestations in the physical world, for everything has its cycle of beginning, duration and end. The Western world has become adept at "time management," a concept earlier people would have found absurd. The modern world runs on a schedule, and if we want to participate successfully we have to learn to manage our time. One of the first rules of spiritual life is to observe punctuality. To do otherwise is to show disrespect for others.

Nonetheless, time can be a brutal taskmaster, and if we aren't careful it can rule us and ruin us. The spiritual rhythms of life are in the spaces between events. We need to learn how to slow down and appreciate these spaces. We need also to learn that there are other cycles and rhythms that a clock cannot measure. To live a sacred life we must tune in to the rhythms of the sun, moon, Earth and seasons. This movement of the heavenly bodies is a rhythmic measure—a kind of cosmic procession or dance—that gives birth to sacred time.

All cultures of the past recognized the importance of making certain moments especially auspicious and festive in order to promote a feeling of sanctity and holiness. The word *holiday* means "holy day." Though it may be true that we think of holidays nowadays as merely "time off" for relaxation or "letting go," we can enhance our experience of sacred culture by becoming cognizant of the uplifting qualities of certain moments in the cycles and rhythms of time.

From this perspective, we find that each day, week, month, season and year has its especially sacred moments—times that stand out due to a special quality that helps us attune ourselves to the divinity in life. These moments give opportunities to develop feelings of reverence, wonder and devotion. The beloved writer Tasha Tudor called these special moments, "times to keep"—times to pause in the business of living and connect ourselves lovingly to the inner significance of each "holy day."

All spiritual traditions have looked upon morning as a special time for prayer and meditation. The hours before sunrise are especially favorable for inner work. The actual moment of the sunrise is a unique time in the daily cycle when the Earth is flooded with the radiant life-giving energies of our "day star." All ancient peoples revered the sun as the external aspect of divinity, not because they were foolish or idolatrous, but because they recognized the sun as the source of all life on our planet. The sun is the original trinity of life, light and warmth. Today many people continue to revere the sun—not out of idolatry, but because it *represents* divine life. It is the most obvious manifestation of the principle of divine radiance and is the giver of life to the Earth. Early Christians believed that Christ was an emanation of the Solar Logos, or spiritual Being within the sun. In Christian metaphysics, the Archangel Michael is traditionally considered the ruler of the "sun sphere" and makes his home, along with the archangels and the angelic host, within the spiritual aura of the sun.

Evening is also a sacred time. Prayers have always traditionally been recited and devotions said in the evening. These times of evening prayer were called "vespers," meaning *twilight*. A good practice is to remind oneself to link up in thought to the higher beings through prayer and meditation at nine o'clock, noon, three, and six. These times correspond to the four cardinal points in the yearly cycle—the equinoxes and solstices—which are the most sacred moments of the year.

The cardinal points are the first day of winter, spring, summer and autumn. In the Christian tradition they are associated with Christmas, Easter, St. John's Day and Michaelmas. All ancient cultures have had festivals linked to these times of year, which are truly sacred moments in the Earth's journey around the sun. These moments are reminders of the eternal interplay of light and dark, and represent the triumph of the light in the human soul over the darkness of ignorance and materialism.

We are all familiar with the lunar cycle—phases of the moon from new moon to full moon and back again—but our culture tends to place little importance in it. However, by working with the lunar cycle, we can learn a great deal about ourselves and the influence of the cosmos in our lives. Since early times, men and women have planted and harvested according to the lunar cycle. Farmers' almanacs have always emphasized the importance of timing in regard to planting and harvest in harmony with these cycles. Mia and I noticed a long time ago that we could accomplish much more during the two weeks of the waxing moon, particularly the last five days before the full moon. We found that the period of the waning moon was an easier time to relax and let go of responsibilities.

The period of the waxing moon is also the most auspicious time to do inner work. During this phase, there is a gradual crescendo of life force. At the exact moment of the full moon, our planet is bathed in a flood of spiritual energy, a shower of solar and stellar forces. Recognizing this, many groups around the world gather for meditation and prayer at the full moon, when conditions are at their peak for releasing waves of spiritual light through the denser ethers interpenetrating the physical dimension of life.

The full moon is an image of the alchemists' goal, the transmutation of *luna,* or silver, into *sol,* or gold. The moon represents the soul. As we transform our feelings into the gold of inner radiance, the soul becomes a mirror that perfectly reflects the brilliance of the spirit, represented by the sun. At the moment of the full moon, the moon becomes a kind of "cosmic mirror," which fully reflects the sun's radiance. Thus the full moon is an image of the Philosopher's Stone, the inner power that transmutes our psyche into the divine image. The soul transformed may be symbolized as a mirror that reflects the spirit's brilliance. When our soul is always "at the full"—that is, when our feelings are transformed so that we can sustain the radiance of inner light pictured cosmically at the moment of the full moon—we have achieved that measure of enlightenment referred to as the Philosopher's Stone.

SINCERITY IS MORE IMPORTANT THAN RITUAL

It is helpful to work with the festivals and auspicious moments of the year in order to augment our awareness of sacred living. However, we should not substitute external observances for the immediacy of our actual inner experiences. Although the use of ritual can enhance our experience of the sacred, it is well to remember that the important element in any observance is the feeling and awareness produced, not the ritual itself. Otherwise, we tend toward a slavish observance of external forms, which may come to lose their inner meaning. Leo Tolstoy elegantly makes the point in his story of the three old hermits:

An orthodox bishop has learned of three old monks who live alone on an island and who do not recite their prayers properly. The bishop goes to visit them and finds the three hermits living a simple existence, ceaselessly worshipping God. The bishop asks them what prayers they use. "We are simple souls, holy Father," the three old hermits reply. "Our prayer is simply this: 'O, God, Thou art Three, we are three, have mercy on us.'" The bishop tells the hermits that their prayer will never do, and he proceeds to teach them the proper prayers of the orthodox liturgy. Then he returns to his boat and begins to sail away. Much to his surprise, as his boat leaves shore, the bishop notices the three old hermits running toward him across the surface of the water. They came up along side the boat and plead, "Holy Father, we have forgotten the prayers you taught us. Please tell us again." Whereupon the bishop, duly humbled, replies that they should continue with their old form of prayer. As Tolstoy's story eloquently reminds us, it is the sincerity and earnestness of our efforts that matter most, not the form in which we clothe them.

THE GRAIL AND THE BUTTERFLY AS IMAGES OF THE SOUL

Ancient alchemical texts sometimes speak of "fixing the volatile," which refers to capturing the life force, or "energy essence," of the divine spark. One of the great epics of Western spirituality is the story of Parzival, the young knight who goes in quest of the Grail—the legendary cup that caught the blood of Christ at the crucifixion. The Grail represents the "chalice" the soul creates in order to hold the energies of enlightenment, the frequencies of the higher self. As we expand the light in our minds and the love in our hearts, our souls become living vessels through which flows the radiance of our spiritual essence. The path of inner unfolding is the path of "discovering" the Grail. Actually, the Grail is not so much *found* as it is *fashioned*. We fashion our grail chalice when we forge our minds and hearts into vessels fit to hold the immortal essence of the divine spark. We most easily accomplish this by living in attunement with the sacred universal laws.

Perhaps the most perfect symbol of the soul's metamorphosis is the butterfly. The lowly caterpillar devours living things, leaving a trail of waste and destruction—the hallmark of a true pest. Then some mysterious urge prompts it to wrap itself in a fine substance which it produces from within itself—a substance that it weaves from out of its own hidden powers. Within the secret world of the cocoon, it undergoes a miraculous development, emerging in time as an entirely new creature, utterly different from the caterpillar it once was. Not only is the butterfly a marvel of grace and beauty—seemingly a winged flower—but it is beneficial as well, for it serves to pollinate many plants, giving life to future generations.

The butterfly is nature's eternal emblem of the human soul and the miracle of soul alchemy. Within the human heart is an urge to grow out of the ugly stage of "caterpillar"—the greedy, destructive pest—and become a creature of beauty and grace. Beyond that, the butterfly teaches us that it is possible to grow wings, speaking symbolically, and fly. This beautiful creature is the promise of our happy future. The butterfly is a symbol of the soul that emerges from the darkness of ignorance and sorrow and is reborn into the light of higher truth. Many of us still "crawl on our stomachs," ravaging our way through life, leaving a trail of destruction in our wake. If we aspire to become like a butterfly, there is no other way but to stop living like a caterpillar.

The inner activity of the caterpillar in the cocoon represents prayer, meditation, contemplation and study. Prayer is a dialogue between the sacred in ourselves and the sacred in the cosmos. Prayer builds a bridge of light to our immortal selves. By prayer and meditation we come to know who we are.

Regardless of whether we call it God, Christ, the Buddha Nature, the Absolute, Atma, the Supreme or Universal Consciousness, there exists a fountain of radiant light within each soul. Contact with this center of our being brings joy and strength for life. This is the source of wisdom, love and power—the imprisoned splendor that patiently awaits release.

NOTHING TAKES THE PLACE OF DIRECT EXPERIENCE

One of the first teachers I had was an Indonesian Buddhist named Tom, who worked for a large multinational corporation. As a young man he had healed himself of a severe illness by meditation, breathing exercises and yoga. One of the things that impressed me most about him, in addition to his gentleness and unassuming manner, was his extraordinary power of concentration. He told me that it was good to read books on spiritual subjects, but advised that they could only take one so far. Nothing could take the place of experience.

Actual spiritual experience can only come as a result of living the truths, and by the practice of meditation and prayer. A person lacking experience in spiritual matters is like someone who has read dozens of books about Mozart, and knows almost everything about his life, but has never actually heard his music. Only when you have heard his music will you know the greatness of Mozart. Similarly, only through expanding your inner life through periods of contemplation will you begin to experience the bright energy of the indwelling spark.

There exist in all human beings dormant qualities that, when awakened, will grant us higher perception—direct vision of spiritual truth. We all have the capacity to become conscious in the spiritual dimensions, to be reborn onto higher planes of existence. The means to awaken these slumbering organs of enlightenment is by a transformation of the forces of thinking and feeling.

For this reason thinking and feeling are really sacred processes and deserve our full attention. The time-honored methods of prayer, meditation and contemplation are means to transform thinking and feeling, and to unfold the qualities of our inner self. Prayer and meditation elevate our consciousness and put us in touch with forces that heal and transform. They represent a higher form of breathing—a reciprocal give and take with the divine atmosphere of a higher world of which our souls and spirits are a part.

We need both the inner practice of meditation and a life of practical usefulness in the world in order to develop in a balanced way. This was symbolized in the ancient Greek myth of Demeter—goddess of the harvest—and Persephone, mentioned earlier in connection to the ancient Mystery schools. When the divine Demeter visits the town of Eleusis, she disguises herself as an old woman. The goddess is invited into the home of a woman named Metaneira, to help tend Metaneira's infant son, Demophon. The goddess decides to make Demophon immortal. When no one sees, she bathes the child with ambrosia, the nectar of the gods that grants immortality. At night, when the household is asleep, she places the infant boy in the red hot heart of the fire.

These two actions symbolize the complementary activities of meditation, and our daily experience of "living in the world." "Bathing with ambrosia" is what we do when we meditate. We immerse ourselves in the luminous thoughts—the words of power—of the world's wisdom traditions. This transforms us inwardly, in our soul body. The act of being placed in the fire represents *living in the world* with its trials and challenges, which test our mettle and help us stabilize the higher frequencies we contact while we meditate. The symbolism of the ancient myth informs us that the final result of these two processes, when taken to their ultimate course, will be our becoming immortal. Not necessarily in our physical bodies, but more important, in our *consciousness.* When we elevate the frequencies of our inner life and manifest the forces that stream from our center, we unfold the awareness of our divine spark, the immortal self. Initiation does not have to be an ordeal. It is simply the opportunity to demonstrate self-mastery. The outcome of initiation is a triumphant, harmonious and joyous display of the inner glory we all possess.

EXPERIENCING THE INNER WORLDS

Many people who become interested in spiritual matters find it difficult to shake the materialistic bias of our culture. They would like to believe in the reality of the "higher worlds," but can't seem to do it. If one practices meditation for a long period of time, the conviction will gradually arise as a result of inner experience that the inner dimensions are authentic. Another way to have absolute certainty of the higher worlds is to have an "out-of-body experience." Perhaps nothing is else is so persuasive.

When I was nineteen I was reading a book that described exercises in "astral projection"—the technique of the soul, or "astral body," lifting out of the physical body while one remains fully conscious of the experience. I tried the exercise for several weeks and one afternoon I actually began to "lift out." I was so startled by the experience that I felt momentary panic and immediately returned to my physical body. After that I stopped experimenting.

Several years later I had an out-of-body experience involuntarily. I was living in Europe and staying in a hotel. One night I was having difficulty sleeping due to indigestion. As I lingered in that drowsy state between wakefulness and sleep, I felt myself slip out of my physical body. Suddenly wide awake, I was thrilled to be experiencing the subtle dimension consciously. I realized that I was moving fluidly about in the denser levels of what is sometimes called the "etheric plane." I recognized the familiar physical environment, but in my subtle form it offered no resistance. I was quite literally going through the walls. The experience only lasted a minute or two, but it was exhilarating to say the least. Nothing is so convincing of the reality of the spiritual worlds as an experience like this one.

In the unusual book by Greta Woodrew entitled *On a Slide of Light*, she describes her friendship with Helen Keller, who was quite elderly at the time. Helen Keller revealed to Greta Woodrew that she had become an "expert" in out-of-body projection and spent a good deal of time exploring the inner planes. Although Helen Keller lacked the sense of physical sight, she was free to perceive the multidimensional aspects of the universe through conscious activity in her subtle body. We are assured by the great spiritual guides of the human race that these experiences are the fruit of prayer, meditation and an active inner life.

Jacques Lusseyran was a leader of the French resistance against the Nazi occupation during the Second World War. He displayed daring leadership abilities and was the one his companions called upon to test if new applicants were sincere, or if they might be potential traitors to the cause. What made all this especially remarkable was that Jacques Lusseyran was blind!

Jacques had lost his eyesight in a school accident when he was eight years old. During the years that followed he developed clairvoyant sight—the ability to "see" and perceive through inner-sensory organs of cognition that lie dormant in most of us. Through the intensity of his inner life, Jacques Lusseyran unfolded these higher faculties. The "gifts" of "extrasensory perception" that he displayed are within the reach of all human beings. By going into the inner temple of our souls in periods of prayer and meditation all of us can gradually unfold the spiritual organs of perception that reveal the existence of a "higher world"—our true place of origin.

These spiritual organs are the chakras, or energy vortices, that are part of the subtle human energy system along the spinal column. Chakra means *wheel*, or *lotus*. Each chakra has a different number of petals; each petal corresponds to a faculty or mode of intelligence, such as the ability to know what others are feeling, or the power to act boldly and fearlessly. There are many chakras, but seven principal ones. The three lower chakras, related to survival, procreation and instinctive will, are highly developed in all human beings. The development of the higher four chakras—located approximately at the heart, the throat, the brow, and the crown of the head—is the task of all human beings now and in the future.

The twelve-petaled heart chakra has special importance for our time, because its proper development brings about compassion and empathy with all of life. It is through the heart chakra that we enter dimensions of heavenly happiness. This center of spiritual awareness, when fully formed, is a portal that will open up a world of divine splendor. It is essential to form an image in meditation of one's heart center. Traditionally, the lotus, rose, or lily are recommended. When you focus the mind on such an image every day for years, you build up a powerful etheric vortex. Combined with elevated thoughts and affirmations, such exercises stimulate a gradual transformation. You begin to weave into your subtle body the substance of your higher nature, which gradually brings about spiritual perceptions and experiences.

The best way to develop these higher centers is by the practice of soul alchemy, the cultivation of virtue. When we refrain from anger and irritability—developing gentleness in our behavior, speech and actions—we allow these higher organs of spiritual awareness to unfold properly. As we develop spiritually, the light of our higher nature begins to pulsate through the chakras. The lotus petals begin to spin or revolve, and we discover that we are beginning to see and hear in the subtle dimensions. These higher faculties are the promise of future gifts and powers that include telepathy, clairvoyance and higher levels of compassion. One of the most beautiful results of developing these sense organs of the soul is *the ability to feel joy*. When we can sustain the feeling of joy and serenity through maintaining a loving attitude, we will have transformed ourselves.

True seekers of the spirit know that the powers are not ends in themselves, but natural byproducts of inner developing. True spiritual masters have always emphasized that the real work is the growth of virtue, goodness and the moral qualities inherent in our deeper nature. A story from India illustrates the folly of focusing on powers and miracles rather than the true goal of liberation and enlightenment.

A yogi has practiced for years until he has learned how to walk on the surface of the river. He goes to a high master and proudly demonstrates his skill. "How long have you spent learning to do this?" the great master asks the yogi. "Ten years, master," he replies. "You fool," rebukes the master. "Why waste all that time and energy learning to walk on water when for a dollar you can take the boat?"

We love the glamour and the mystique of the miracles brought on by inner efforts. Great teachers emphasize, however, that the important thing is to live a good life.

The Diamond Self

A story from India tells that when the gods created the world and the human race they wanted to give people a wealth of treasures to enjoy. The greatest treasure of all they hid in a place where it would be difficult to find—a place where people would not think to look. So they took the greatest treasure of all, the priceless jewel of their divine nature—the very spark that was of the same immortal substance as that of which the gods were made—and this they hid within the hearts of all human beings.

The Indian spiritual teacher H. W. L. Poonja—affectionately called Papaji—tells the following story to illustrate this truth. A master pickpocket saw a man buy the perfect diamond, one the pickpocket yearned to have. When the man bought a train ticket to Madras, so did the pickpocket. They ended up in the same compartment. The pickpocket went through all the man's luggage and clothing when he was asleep, but he could not find the diamond. When the train reached Madras, the pickpocket approached the man on the platform. "Excuse me sir," he said. "I am a master pickpocket. I have tried everything without success. You have arrived now at your destination. I will not bother you, but I must know where you hid the diamond."

The man said, "I saw you watch me buy the diamond. When you showed up on the train, I knew you were after the diamond. I thought you must be very clever, and I wondered where I could hide this diamond that you would never search. So I hid it in your own pocket."

"The highest revelation," said Emerson, "is that God is in every man." It is this divine spark, the seed of immortality and divinity, which is gradually discovered through right living. The powers of this jewel are released as we grow inwardly through the process of prayer and meditation, and by living in a manner that serves and assists others. In our essential nature we are already perfect, whole and complete. Our deeper self does not need improvement. It is our personality that needs to be transformed into the "temple" of the spirit. When our thoughts, feelings and actions are harmonized with the frequencies of our immortal nature, the higher self expresses itself in and through us. Our higher self has never abandoned us. Most of us have abandoned it. Our task is to make our personalities fit dwelling places for the eternal light. The greatest achievement, the greatest success and the greatest miracle of any life is the discovery of one's immortal indwelling presence.

THE ALCHEMICAL WEDDING

The secret of alchemy is the transmuting of soul substance. We replace dark thoughts with thoughts that shine with wisdom. We replace heavy, discordant emotions with gratitude, love, appreciation and the joy that streams from the eternal light within us. Our actions become a mirror of these elevated frequencies of mind and heart. When this process is carried far enough, a miraculous transformation occurs, which is sometimes referred to as the "alchemical wedding," or the mystical marriage.

As described in Chapter Five, the individuality—or higher self— can be represented as an equilateral triangle pointing downward. The three sides of the triangle represent love, wisdom and strength (or love, light and life). The personality may be depicted as a triangle pointing upward. The sides of this triangle refer to the faculties of thought, feeling and will. Spiritual unfolding leads to the union of these two triangles, forming the six-pointed Seal of Solomon. This occurs as we learn to think, feel and act under the inspiration of the deeper self—the divinity within us. When the will to transform ourselves grows strong enough it creates an opening in consciousness for the descent of the divine self into the personality. This is the alchemical wedding—the union of our deeper self with our personality.

Sacred geometry reveals this process in the image of the star tetrahedron (see diagram). The star tetrahedron is composed of two interlocking tetrahedrons. The downward-pointing tetrahedron represents the higher self, or individuality. The upward pointing tetrahedron is the personality. The four sides of the "higher" tetrahedron represent the spiritual attributes of wisdom, intuition, compassion and strength. The sides of the "lower" tetrahedron stand for the faculties of imagination, intellect, feeling and will. Jesus referred to these four principles when he gave the commandment to "love God with all your heart, mind, soul and strength." Each of us is a point of consciousness—the "I"—that links spirit and matter. When we fuse these two tetrahedrons by our aspiration to a higher life, we will literally be living on a higher plane of being.

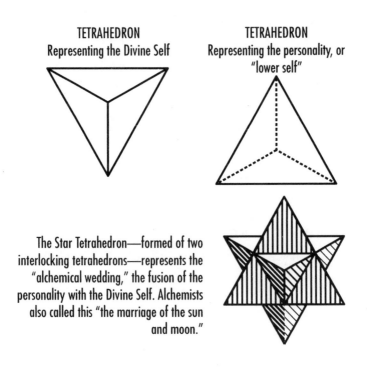

TETRAHEDRON
Representing the Divine Self

TETRAHEDRON
Representing the personality, or "lower self"

The Star Tetrahedron—formed of two interlocking tetrahedrons—represents the "alchemical wedding," the fusion of the personality with the Divine Self. Alchemists also called this "the marriage of the sun and moon."

The star tetrahedron is a geometrical image of the sacred process often called *ascension*. As the fusion of the two tetrahedrons suggests, ascension involves two simultaneous activities or orientations to our inner forces. We raise the frequencies of our consciousness while at the same time we "anchor" a stream of spiritual energy that flows from our deeper self. In alchemical terms, we transmute substance while crystallizing spirit. The alchemical wedding raises Earth to Heaven and brings Heaven into the Earth.

The star tetrahedron is one of the most profound of all symbols. It is the Seal of Solomon seen in three-dimensional form—an emblem of the initiate, saint or master. It represents the fusion of our personality with our immortal spirit. In its highest sense, the star tetrahedron stands for the illumination of our consciousness and the overcoming of death.

The Alchemy of Eternal Life

Each of us has a Sleeping Beauty in our souls. The prince whose kiss awakens Beauty is our aspiration to a higher life. As we make contact with our spirit presence, the light in our minds and the love in our hearts increase. The source of life within us is an unquenchable reservoir of energy, intelligence and power. An ever-flowing spring is a beautiful symbol of this life-source. When we tap this wellspring through meditation, we release a stream of light. The light from this inner fountain becomes active in our own affairs when we express it through our words and actions.

The immortal spiritual jewel at the core of our being is like a tiny sun that radiates and gives unceasingly. This pulsating star of light within us vibrates at a very high frequency—beyond the discord of earthly conflict. To approach this center we must resonate at a high frequency in our thoughts and feelings. Those frequencies are love, wisdom, light, harmony and all the virtues of the enlightened consciousness. We know when we are beginning to resonate at these levels because we will experience joy and light in our consciousness. From the higher self radiates an endless stream of blessing. The soul is the chalice that receives the light that flows from the spiritual levels of existence. It is the symbolic Holy Grail that captures the life force and pours it out in loving service upon Earth.

The most valuable treasures in life are not material. In the words of the Little Prince, "That which is essential is invisible to the eye." The elements of highest value in life are the light of wisdom in the mind and the warmth of love in the heart. These are the heavenly treasures of ultimate worth. Just as all spectral colors are contained in the light, so are all virtues found within the light of our spirit, the light that streams through the soul in its most exalted moments.

Your progress and success in life for all time to come depends on the quality of your inner life—of your thoughts, feelings, moods and reflections. By daily periods of meditation and inner tranquillity, you begin to weave a garment of light and beauty within you. Tibetan Buddhists call this garment of light the Rainbow Body. In the Bible it is called the Body of Light or the Robe of Glory. Referring by analogy to the spiritual basis of the Body of Glory, Saint Paul said, "If there is a physical body, there is also a spiritual body." The elements that fashion the Rainbow Body, or "light body," are the sublime thoughts and feelings produced by the seeking of our hearts and questing of our minds. We weave our light body—our luminous rainbow aura—by our aspiration to beauty, goodness, and truth. Every new affirmation of our sacred self is a thread woven into the fabric of our body of immortality and enlightenment. The soul thus transfigured becomes the light body.

Artists have traditionally depicted this divine aura—known variously as the light body, the Rainbow Body, or the Rainbow Bridge—as the golden halo around an illumined saint. By inspired thoughts and sacred feelings we build the rainbow bridge of light that unites our physical brain to our immortal self, the divine presence within us.

In our Body of Light, or light body, we can travel at the speed of thought. Nothing of a material nature can obstruct us. Our light body will eventually become the vehicle in which we explore the vastness of space and the outer reaches of the universe. We build our light body by our best thoughts and deeds, our finest sentiments and imaginations. It is a work of many lifetimes, but the result is the creation of the garment of our immortality.

When we work consciously on creating the best within ourselves, like the butterfly, we enact the great transformation. We accomplish the miracle of soul alchemy and turn our souls into vessels of light. In so doing, we forge a bright future for ourselves and those we love.

Exercises in Sacred Living:
Activating the Alchemy of Inner Unfolding

In order to make progress in one's inner work, it is essential to set aside time for this purpose, even if for only five minutes a day. Those who establish regular time for daily periods of prayer and contemplation often find that this quiet inner work is as necessary as eating or sleeping. The ideal is to reach the stage where making time is not an effort, but naturally becomes an essential part of the day.

There are dozens of good books on meditation, some of which you can find at any well-stocked bookstore. Generally speaking, the goal for most people, at least at first, should not be emptying the mind. A better approach is to focus the mind through exercises in concentration, visualization, prayer and affirmation. Choose an uplifting thought, affirmation, or sacred image. Concentrate on it to the exclusion of all else. This is the first stage of meditation as most commonly practiced. Regarding meditative styles and techniques, much depends on one's temperament and philosophical inclinations. With practice, you will settle upon a meditative approach most suitable to your temperament and personality.

Meditation opens a window into the spiritual world. If meditation becomes a regular practice, one gradually comes to realize that the world one enters in deep contemplation is not fantasy or an illusion, but is a subtle dimension of existence that is in fact our true home and place of origin. The day is coming when people will wake up to the fact that they are not human beings having occasional spiritual experiences, but spiritual beings experiencing life on Earth.

Activity Number One

Find a quiet corner, relax, breathe calmly and deeply. Focus your mind upon an uplifting thought or a beautiful image—perhaps a lily, lotus or a rose. Imagine yourself sitting beside a bubbling fountain in a paradisal garden. Picture the splendor of the scenery in vivid detail. An angel comes gently near and smiles. You absorb the healing, vitalizing energies that stream from the heart and head of this glorious being of love, wisdom and strength. Imagine that you are being transformed into the brilliance that lies within you as a seed—the perfection represented by the angel—an image of your own Higher Self. Slowly you are metamorphosing into this light being, becoming like the butterfly, graceful, happy and free. Resolve to express these qualities in your relationships, then open your eyes, smile and pick up the threads of living with a refreshed mind and a renewed heart.

Activity Number Two

This is an ancient method of mindfulness that is employed in both Eastern and Western traditions. Before retiring, mentally go back through the course of your day's experiences. This retrospective should be done from that moment backwards—almost like watching a film in reverse—until the moment you woke up. Primarily observe yourself and your reactions to people and events. What were your emotional responses? What did you say? Observe yourself from the standpoint of your higher self. Don't condemn yourself if you acted foolishly. Simply take note of areas where you would like to improve.

Not only will this exercise awaken your deeper self, but you will find that you fall asleep more easily and rapidly!

Affirmations

"I am a luminous, immortal being of limitless splendor and light."

"My higher self is perfect. I am capable of infinite expansion towards the light."

"All good qualities exist now in my higher consciousness. I am in touch with this golden center of celestial perfection. I express these qualities in my life."

"Every new affirmation of my celestial being is the beginning of a better life"

CHAPTER TWELVE

THE ALCHEMY OF LIGHT AND LOVE

"The sun shines not on us, but in us."

– John Muir

"Real isn't how you are made," said the Skin Horse.
"It's a thing that happens to you.
When a child loves you for a long, long time, not just
to play with, but REALLY loves you, then you become Real."

– Margery Williams, *The Velveteen Rabbit*

"Love conquers all things."

– Virgil

When I lived in Rome, one of my favorite destinations was the Pantheon. Constructed nearly 2,000 years ago, the Pantheon is sometimes described as the world's oldest continually-used building. Today the Pantheon is a Catholic church. Originally it was a temple dedicated to the chief gods and goddesses of antiquity. Hence the term "pantheon," which means "place of all the divinities."

It was always thrilling to stand inside the Pantheon. The form of this ancient temple seemed a lesson in understanding the universe—a scripture in stone.

The Pantheon's circular architecture conjures a sense of universality and inclusiveness. The circle, capable of infinite expansion from its center, has the potential to embrace all things. Thus it represents the universal life. The Pantheon's interior is illumined by a large circular window at the apex of the dome. This window signifies the vault of the heavens and the cosmic fountain or matrix from which all light springs. It represents also the crown chakra, the highest energy center at the top of the head through which flows pure light from our divine self. The light streaming into the Pantheon conveys an image of the illumination of our own temple—our soul and physical body—by the radiance of the divine self. It was only natural that the ancients would place great emphasis on light, for light is the most obvious and compelling revelation of divinity.

Light is the creative principle in nature. According to religion, the first emanation of the divine world was light. In Genesis this is expressed when God said, "Let there be light." What we call matter, upon close examination, displays the properties and characteristics of light. Quantum physics now declares that matter really is "condensed" light—a dance of pulsing, luminous waves. Physicist David Bohm echoes the ancient sages when he states that "All matter is frozen light." Metaphysics has always taught that light is the primordial element, and that "spirit" and "matter" are polarized expressions of this one divine principle. So-called matter is really standing waves of "congealed" light. The universe is more like a luminous thought than a solid mass.

Light has a dual meaning. Used as a noun, *light* is radiance or illumination. Used as an adjective, it refers to the absence of weight. Thus it is associated both with intelligence (the light of knowledge) and with freedom (the lack of burdens). What we call enlightenment—or soul alchemy—is a process of introducing more radiance into our thinking and our emotions, which will result in light-filled actions. It is a process of illumination and liberation. Our thoughts, feelings and intentions determine the quality and quantity of the light we emanate and express in our lives. Light elevates us and makes us shine. All blessings are contained within the light.

Even food is essentially light. Vitamins and minerals exist in their primary state as the energy of sunlight. Plants are the foundation of the food chain because plants transform sunlight into chlorophyll through photosynthesis. The bottom of the food chain is made up of single cell plants, like blue-green algae. Food has really two essential components: the cellulose, or cell matter, which provides the bulk that our bodies use to rebuild tissue; and the energy or life component, which is light. The lower we eat on the food chain, and the purer and less processed our foods, the closer we are to ingesting pure light.

COLOR = THE SUFFERINGS OF THE LIGHT

All the colors of the spectrum spring from the interrelation of light and darkness—of spirit and matter. Color represents the living power of the soul. The soul is the child that is born of the union of spirit and matter. The more light we emanate, the more vibrant will be our soul's colors. Clairvoyants see these colors in the aura. Some medical intuitives can diagnose our health from the colors in our energy field. As we work to improve our inner lives, we enhance the beauty of our soul's emanations. We create a spectrum of living light in our consciousness. This is the way of transformation—the path of light.

Color is differentiated light. Light is the union of all colors. The poet-scientist Goethe said that "Colors are the deeds and the sufferings of the light." Goethe's saying refers to the fact that color is the expression of the universal soul, whose descent into matter resulted in its "deeds and sufferings." As the pure undifferentiated light of the universal creator spirit descended into matter, it took upon itself a garment of shining, colorful rays.

If we could see clairvoyantly, we would know that everything, even minerals and rocks, are bathed in and radiate light. If we could raise our consciousness sufficiently we would hear symphonies in the light. Colors would each have a perfume as well as a sound. Color has a profound influence on our moods and feelings. Because colors sway our feelings and our feelings prompt us to act, colors directly impact our behavior.

Just one of many clinically proven examples of the effects of color on consciousness is the use of "bubble gum pink" in correctional institutions. When necessary, inmates are placed in specially painted rooms in order to calm them. It has been found consistently that in a matter of seconds, "bubble gum pink" influences people to relax. The effects are as much physical as psychological, acting directly on the muscular system. Bubble gum pink has been proven to calm nerves and is now widely used to reduce aggressive behavior.

In order to create a culture based on wisdom, we will have to grow in our knowledge and perception of how colors influence our inner life and our activities. In the future, it is likely that we will move away from wearing dark, drab colors, replacing them with vibrant pastels that reflect elevated emotional states. By choosing to surround ourselves with colors that have a positive effect on our moods and actions, we harmonize and improve our lives.

THE HEALING LIGHT

The therapeutic value of sunlight has been used in treatment since earliest times. In ancient Greece, Pythagoras employed exposure to the sun's rays as a means of healing. The classical Greek physicians, Herodotus and Galen—and in medieval Spain, Avicenna—all advocated solar baths and sun therapy. Since the 1880s, ultraviolet light has been used for its antibacterial properties in the treatment of disease. By the end of the nineteenth century, doctors discovered that rickets could be effectively treated by vitamin D contained in sunlight. At about the same time, the Danish scientist Niels Finsen discovered that the sun's rays diminished the symptoms caused by tuberculosis. In 1903 he won the Nobel prize for his innovative work using ultra-violet and solar light in healing.

Lack of sunlight affects our moods. The common malady related to sunlight deficiency has been given the clinical name of Seasonal Affective Disorder (SAD), which is especially commonplace in areas such as the Pacific Northwest, where the sun may rarely be seen for months. It is now universally recognized that the prolonged absence of sunlight can lead to depression.

A renaissance in healing using light and color therapy is currently taking place. In his book, *Light: Medicine of the Future*, the medical pioneer and visionary, Jacob Liberman, describes the healing value and potential of light. He calls light "the final frontier" and says that "Our total development is dependent on the quality and specific aspects of universal light to which we are receptive." Dr. Liberman makes an eloquent case for the emerging medical technologies that employ light. "Today," he writes, "light and its component colors are being used in almost every aspect of science and medicine." He goes on to predict that "Invasive medical approaches to treatment will become outdated as we enter the light age. Scalpels will be replaced by lasers, chemotherapy by phototherapy (light therapy), prescription drugs by prescription colors, acupuncture needles by needles of light, eye glasses by healthy eyes. Cancer will be a disease of the past; health and longevity will be the norm of the future."

The Fountain of Youth

It may not be possible to live forever in the physical body, but we can no doubt greatly prolong our life on Earth. Our bodies age on a cellular level when the cells do not continue replicating themselves. The origin of this aging process is in our minds.

Seeking to defeat the aging process, men and women since ancient times have searched for the legendary "fountain of youth." The fountain of youth will not be found in the physical world. It is within us that its eternal waters flow. The fountain of youth is another name for the alchemical Elixir of Life. It is a stream of love and joyous feeling that flows perpetually from our higher consciousness—our deeper self. When this light transforms our feelings into joy and inner buoyancy, we will taste the fabled Elixir of Life. By inspired thoughts and sacred feelings we bathe our souls in this eternal light. By affirming the reality of our deeper self we can overcome the body's subconscious death wish, strengthen the immune system and enhance the radiant health of our etheric and physical organisms.

On a subatomic level, the substance of our bodies—electrons, protons, neutrons and quarks—are wave frequencies of pure undulating energy. What we call physical matter is really "frozen light." We are literally *light beings* who have been hypnotized and stupefied by misinterpreting the messages that come to us through our senses. We embrace our own immortality as we affirm the truth of our divine origin and luminous destiny.

The universe we inhabit is a field of light, an ocean of energy. Because we tend to identify with the physical body and with past errors, we forget that we are really light. Instead of soaring, we slump beneath the weight of our burdens. As we spiritualize our consciousness and fashion our light bodies, we learn to live as do the great masters, gliding on the sea of light the way a swan glides on the surface of a pond.

In our deeper selves we are already immortal. No external doctrine that we might embrace is going to confer eternal life on us. Immortality was bestowed on us by our Creator when the celestial beings forged our spirits out of the eternal "breath" of the divine. Each of us is a spark or ray of divine light. It might truthfully be said that we are light in slow motion.

The fountain of youth is the stream of golden light that originates from the divine spark in our hearts. We plunge into these "living waters" when we immerse ourselves in inspired thoughts and feelings. As we resurrect our minds and elevate our consciousness, increased life force streams through the etheric field, thereby enhancing the vitality of our physical organisms.

THE PINEAL GLAND AND THE THIRD EYE

The pineal gland has always been of interest to philosophers, and science is now exploring this unique portion of the brain. Sixteenth century French philosopher René Descartes—famous for his axiom, "I think, therefore I am"—said that the pineal gland was the seat of the soul. The pea-sized pineal gland—located behind the forehead between the right and left brain hemispheres—is sensitive to light perceived by the eyes. It translates the light coming from the eyes into hormone signals that regulate many body functions.

It is now known that the pineal gland secretes the powerful hormone called melatonin. Melatonin is released into the bloodstream by the pineal gland in response to light perceived through the eyes. Melatonin is released at night and is suppressed during the day. Researchers say melatonin affects every cell in the body. It plays a role in virtually every body function including growth, temperature and reproduction. Some scientists are now concluding that the pineal gland—and melatonin—directly influence (or delay) the aging process. It is now believed melatonin increases longevity and that aging is caused by a deterioration in the pineal gland's ability to manufacture this hormone.

The pineal gland is associated with a more subtle energy center in the etheric or vital body. The etheric body is an aura of light pulsating within or "behind" our physical form. This energy system forms the vital "lattice work" or underpinning for the physical body and circulates life energy through a complex network of undulating vital currents. Physics recognizes that there are light-wave frequencies above that of visible light on the electromagnetic spectrum. This fact in nature is symbolic of the subtle qualities of light that emanate from the soul and spirit dimensions, which include the etheric energy field. These invisible light-wave frequencies correspond to the most luminous, yet subtle, radiations of thought and emotion. Sages tell us that as we grow and develop spiritually, we gradually intensify this subtle energy so that even our physical bodies become radiant.

The etheric center in the region of the pineal gland is the "Third Eye" described in many sacred texts. The Third Eye confers clairvoyance and spiritual understanding. Christ said that "When your eye is single, your whole body will be full of light." Perhaps he was referring to the unfolding of the Third Eye, which occurs as a result of an intense inner life and the flowering of soul virtues. The pineal gland is not identical to the Third Eye, but is the physical gland that corresponds to this more subtle energy center in the etheric or vital body. The Third Eye is often called the "brow chakra."

The Third Eye, linked to the pineal gland, is the organ of spiritual vision. When this center is fully activated, its petals unfold and begin to revolve or spin. As a result we begin to see in the spiritual world. Those who open the Third Eye become seers. Through this "window of the soul," we will one day perceive angels and higher beings that dwell within the subtle dimensions of universal life.

Ages ago, our eyes were formed by exposure to light. Without the presence of light, we would not have developed the physical organs of sight. Just as physical light perceived by the eyes gives the cue to the pineal gland in regulating bodily processes, *spiritual light* streaming through our inspired thoughts influences and regulates our energy field through the medium of the Third Eye and the other chakras. The spiritual light that we absorb through our meditations will fashion the higher spiritual organs that grant clairvoyance.

THE YOGA OF LIGHT

The healing of the future will include a highly developed science and art of utilizing light and color rays in treatment. Modern science is validating the effectiveness of sunlight in healing. Full-spectrum light has been shown to be effective in relieving depressed moods. Sunlight is even more powerful. All the pure spectrum colors influence us mentally, emotionally and physically. Although we can benefit by the application of specific colors, we can allow our bodies to select what they need from the spectrum by exposing ourselves judiciously to direct sunlight at sunrise, early morning or sunset.

The medical pioneer John Ott believed that human beings have "solar energy cells" all over the body that can directly produce carbohydrates, proteins, and even DNA directly from sunlight. In this way, it would appear that human beings share with plants the ability to synthesize light. Through a process not fully understood by science, we transform sunlight into the matter of our bodies. This sheds light on an ancient Persian legend about the origins of human nutrition. When Zarathustra—founder of ancient Persian culture—asked the Sun Spirit, Ahura Mazda, what the first human being ate, he replied that "He ate fire and drank light."

The use of sunlight in therapy suggests that the sun may also influence our spiritual development. The sun is the source of all terrestrial life and is an image of the spiritual light that gives life to our souls. No wonder the ancients revered the sun as the most obvious manifestation of divinity perceivable by our senses. Of course, the sun is not God, but it embodies like nothing else the divine qualities of light, life and warmth. The light of the sun is a perpetual reminder of the light of the spirit.

The inspired teachers Peter Deunov and Michael Aivanhov reintroduced to the world the "yoga of the sun," which Aivanhov called "Surya Yoga" from the Sanskrit word, *surya,* meaning sun. Central to the practice of Surya Yoga is greeting the sun at dawn. The radiance of the sun contains profound mysteries, the understanding of which can assist us in our evolution. Science has yet to comprehend the full glory and significance of the sun. The ancient wisdom has always insisted that behind the sun is a majestic Being—the Divine Logos.

In addition to the benefits of greeting the sun at dawn, Peter Deunov and Mikhael Aivanhov advised spiritual seekers to work imaginatively with light. They suggested exercises in which one thinks of light, and visualizes the whole universe bathed in light. The light contains all gifts, virtues, and powers. By concentrating on light, modeling ourselves on light, we will be led to the fountain of joy and peace within ourselves. Those who love the light begin to shine with an inner intensity.

Our future development is intimately connected to light. We grow spiritually in proportion to the light that we emanate. As we mature, the radiant light of our deeper self begins to shine through the chakras in our subtle body. Light gives us an understanding of how to live joyfully. Light moves swiftly because it has no burdens; it is joyful and unfettered. Light bathes everything with its all-pervasive emanations; yet it leaves everything free. In India, light is personified as the goddess Jyoti. She is ever joyful and loving. Light teaches us how to find joy.

Angels and spiritual beings have always been described in terms of their light—which is often characterized as an almost blinding radiance. So luminous was Christ at the moment of his transfiguration that the disciples had to shield their eyes. *Deva*, the Sanskrit term for angel, means "shining one."

By filling our minds with the inspired thoughts from the world's wisdom traditions, we attune ourselves to the light of the spirit, the sun in our hearts. Perhaps there is no greater practice, no greater aspiration, than to seek to embody the light, warmth and life that finds its most visible expression in the sun.

Light is closely related to love. They are expressions of the same force. The radiance of light and the warmth of love spring from the fire of our spirit. When expressed through the mind, spiritual energy becomes intelligence, or wisdom. This inner beauty expressed through the heart becomes the warmth of love and joy. Our spiritual essence is both radiance and warmth—wisdom and love.

Light and love are twin children of the divine. Light is the brilliant emanation of the primordial Being, expressing as cosmic intelligence. Light is synonymous with wisdom. But wisdom without love can be a cold light, bringing knowledge, but not necessarily contentment. Only love—the joy within the light—can bring happiness. In order to be happy, we must love. Perhaps it is true that love can be blind. But love guided by the light of wisdom is the greatest power in the world. In fact, we need both wisdom and love, for these are the essence of the spirit.

THE VELOCITY OF LOVE

Several years ago, Suzanne Ciani composed a lovely melody entitled *The Velocity of Love*. We often hear references to the speed of light, but rarely think in terms of love having velocity. Her song made me think. Does love have a velocity? If so, is it greater than the speed of light?

We know that love can heal, and that young children deprived of love begin to wither and die. What other unknown powers and qualities might love contain? In her inspired book, *Mary's Message to the World*, Annie Kirkwood describes the undiscovered powers of love that will become known in the near future. She affirms that love has a velocity greater than that of light. She even makes the startling statement that it will be possible to heat our homes with the energy of love! Love has a measurable vibrational field. Love can penetrate even the most formidable barriers. There is no place that love cannot go. Love is the quintessence of life itself.

The saintly Hilda Charlton, mentioned in Chapter Seven, lived her life as an expression of love. Her lectures and talks were imbued with an almost tangible energy of love, which changed the destinies of her listeners. Her life story is full of charming anecdotes about love's power. In her twenties she resolved to overcome her fear of snakes by consciously sending out love to snakes everywhere. One morning shortly after her decision to love snakes, she came upon a coiled rattler on a mountain in northern California. Although the rattler was poised to strike, Hilda stepped fearlessly over it and continued on her way.

Many years later, when she was living in New York City, Hilda saw a TV show with Uri Geller bending spoons. "We can bend spoons with love," she exclaimed, overflowing with childlike enthusiasm. Hilda and some of her students sat around the room and began bending spoons simply by sending them love. Remarked a student years later: "There's still not a normal spoon in the house."

In his book, *The Fruit of Your Thoughts*, John Roberts paraphrases Peter Rosen's words on loving and enlightened living: "We evolve spiritually by developing the courage to love, which rids us of fear. Recognize and accept that God is the one energy that fills us all. Just be yourself. We don't have to prove that we are loving. Love is our energy. We show this through our respect and courage. With nothing to defend and nothing to lose, we can be like the Master and exude peace. Silence speaks loudly.... There is no danger when you are safely cradled in the arms of love.... Remind yourself to be relaxed, loving and kind today."

If we embrace the love and light of our deeper self, we can alter our destiny. By loving actions we can dissolve potential dangers on our path. This is one of the meanings of divine grace. We can activate the power of divine grace when we consistently express the magic of love. When we fill our minds with the wisdom of luminous thinking, the petals of our hearts begin to blossom. Just as plants turn toward the light of the sun, so do our hearts open to the sun of love that shines eternally from our divine self.

THE LOVE OF LITTLE FLOWER

Saint Therese of Lisieux—affectionately known as Little Flower—lived in France near the end of the last century, passing on in 1897 at the tender age of 24. Although she rarely left the cloister and was almost unknown during her life, she is today one of the world's most beloved saints. Her autobiography has sold many millions of copies throughout the world and has inspired innumerable people with its simple tale of devotion and love. In her book she describes feeling "beside myself with joy" when she finally realized her purpose on Earth. "I've found my vocation, and my vocation is love... To be nothing else but love." Little Flower goes on to describe how she means to live her vocation. "Love needs to be proved by action. Well, even a child can scatter flowers, to scent the throne-room with their fragrance; even a little child can sing.... That shall be my life, to scatter flowers....

here by a smiling look, there by a kindly word, always doing the tiniest things right, and doing it for love.... And as I scatter my flowers I shall be singing; how could one be sad when occupied so pleasantly?"

Despite her enthusiasm and devotion, the path of Little Flower was not always easy. In her intimate confidings, Saint Therese reveals the struggle of her heart to love in the face of the foibles, pettiness and misunderstanding of those around her. She writes that "...love means putting up with other people's shortcomings, feeling no surprise at their weaknesses, finding encouragement even in the slightest evidence of good qualities in them.... it (is) no good leaving charity locked up in the depths of your heart." The simple loving way of Little Flower has been an inspiration to millions. It is not easy to love in a world so full of hatred, cruelty and wrongdoing. But it is possible when we commit ourselves, as did Therese, to manifest a loving spirit. So great was her love that Therese vowed to spend her Heaven doing good on Earth. Like so many of the saints and heavenly masters, she remains very close to humanity. To this day, numerous miracles have been attributed to the intervention of Little Flower in the lives of those open to her influence.

LOVE - THE KEY TO SACRED LIVING

The greatest mystery and the greatest power in life is that of love. It is the greatest power because it is stronger than any emotion, and can transform the most wretched individual and redeem the most difficult circumstances. It is the greatest mystery, for we know so little about the higher nature of love and have only begun in a fumbling fashion to express it.

The Greeks had several words to express different manifestations of love. Sexual love was *Eros*. *Philia* meant a love as might be shared between long-time friends, or by members of the same family who felt strong feelings of kinship. *Agape* referred to the highest form of love—an ideal, transcendent, spiritual love.

Christ said to love God with all your mind, heart, soul and strength, and to love your neighbor as yourself. A saintly love as expressed by Jesus, Buddha and Saint Francis is indeed rare. Yet many individuals have reached a point in their development where love for others—and the ideal of expressing love—is becoming the prime motivating force in their lives. Love gives hope to all. It is the promise that keeps one striving, growing and becoming.

When I was a teenager, I sometimes reflected on the words that my "angel presence" spoke to me when I was five years old. "You are on Earth to learn to love." I thought then that it was an easy thing to love. Only with the tests and challenges of adult life did I realize that to love was not as simple as my youthful idealism had believed. The mind is always coming up with a multitude of reasons why we shouldn't love. If we focus on the differences and the abrasive little peculiarities of human personality, we're likely to throw up our arms in exasperation. If we care to look, we can always find a significant number of "revolting specimens" in the world. The harsh experiences and disappointments of life can easily make us bitter, but only by loving can we free ourselves from negative emotions and the shackles of our critical mind.

I know two women who are an inspiring example of the power of love. Marge and Mary are "getting up in years" but are very youthful in spirit. A few years ago they decided to go to Britain together. They rented a car and spent two weeks touring Ireland, Scotland, Wales and England. They are both strong and independent personalities, and held differing opinions of how to "have a good time" on their vacation abroad. When they returned one could see that they had sometimes rubbed on each others nerves.

A year later Marge had a stroke and a heart attack, followed by quadruple bypass surgery. There was a great outpouring of affection for her from her community of friends. One of the most steadfast, loyal and attentive was Mary. She was at Marge's side day and night. It was heartwarming to see the bond of love they shared. Marge was soon back on her feet after a recovery that was a miracle in its own right. I saw them together one evening and Mary jokingly "complained" of all she did to help Marge when she was bed-ridden. She smiled at Marge, then added with a gleam in her eyes, "But would I do it again?" She paused a moment, then warmly exclaimed, "You bet I would!"

The difficulties we experience are often the stepping stones of our progress. The alchemical key to our unfolding is the manner in which we respond to life's challenges. As a friend of mine, Alan Greene, so wisely said, "It is not how much we have suffered that matters most, but how much we have loved." Love is a power that can transform the sorrowful experiences of life.

Much of the suffering people experience is due to a misunderstanding of love. "The misfortunes of people today," said Peter Deunov, "are due to the fact that they do not manifest their love, but rather expect others to love them. The disenchantment of people is due to the fact that they expect to be loved. Those who want the love of others, but do not give of themselves, cannot be loved. Let them first give their love and it will be given unto them. Unless you first give your heart, you will always be far from love.... as soon as you find love, you will know the inner meaning of life. In this way you will love everything in the world; animals, plants and even every stone. Love everything but do not strive to possess anything." Love thrives in an atmosphere of freedom. In the presence of force, love withers. Writes Kahlil Gibran: "Love one another but make not a bond of love: let it rather be a moving sea between the shores of your soul."

Perhaps if we comprehended the factors of destiny that have shaped people—the reason the criminal and the arms dealer and the homeless man have become who they are—we would understand rather than stand in judgment. Judgment is a form of mental compensation that makes us feel superior to others. When we judge, we arrogantly *stand over* another—the very opposite of *under-standing*. When we judge others, we diminish ourselves. We fall from grace. When we can truly understand, compassion awakens in our hearts. Understanding is the fountain from which love flows. When love awakens, we find the source of peace. Peace enters our heart on the wings of understanding.

We Become What We Love

The alchemists worked with sulfur in order to create the Philosopher's Stone. The alchemical sulfur represents the fire of the spirit—the flame of love. With fiery sparks from the heart of love, humanity will kindle a sacred culture, a culture of light. Those who focus on light-filled thoughts kindle a flame within their consciousness, which can grow in intensity and illuminate the whole of life. Such people become beacons of light in the subtle dimensions. As one sends forth loving emanations, she or he is bathed in ethereal light. When one releases the light, one receives it.

Love is always expressed through giving. Giving is the spontaneous outgrowth of love. For love to transform the world, it must shine through our generosity. The ancient Egyptian image mentioned in Chapter Four, of the sun with many rays—and a hand on the end of each ray—is a beautiful picture of the givingness of light and love. The sun is the heart of our solar system. It overflows with generosity and love, and gives life to all by its constant outpouring of warmth and light.

When we love something, we begin to resemble it. If we love art, music, athletics, literature or anything—we may begin to acquire skills and talents in that area. Love awakens slumbering faculties, even genius. If you want to obtain anything of value in life, you must love it, because love is the most magnetic force in existence. Mastery in any area of life is the fruit of love.

The mysterious motive power at the core of human feeling is love. Love gives vitality to life. It is the driving force in human evolution. Within nature, love is the divine play of all elements and all creatures—the heavenly *Lila*, or dance, of Indian mythology.

In human relationships love is the rhythmic dance of giving and receiving—of balanced, kind-hearted exchanges. Expressing goodwill and helpfulness liberates one from the prison of loneliness and despair. Love is also the most important element in any spiritual practice. "Without love," said White Eagle, "we cannot know the meaning and mystery of God." In the words of Sai Baba, "Begin the day with love, fill the day with love, end the day with love. This is the way to God-consciousness."

Love gives value to life. Wealth without love is meaningless. Love transforms us and gives us more abundant life. Love is also the source of happiness. The more love we infuse into our labors, the more happiness we experience. The feeling of love in the heart is the origin of contentment in life. Love is the wellspring of human joy. "The love planted in your hearts by the divine beings," says White Eagle, "is infinite power, supreme happiness; it is heavenly joy."

The power to forgive and to grow beyond pain is the power of love. Love enables us to overcome the anguish of loss. "From suffering

I have learned this," wrote Mechtild of Magdeburg, "that whoever is sore wounded by love will never be made whole unless she embraces the very same love which wounded her." The secret of the alchemy of our souls is never to allow the currents of love to dry up. Love restores the wounded soul, for love is alive.

Love Is Stronger Than Death

One of the most beautiful and loving relationships that has come down to us from the past is that of Robert Browning and Elizabeth Barret Browning, two of England's most significant nineteenth century poets. Elizabeth was petite, and because of her olive complexion, Robert affectionately called her "my little Portuguese." Her famous verses published under the title *Sonnets From the Portuguese* have always been among the world's most beloved poems.

When Elizabeth's health deteriorated, Robert arranged for them to travel to Italy in the hope that the warmer climate would restore her. Her health returned and they decided to live in Italy. They built a home in Florence where they spent the happiest years of their life together. But in June of 1861, Elizabeth again became ill. This time Robert knew intuitively that she would not recover. All night he sat beside her bed, praying passionately, imploring her not to leave him. Occasionally she would recover from her sleep and gently smile or whisper a word of hope until she was too weak even for that. Late at night she recovered enough to ask him to hold her one last time. She could barely whisper the words, "Hold me, beloved." He lifted her from the bed and carried her to the chair by the window, cradling her gently in his arms until dawn. As the first light of the new day touched the sky, he kissed her on her cold lips one last time. She stirred from her deep sleep and whispered her final words, "It is beautiful," then passed away.

Through his grief Robert Browning wrote one of his greatest poems, *Prospice* (look forward), in which he scribed his conviction that love is eternal and that he would one day again hold his beloved in his arms. He wrote, "Oh thou soul of my soul! I shall clasp thee again." No doubt he was inspired by the lines of one of Elizabeth's most universally loved poems, written for him and published in *Sonnets From the Portuguese*.

"I love thee with the breath,

Smiles, tears, of all my life! —and if God choose,

I shall love thee better after death."

Robert and Elizabeth Barret Browning knew what all mystics, saints and visionary poets have known—that love is an eternal force that overcomes death. Truly, those who love never die.

THE SECRET OF ENLIGHTENMENT

Love transforms the experience of human life. Love is an elevated state of consciousness that is always expressed in harmonious actions and gestures. The feeling of expansion and well-being that comes when we experience love in our hearts is its own reward. Mikhael Aivhanov expressed these words about the power of love: "Our hearts must be full of love for human beings because they are all our brothers and sisters. We must think of them and help them without expecting the slightest reward, for, in reality, our reward is already given to us in that inner sense of expansion, that extraordinary sensation of warmth that fills us when we love. This is a marvelous reward; life contains none greater."

The essence of enlightenment is to raise the vibrations of your love. The enlightened person loves everyone, just as the sun shines on the saint and the criminal with equal radiance. Divine love is universal. When we can expand our love to include the universe, we will touch the consciousness of our divine self. Notice how you feel when you are experiencing a heightened state of love. Imagine experiencing that feeling without the object of your love being there. Cultivate that feeling irrespective of an object. Imagine holding that feeling and emanating it steadily. When we can maintain the feeling of love in our hearts—free of any object, without demanding that our love be reciprocated—our lives will be forever transformed. We will stand on the threshold of the deepest mysteries. We are then ready to enter a new consciousness, symbolized in the ancient Mystery teachings as the inner precincts of the temple. Wherever we go, we will be emissaries of a sacred culture—a culture of love.

In Chapter One we told the story of Narada and Krishna, and the glass of water that Krishna asked Narada to fetch. This "glass of water" may be seen as a metaphor for *the water of life*. What is the water of life? It is the spiritual emanation of rainbow light, infused with love, that streams from the celestial dimensions into mind, soul and body. This "water" is the divine radiance, the "river of light," that streams from the universal source, the primordial fountainhead. This heavenly water brings understanding and quenches the soul's thirst—the longing for the light that fulfills us. When we drink from this celestial fountain that streams into us from our own divine self, our thirst will be forever quenched. This "ambrosia of the gods"—the light of Heaven imbued with love—lifts us into a new state of being. A day will come when science understands love to be a cosmic force that flows through all dimensions of life. We are all living links in a chain, an unending circuit of divine energy. The divine circulatory flow is really the stream of love through all manifestations of universal existence. Love is the essence of soul alchemy—the transmutation of our psyches into the divine image. Love is the supreme light and energy that makes life possible.

The driving force of our evolution as souls is love. We grow as we learn love's evolutionary lessons. The drop of elixir extracted from the grinding wheels of destiny is wisdom-filled love—the quintessence of experience. Light and love give wings to the mind and the imagination, enabling the soul to rise to a higher state of awareness and behold the image of its own divinity.

Life without love is a wasteland. Where kindness is expressed a fountain bursts forth and an oasis comes to life. When the Earth is filled with countless of these fountains of light—these springs of kindness—then the Earth will become once again a garden. We help create the coming culture of beauty each time we express wisdom and love in our actions.

In an age to come, humanity will resolve all conflicting tones and discord into a vibrant harmony. It was this vision that inspired Beethoven to write the choral finale to his Ninth Symphony, the famous *Ode to Joy*. Already a fortunate few on Earth can hear the faint strains of the new music sounding in the depths of their consciousness. These are the advance guard of the coming race of enlightened humanity. In the future we will move to the rhythms and give voice to the inspirations of light-filled love. It is this world that seeks to come to birth through humankind.

Christ gave the secret to enlightenment and liberation when he said, "Love one another as I have loved you." St. John the Divine echoed these words, writing, "Let us love one another, for love is of God.... If we love one another, God lives in us, and divine love is perfected in us." These words are the capstone on the monument to wisdom entrusted to us by the ancient world. They are a revelation illuminating our path into the future. Love is the key that unlocks the portals to Heaven on Earth. When we vibrate to the melody of love, we resonate in harmony with the universe.

When we finally walk in harmony with the rhythms of this celestial power, we will give expression to the vision of the immortal Italian poet Dante Alighieri, when he wrote the final words of his *Divine Comedy*, "My will and my desire were turned by love, the love that moves the sun and the other stars." As we harmonize ourselves with the divine rhythms—which find expression in the sacred laws—we will join Heaven and Earth. Through us will stream life-giving powers. These forces will build a civilization infused with light, love and truth. We will become creators of a sacred culture, living in ways that bring new life to the Earth.

Exercises in Sacred Living:
Activating the Alchemy of Light and Love

Activity Number One

Sit comfortably in your favorite chair. Imagine that your real being is weightless and luminous. Even your physical body is fundamentally composed of light. Affirm that the universe we live in is a light-wave universe. Your thoughts are subtle frequencies of light.

Visualize a star of light or a radiant sun above your head. This represents your higher self—who you are in essence. (It is helpful to picture this star above you often during the day and during times of meditation and inner quiet.) Imagine that streams of wisdom, love and strength flow from this star into your mind, heart and physical body. All the cells of your body are bathed in this beautiful, healing light. Darkness vanishes. You are in perfect health—an eternal being of light, now and forevermore.

Activity Number Two

Stand in front of an open window and breathe deeply. Picture the golden star of your higher self just above you. Imagine that on each inbreath you are pulling in a stream of golden light from this star. The stream of light flows down into the region of your heart. As you gently breathe out, imagine that this light is streaming forth in all directions as love from your heart. Imagine that it is stimulating the light in the minds and the warmth in the hearts of all creatures every-where. You can do this exercise as often as you like. You should find that it has a tremendous power to stimulate your own inner unfold-ing.

Activity Number Three

Relax in your customary place of quiet and meditation. Breathe slowly and deeply, mentally repeating affirmations or prayers that help you achieve a calm and uplifted state of mind. Then picture yourself in a vast meadow of grass and flowers. These can be tulips, lilies, irises, roses or any flower you desire. See yourself walking through the meadow towards a hill in the direction of the sunrise. Just as you reach the top of the hill the sun appears in all its bril-liance above the horizon. In the valley beneath you, spread before your delighted and astounded eyes, is a serene community of the future. In the center of the valley is a glorious temple that appears to built of purest, gleaming gold. You have entered the Earth of a future epoch—a golden age of universal peace, goodwill and prosperity. All nations have learned to live in amity, and blood is no longer shed upon the Earth.

Picture in great detail the wonderful and inspiring advances of this enlightened civilization. What will the architecture be like? What are people wearing? Picture the health and happiness of all the people you see. Know that you are a beloved member of this coming, illumi-nated humanity.

Exercises like this one help to build the thoughtform of the new civilization and strengthen your own subconscious assurance of better times to come.

Activity Number Four

When you put together a puzzle, there is a defining moment when suddenly the entire picture can be visualized. Each of the preceding chapters is a piece of a puzzle whose entirety forms a complete image—an image of a harmonious life characterized by light, kindness and gentle strength.

When you have completed this book, you may wish to read it again immediately in order to absorb these principles of sacred living more deeply into your mind. To derive maximum benefit, it is suggested that you spend a week focusing on each chapter.

An excellent practice is to read a chapter in the morning as soon as you awake, and again in the evening before retiring. As you do so, your understanding will increase. The light in your mind will grow as you imprint these ideas into your heart through concentration and reflection.

Keep a notebook or diary of your insights and recollections. Reflect on your daily experiences and interactions in the light of each of the celestial laws. In some areas you will be stronger than others. For instance, you may tend to be an "idea person," always thinking and conceptualizing, but not very effective in getting things done and carrying through with decisions. If that is the case, spend more time on chapter four, the alchemy of action. Work more intensively with the affirmations at the end of that chapter, and make up affirmations of your own that will develop in your personality the qualities you desire.

It is especially effective if you work with these ideas in a small study group formed for this purpose. Each member will have unique insights and experiences that will add to the understanding of everyone. It is possible to think these truths deeply into the subconscious mind where they become a permanent feature of character. Each individual who does so will be performing a work upon themselves that will benefit everyone. The more people who grasp and apply the deeper truths—the laws of soul alchemy—the sooner humankind can solve its problems and enter a more harmonious era.

Affirmations

"I am a ray of luminous light—happy, brilliant, and weightless."

"I live in the light. I am a child of limitless light and universal love."

"I transform my environment into a kingdom of light and happiness. May all those with whom I am and ever will be in contact with be blessed."

"May my heart shine with love for all beings."

THE COMING GOLDEN AGE

The world today is in the midst of unprecedented turmoil and upheaval. At the same time, there is recognition of a global spiritual awakening—often referred to as a shift in human perception. These seemingly contrary developments should come as no surprise, for we stand at a historical turning point. It is as if we have entered the turbulent waters where two oceans meet. The human race is moving out of one experience into an entirely new world, with fresh currents leading us to undiscovered possibilities. If we can solve our present challenges, we will find ourselves on the threshold of a new era in human understanding and achievement. In order to move through the current crisis, there must be a core group of individuals—a vanguard—who can lead the way into more peaceful waters.

The coming transformation in consciousness is often described as a collective experience that will be made by the entire human race. But the human race is made up of individuals. Just as children must learn to walk on their own, so must we, as individuals, take the first steps into a more enlightened life. What is required is a sufficient number of daring individuals with awakened hearts and pioneer spirits—men and women who can anchor the new consciousness in their daily lives. Only a small amount of leaven is needed to make a loaf of bread rise. The same is true of humanity. Even a minority of individuals dedicated to the creation of a sacred culture can elevate and transform our current civilization.

It is interesting from the standpoint of alchemy that the ages of the Earth and humanity are often classified according to minerals, or metals. Thus we have the "Stone Age," the "Iron Age," the "Bronze Age." In the metaphysical traditions of both East and West, there is mention of a prophesied golden age. According to these traditions, humanity will soon enter a time of spiritual beatitude and material prosperity. Of course, our entrance into this era is contingent upon our solving the problems that face us. Our path into the golden age can be strewn with apocalyptic upheaval or blessed with gentle awakenings. It is up to us. If the current violent and destructive trends hold sway, we may have to pass through an "ordeal by fire"—the "tribulation" prophesied by several Biblical prophets, including Daniel, St. John and Jesus.

Regardless of the manner in which humanity makes the transition into the new era, the coming golden age will be the culmination of a process of inner transformation and awakening. It will be the result of soul alchemy. What will this coming golden age be like? Although the details elude us, it can be helpful and encouraging to create mental images of this coming era of sacred living.

In the *Book of Revelation*, St. John describes the vision he was given of the promised era. He says there will be "a new Heaven and a new Earth." The "new Heaven" is a new way of thinking, a new philosophy. It will be a philosophy of life, love and harmony. The "new Earth" refers to a new way of behaving and interacting—a return to sacred living. Humanity will act in new and enlightened ways. We will create a culture of love, goodness and great beauty. Each of us will feel it our mission to spiritualize and make beautiful the little patch of Earth on which we live. Our task will be to make the Earth a sacred place. We will be alchemists, transforming our lives into manifestations of wisdom and love.

First and foremost, human beings will learn to live together in peace and harmony. The ancient prophecy will be fulfilled and we will "beat swords into plowshares," putting to an end the horrors of war. The wanton shedding of blood will become a distant memory. The emergence of peace among nations will lead to an era of unprecedented prosperity. Disagreements will be settled amicably through discussion and ongoing dialogue. In living harmoniously, humanity will recognize the sanctity of life. As people come to know the laws that govern life, we will realize that those who hurt others hurt themselves. Crime will disappear as people comprehend the reciprocity at the heart of all action. Populations will not crowd into dense, dirty cities but will be spread out through the plains, forests and meadows of Earth. Cities will not be characterized, as they are now, by pockets of prosperity surrounded by neighborhoods of misery and want. Communities will become places of beauty. Poverty will be eliminated, as will the scourge of disease. The common life span of humans will be double or triple what it is today. Our relationship to the animal kingdom will improve dramatically and the four-legged creatures will no longer live in fear of humans. The Earth will cease to be a "vale of sorrows," becoming instead a place of comfort and joy.

Technology will take the path of spiritual science. We will discover laws and principles previously unknown. Homes will be solar powered. Vehicles of transportation will run on a new fuel—akin to solar or magnetic power—that utilizes the pranic life force within the etheric element. Pollution caused by fossil fuels will be eliminated. The air, soil and water will be regenerated. The power of corporate and government syndicates that seek to enslave humanity will be broken. With the triumph of the spirit, tyranny will come to an end.

All will master the law of causation and each individual will become master of his or her destiny. We will unfold our full spiritual potential, developing and manifesting the spectrum of powers inherent within our eternal divine spark. People will develop the gifts of the spirit, including telepathy, clairvoyance, heightened intuition, the ability to heal, and advanced forms of mind and spirit power. The true history of the Earth will be known and humanity will take its place within the universal community of angels and enlightened beings. We will join the hierarchy of glorified souls, growing towards perfection.

As more individuals are inspired to bring the light and love of their true selves into expression, we will find our way into the new era. This is the "great work"—the alchemists' *magnum opus*—that all human beings are called to do. Each of us is meant to transform our own soul into a "jewel." St. John used the idea of twelve-fold perfection in his Book of Revelation in the image of the twelve foundation stones of the sacred city. The creation of a sacred culture—epitomized as the sacred city of Revelation—is reflected in the image of the Philosopher's Stone, the jewel of our immortal self. This jewel may be visualized as having twelve facets. Each facet represents one of the twelve alchemical laws described in this book. Thus, it is a synthesis of the various perspectives of sacred living—a single gem of indescribable brilliance.

An image of this twelvefold perfection is the *dodecahedron*, pictured below and at the beginning of each chapter of this book. The dodecahedron is one of the five geometric shapes known collectively as the "Platonic solids." Plato, the illustrious Athenian philosopher for whom these shapes were named, said that God used the dodecahedron when he created the world and set the constellations in the Heavens. Both Plato and Pythagoras before him claimed that the twelve-faced symmetrical solid known as the dodecahedron was the foundation of the universe. We might think of it as the foundation stone to the construction of our own inner temple of enlightenment. This image is a fitting symbol for the jewel of our inner self—our true divine nature—which shines with an eternal star-like brilliance. It represents the Philosopher's Stone, the alchemist's key to personal and cultural transformation.

As we unfold our hidden splendor—the secret of our soul—we discover the abundant life of the spirit. As this new life streams into us, it transmutes the very substance of our tissues and cells, even our DNA itself. We find that the Elixir of Life is an essence, a radiance, produced by our own consciousness, which can penetrate right into our bones. We enact the great work of transmutation, of soul alchemy, when we express harmony in our lives and our relationships.

The golden light that emanates from those who seek to live a sacred life will create the coming era of enlightenment. The new culture itself will become the "gold" produced by the alchemy of soul transformation. Each of us will consciously dance the path of initiation—the way of soul evolution into divine stature—which leads across the threshold of immortality. On this path, each will answer affirmatively Christ's words when he echoed the Psalmist, "Know you not that you are gods?" The golden age is dawning, and the eternal mysteries will soon flower in the hearts of humanity, bringing enlightenment, understanding and happiness to hungry souls.

There is a transcendent wisdom that underlies our universe. It bursts forth from an eternal spring that streams out of the heart of the world. The living water from this fountain is the source of life and light that sustains all creatures. Humanity's age-long thirst will be quenched when it finds this water of life. In so doing, we will come to understand the great laws that govern existence. The living synthesis of all these laws is love. May enough people discover and apply these truths, so that we may begin to transform this Earth into the garden it is meant to become.

Meditative Verse

More radiant than the sun,
Purer than the snow,
Finer than the ether,
is the Self,
The Spirit in my heart.
This Self am I.
I am this Self.

— *The Bhagavad Gita*

SUGGESTED READING

Aivanhov, Omraam M. *The Book of Divine Magic.* France: Editions Prosveta, 1989.

———1990. *Golden Rules for Everyday Life.* France: Editions Prosveta.

Anderson, Greg. *The 22 (Non-Negotiable) Laws of Wellness.* New York: Harper Collins, 1995.

Bergh, Kirsten Savitri. *She Would Draw Flowers.* Minneapolis, Minnesota: Linda Bergh. 1997. (To obtain copies, contact *Amazon.com Books* or number listed below)

Brinkley, Dannion. *Saved By the Light.* New York: Villard Books, 1995.

Burnham, Sophie. *Book of Angels.* New York: Ballantine, 1990, 1994.

Canfield, Jack and Hansen, Mark Victor. *Chicken Soup For the Soul.* Deerfield Beach, Florida: Health Communications, 1993.

Carter, Forrest. *The Education of LittleTree.* Albuquerque, NM: University of New Mexico Press, 1976.

Charlton, Hilda. *Saints Alive.* Woodstock, NY: Golden Quest, 1989.

Clark, Glenn. *The Man Who Tapped the Secrets of the Universe.* Swannanoa, Virginia: University of Science and Philosophy, 1946.

Cohen, Alan. *The Dragon Doesn't Live Here Anymore.* New York: Fawcett Columbine, 1981.

Dyer, Wayne. *A Promise is a Promise.* Carlsbad, Calif.: Hay House, 1996.

Easwaran, Eknath. Editor, *The Dhammapada.* Tomales, Calif.: Nilgiri Press, 1985.

Hamilton, Edith. *Mythology.* New York: Penguin Meridian, 1969.

Hanh, Thich Nhat. *Being Peace.* Berkeley: Parallax Press, 1987, 1996.

Hay, Louise. *You Can Heal Your Life.* Carlsbad, Calif.: Hay House, 1984, 1987.

Holmes, Ernest. *Science of Mind.* New York: G.P. Putnam and Sons, 1938, 1966.

Hunt, Valerie. *Infinite Mind: Science of the Human Vibrations of Consciousness.* Malibu, California: Malibu Publishing Co., 1996.

Isherwood, Christopher and Swami Prabhavananda. *The Song of God: The Bhagavad Gita.* New York: Penguin Books, 1944, 1972.

King, Serge. *Mastering Your Hidden Self*. Wheaton, Illinois: Quest Books, 1985.

Klocek, Dennis. *Seeking Spirit Vision*. Fair Oaks, Calif: Rudolf Steiner College Press: 1998.

Liberman, Jacob. *Light: Medicine of the Future*. Santa Fe: Bear and Company, 1991.

Lorimer, David. *Prophet For Our Times: The Life and Teachings of Peter Deunov*. Rockport, Massachusetts: Element Books, 1991.

Lusseyran, Jacques. *And There Was Light*. California: Atrium, 1986

Markides, Kyriacos. *The Magus of Strovolos*. New York: Arcana/Penguin, 1985.

Maybury, Richard J. *Whatever happened to Justice*. Placerville, California: Bluestocking Press, 1992.

Myss, Caroline. *Anatomy of the Spirit*. New York: Harmony Books, 1996.

Nicholl, Donald. *Holiness*. New York: Paulist Press, 1981, 1987.

Prophet, Elizabeth Clare. *Reincarnation, the Missing Link in Christianity*. Corwin Springs, Montana: Summit University Press. 1997.

Roberts, John. *The Fruit of Your Thoughts*. Boise: Roaring Lion Publishers, 1997.

———— 1998. *The Moth Comes to the Flame: Conversations Between Seeker and Sage*. Boise: Roaring Lion Publishing:

Rosen, Peter. *Luminous Life*. Gatlinburg, Tenn.: Roaring Lion Publishers, 1995.

Russell, Lao. *God Will Work With You But Not For You*. Waynesboro, Virginia: University of Science and Philosophy, 1955.

Sardello, Robert. *Love and the Soul*. New York: Harper Collins, 1995.

Steiner, Rudolf. *Knowledge of Higher Worlds and its Attainment*. New York: Anthroposophic Press, 1947.

White Eagle. *Wisdom From White Eagle*. Hampshire, England: White Eagle Publishing Trust, 1967.

———— 1972. *The Quiet Mind*. Hampshire, England: White Eagle Publishing Trust.

Zitko, John. *Lemurian Theo-Christic Conception*. Benson, Arizona: World University. 1964.

To order any of the above titles, consult your local bookstore, or call (520) 445-5056.

About the Author

Emory John Michael has spent many years living and traveling abroad—much of that time in Europe and South America. He has a degree in education and has taught students of all ages in a variety of settings and countries. While living in Europe, he taught English as a second language in Rome, Spain, and Switzerland. His first book, *Queen of the Sun*, has been translated into nine foreign languages. He has appeared on radio and TV shows across the country, and teaches classes and seminars on the material in his books.

Mr. Michael and his talented wife, Mia, own a book and gift store in Prescott, Arizona. When not writing, playing music, or traveling, he enjoys exploring the National Forest by their home—a high desert treasure-trove of natural splendors. Mr. Michael publishes a quarterly newsletter, called *The Oracle*.

To be on Emory John Michael's mailing list and receive his quarterly newsletter, please send $16.00 to Mountain Rose Publishing, P.O. Box 2738, Prescott, AZ 86302

ORDER FORM

Mountain Rose Publishing Company
PO Box 2738
Prescott, AZ 86302
(520)445-5056
Fax: (520) 778-1601

To order more copies of *The Alchemy of Sacred Living,* or Emory John Michael's exciting spiritual adventure *Queen of the Sun,* fill in the information below and send it in with a check, or just pick up the phone and order with a credit card. Call (520) 445-5056.

_____   THE ALCHEMY OF SACRED LIVING   @ $14.95

_____   QUEEN OF THE SUN   @ $12.95

Shipping: $3.00 first book   _____

$1.00 second book   _____

$0.50 each additional book   _____

TOTAL   _____

Name: _____

Address: _____

_____

Phone _____

• To speed up phone orders, please have your credit card number ready.

Mountain Rose Publishing
PO Box 284
Santa Cruz, CA 95061